The Literary Galaxy of
STAR TREK

The Literary Galaxy of *Star Trek*

An Analysis of References and Themes in the Television Series and Films

JAMES F. BRODERICK

McFarland & Company, Inc., Publishers
Jefferson, North Carolina, and London

LIBRARY OF CONGRESS CATALOGUING-IN-PUBLICATION DATA

Broderick, James F., 1963–
　　The literary galaxy of Star Trek : an analysis of references and themes in the television series and films / James F. Broderick.
　　　p.　　cm.
　　Includes bibliographical references and index.

　　ISBN 0-7864-2571-7 (softcover : 50# alkaline paper) ∞

　　1. Star Trek television programs — Miscellanea.　2. Star Trek films — Miscellanea.　3. Allusions.　I. Title.
PN1992.8.S74B76　2006
791.45'75 — dc22　　　　　　　　　　　　　　　2006008724

British Library cataloguing data are available

©2006 James F. Broderick. All rights reserved

No part of this book may be reproduced or transmitted in any form or by any means, electronic or mechanical, including photocopying or recording, or by any information storage and retrieval system, without permission in writing from the publisher.

On the cover: M31, the Andromeda Galaxy (NASA)

Manufactured in the United States of America

McFarland & Company, Inc., Publishers
　Box 611, Jefferson, North Carolina 28640
　　www.mcfarlandpub.com

Contents

Preface   1

Introduction   5

ONE. The Journey of the Hero   9
TWO. The Quest for Revenge   17
THREE. Leaving Childhood Behind   25
FOUR. The Pain of Love   33
FIVE. The Way of the West   41
SIX. Time Traveling   49
SEVEN. The Ravages of War   57
EIGHT. Return to the Sea   66
NINE. Failure to Communicate   74
TEN. Staying Sane in an Insane World   83
ELEVEN. Mismatched Pairs   92
TWELVE. Reinventing the Self   100

THIRTEEN. Vampirism   109

FOURTEEN. Underneath, We're All the Same   118

FIFTEEN. The Wonders (and Dangers) of Technology   127

SIXTEEN. Fantasy vs. Reality   135

SEVENTEEN. Gods, True and False   145

EIGHTEEN. The Rise of the Machine   153

NINETEEN. That Old Gang of Mine   162

TWENTY. The Quest for Perfection   171

TWENTY-ONE. Growing Old   180

TWENTY-TWO. The Final Journey   188

TWENTY-THREE. Seize the Day   196

TWENTY-FOUR. Socrates Goes to a *Star Trek* Convention   204

Appendix 1. Literary Works (and the Chapters Where They Are Discussed)   213

Appendix 2. Episodes and Films (and the Chapters Where They Are Discussed)   215

Chapter Notes   217

Bibliography   225

Index   229

Preface

For a brief period, almost four decades ago, *Star Trek* was finished. After a three-year run on network television, the series was cancelled and largely unlamented — except for a few holdovers from an eleventh-hour "Save *Star Trek*" campaign. It wasn't until the episodes went into syndication and began showing up daily in re-runs across the country that *Star Trek* the TV show became *Star Trek* the phenomenon. One of the driving forces behind *Trek's* return to prominence was the university campus. College students eagerly sought their daily fix of *Star Trek's* brand of optimism, social commentary, and inter-stellar hook-ups.

And since that time, *Star Trek* has remained a fixture in many dorm rooms, playing regularly on local stations in college towns for the last several decades. In my case, a TV station in Terre Haute, Indiana, showed *Star Trek* at midnight on Sunday nights. Like clockwork, my roommate would flip on the small, black-and-white set and — like all true Trekkers — recite the dialogue in sync with the characters. He loved the show and never missed it.

I wanted to strangle him.

The show, the fans, the whole insular world of *Star Trek* all seemed to me rather, well, weird. I told myself that once I was freed from the cinder-block world of the collegiate dorm, I'd never watch *Star Trek* again.

For 15 years, I kept that promise. I didn't watch a single hour of *Trek*. I immersed myself in the usual post-college obligations: job, marriage, child-raising. And only by accident (though I suppose proponents of fate could find a more causal relationship here) did I find myself watching the Starship *Enterprise* once again sail across my screen. An independent New York–area TV station (I had moved from Indiana years before) began showing re-runs of *Star Trek: The Next Generation*. On Sunday nights. At midnight.

I kept the TV on as background noise while I busied myself finishing paperwork for the coming week. And slowly, steadily, my eye would drift from that stack of papers on my lap to that pretty cool, and suddenly rather smart-seeming, television show. The more I watched, the more I began to see what so many other *Trek* advocates had seen over the years in the original series, the movies and the spin-offs. There was an intelligence at work here, a probing inquisitiveness, a genuine exploration of what contact with alien worlds might yield. The acting was powerful, the stories compelling. But there was something else, too, which appealed to me as a recently-minted Ph.D. in English.

This show was *loaded* with literary references: quotations from great works such as *Hamlet* and *Moby Dick*; appearances by time traveling authors such as Mark Twain and Sherlock Holmes; fantasy sequences where characters imagined themselves caught up in pulp fiction novels; poetry recitations from captains, crewmen, even androids. *Star Trek*, I was discovering, is an English major's treasure trove.

So I followed that thread, noting every literary allusion that I could catch, and the results were daunting. I filled notebooks with notations, and those notes became this book. But in the course of compiling my lexicon of literary *Trek*, I also discovered something else about *Star Trek* which speaks to its enduring significance. Scholars in such areas as philosophy, physics, and religion had also found *Trek* to be treasure troves for *their* disciplines. In that respect, *Star Trek* is somewhat like Walt Whitman's persona-narrator in *Leaves of Grass*, who proclaims "I contain multitudes." At the very least, *Star Trek* seems to bear, comfortably, a multitude of scholarly interpretations.

I was assisted in my pursuit of *Star Trek*'s literary debts by several publications, such as the official fan magazine *Star Trek: Communicator*, and the book-length compilations titled *The Best of Trek* (drawn from a fan-written magazine and numbered serially one through 12), edited by Walter Irwin and G.B. Love. Trek is well-represented on-line, with a number of highly-informed and passionately argued websites, the best of which is "Trekweb" (though the official, Paramount-sponsored site, "StarTrek.Com," has an impressive and user-friendly archive of articles, feature stories, character backgrounds and plot synopses). Many of the principal actors and creative personnel involved in *Trek's* genesis and development have written books about their experience with the franchise. Invaluable insights abound in William Shatner's *Star Trek Memories*, *Star Trek Movie Memories* and *Get a Life!*, as well as Leonard Nimoy's *I Am Not Spock* and his follow-up volume, *I Am Spock*. The single best glimpse behind the scenes is Herb Solow and Robert Justman's *Star Trek: The Inside Story*. Many Trekkers still revere Gene Rodenberry and Stephen Witfield's early but seminal *The Making of Star Trek*. And, of course, *Star Trek* conventions still serve as a fertile ground for the development, debate and dissemination of new interpretations of the *Trek* canon.

The discussion continues. *Star Trek* remains omnipresent through re-runs of the original series and the spin-offs *The Next Generation*, *Deep Space Nine*, *Voyager* and *Enterprise*, DVDs of the shows and the movies, fan-run websites, magazines, a slough of novels, memoirs, short-story contests and conventions large and small. To borrow the title of one of *Star Trek*'s best episodes, when it comes to interpretations of *Star Trek*'s meaning or significance, the sky's the limit.

Writing about *Star Trek* allowed me to live in two worlds simultaneously — the day-to-day world we mere mortals must contend with and the world of the twenty-third century, filled with alien species and intelligent life far beyond our own. I had lots of help navigating through both worlds.

I'd like to thank the staff of the Glen Ridge, New Jersey, Public Library, especially Helen Beckert, for helping to locate hard-to-find source materials. My colleague at New Jersey City University, Bruce Chadwick, once again offered advice on many book-related matters. His counsel was always deeply appreciated. I'm grateful to Darren Miller, a journalistic colleague and friend, for his inspiration and support. Darren helped me solve many vexing writing problems — most of which seemed to occur well past midnight. Thanks also to J.R. Fettinger, whose knowledge *of Star Trek* exceeds my own by light years.

He was generous in sharing his thoughts about all things *Trek*. No first-time convention attendee ever had a better translator. Wayne Blake provided explanations, clarifications and no shortage of strong opinions when I began exploring the fascinating world of *Star Trek*. Lee Anne Sakellerides did some technical trouble-shooting along the way. Without her help, I'd probably still be frantically hitting the space bar.

My daughters Olivia and Maddy contributed to this project in many ways. All writers benefit from new perspectives, and they provided endless ways of looking at our world — present and future.

Most of all, there's Miri: wife, editor, sounding board, inspiration, and co-pilot on our travels through Planet New Jersey. Marrying the smartest person I know turned out to be the smartest thing I ever did. Thanks for a great journey, Miri.

Introduction

First, an admission: the subtitle of this book is somewhat misleading. *Star Trek* does not just make "reference" to literature, *Star Trek* IS literature. Hundreds of novels have been written about the events and characters of the *Star Trek* universe. Dozens of other deeply researched nonfiction books have also been published exploring various aspects of the *Star Trek* universe. Add to that the countless number of essays, magazine articles, websites and fanzines dedicated to the world of *Star Trek*, and even the most narrow-minded critic would be forced to acknowledge the significance of this vast body of literature.

But beyond that impressive collection of writing lies a deeper truth in the statement "*Star Trek* is literature," as Trekkers and casual observers continue to be drawn to *Star Trek* for the same reason one seeks the satisfactions of literature — to discover the depth and complexity of our own world, to help find one's place in the universe.

Like any "classic" work of literature, *Star Trek* shows us heroes and villains seeking love, redemption or vengeance. Thrilling adventure, soul-searing romance, mystical quests and indomitable good humor underlie great literature *and* great *Trek*. Whether riding with Chaucer's pilgrims as they head toward Canterbury, sailing the high seas with the English naval captain Horatio Hornblower or exploring deep space with James Tiberius Kirk & Co., the reader's expectations are the same: a tale which can be enjoyed for its plot and characters, or as a deeper meditation on some aspect of the human condition. Hamlet spent his days wondering what it meant to be human. So too Commander Data, the android who served under *The Next Generation*'s Captain Picard. Their incarnations are separated by five centuries, but their questions and musings about humanity could practically be interchanged.

The stories of *Star Trek* are really no different from any of the tales drawn from "classic" literature. It's true that *Star Trek* exists not just on the page but primarily on TV and in film. But the same can now be said for many of the great and timeless authors of Western Civilization, from Homer to Virginia Woolf, whose works are often introduced to prospective readers on TV and at the movies.

Star Trek not only passes the test as literature, I would also suggest that no other "popular entertainment" draws as much from literary sources, or illuminates as brightly their themes, as *Star Trek*. Just as Shakespeare drew from Boccacio, Melville drew from the Old Testament, and modern horror writers still draw from Edgar Allan Poe and H.P. Lovecraft, *Star Trek* draws from both the letter and the spirit of many canonical authors. In fact, the show's characters themselves often seek comfort or guidance in literature. Captain Kirk shows a surprisingly wide-ranging knowledge of literature throughout the original series and in the subsequent films, including a perfectly timed impromptu recitation of a line from D.H. Lawrence's poem "Whales Weep Not" in *Star Trek IV*, after the humpback whales have been beamed aboard. Captain Picard frequently invokes lines from Shakespeare (the most memorable being his use of a *Hamlet* soliloquy to silence the menacing deity named "Q" after he attacks the character of humanity). Captain Janeway from *Star Trek*: *Voyager* really gets into literature — literally — by entering into novels that are reenacted in the holodeck (called "holonovels"), portraying characters from Victorian-era fiction. Throughout each of the series, major and minor characters often recite or refer to literary works. Jake Sisko, son of *Deep Space Nine*'s Commander Benjamin Sisko, even grows up to be a successful, award-winning writer; his *Collected Stories* wins the Betar Prize for Literature in 2391.[1]

Recognizing the connections between *Star Trek* and literature can open the door to a deeper and more enjoyable experience of all things *Trek*. Obviously, the TV shows, movies and books can be enjoyed simply for their entertainment value. But as William Shatner pointed out in the fan-written tribute volume *Star Trek Lives*:

> I think that the shows on the whole were of very good quality, that in the category of week-to-week television, it was superior. It was also different. In its kind of stories, and its means of storytelling, it lent itself to dualities of meaning, so that there were stories that could be told with significance and yet be entertaining. I think a contribution of that kind of entertainment is very rare today.[2]

Just as viewers of the original *Star Trek* were keenly aware of some important social currents which have been lost — or at least muted — among contemporary viewers (e.g. the Civil Rights movement, the Vietnam War), many fans have never considered the depth and importance of *Trek*'s debt to the literary figures, real and imagined, who transport in and out of the world of *Star Trek*: Mark Twain, Sherlock Holmes, William Shakespeare, even the pulp fiction writers of 1940s San Francisco. Knowing a little about these figures — what they wrote, what they represent — can add a measure of illumination and satisfaction to the *Trek* "canon."

This book explores specifically how *Star Trek* makes use of some familiar stories and themes found in Western literature. It should become clear that the same general fears, joys, problems and possibilities that have appealed to the greatest writers from the beginning of imaginative literature have also generated hundreds of hours of thought-soaked *Trek*. There are dozens of episodes and lots of moments in the movies that borrow, echo, or at least remind one, of "classic" stories from literature. This reliance on the accumulated body of stories which have been retold countless times is in keeping with the philosophical roots of *Star Trek*. Gene Roddenberry, the creator of the series, was deeply committed to humanism,[3] a belief system which emphasizes the worth of the individual rather than the authority of a remote deity (or, as Captain Kirk puts it at the end of *Star Trek V*, "Maybe God isn't out there; maybe he's right here" [pointing to his heart]).[4] One of the pillars of humanism is an embrace of classic literature. Instead of divinely inspired "sacred" texts, humanists turn to the imaginative literature of previous eras for revelations of mankind's dignity and potential. The stories from ancient Greece, Rome, the Italian Renaissance and subsequent literary periods reveal humanity at its best and point the way toward a future which endorses the values of the "humanities"—freedom, justice, equality. Roddenberry often spoke about the future—the 24th century of his own making—as a time when common human vices such as greed, jealousy and cruelty would be gone, replaced by those values illustrated by the great writers, from Aristotle to Orwell. The themes of classic literature are renewed with each voyage of the Starship *Enterprise*.

I have followed no quota system in my selection of *Trek* episodes to discuss. Devout fans of the five different *Trek* series could, no doubt, add lots more episode titles to each of my theme-based chapters. At its core, each *Star Trek* episode can be seen as illustrative of such themes as "Seeking to Know the Mind of God," or "The Limits of Technology." So instead of simply constructing laundry lists of episodes which comprise variations on a theme, I tried to focus on specific episodes which seem most representative, or helpful, in tracing connections between classic literature and *Star Trek*. (I've added a couple of appendices for readers who might want to see where a certain work of literature, or a certain episode, are discussed. The chapters can be read in any sequence, following whatever impulse is motivating you when you pick up the book.) In my ability to select whatever episodes I wanted, I felt somewhat like Q in his omnipotence. But that puckish deity also reminds us of the arrogance of unchecked power and the unreliability of a single perspective. No two *Trek* fans agree on the significance or interpretation of every episode—as any message board at any *Trek* fan website will prove. I merely want to add to the evidence that has already been amassed which testifies to the depth of *Trek*. I welcome disagreements and hope to challenge some widely held interpretations as well.[5]

Spending a little time thinking about the many bridges between *Star Trek* and literature might not change your life. But knowing that such connections exist, and choosing to look more deeply into those connections, is surely, in the words of Mr. Spock, "highly logical." I think it can also prove to be a great deal of fun.

ONE

The Journey of the Hero

Odysseus. Aeneas. Parsifal. Beowulf. King Arthur. Jason. From its very beginnings, and through every subsequent era, western literature has celebrated the achievements of the hero and his (usually, it's *his*—though sometimes it's *her*) quest to achieve some dauntingly difficult task. The canon of "classic" literature features a wide array of brave souls boldly going where no one has gone before. The qualities of heroism — courage, self-sacrifice, ingenuity — have kept readers entranced from the time Homer (or someone much like him) told tales of an intrepid voyager in search of home. The very idea of a hero, some critics have suggested, is embedded in the human psyche, a residual timeprint on the modern mind from our primitive past when (to invoke a time-honored cliché) only the strong survived.

Leaf through any standard literature anthology and you're likely to find the works arranged under section headings copied right from the hero's handbook: "A World of Danger," "Facing the Unknown," "Grace Under Pressure," "The Perils of the Natural World," and the like. Clearly, if there is a root system to the literary family tree of humanity, it is heroism in its many forms.

So where does Jim Kirk figure in all of this?

It's a question that needs asking. Countless fans of *Star Trek* have spoken of the "heroic" acts of James T. Kirk without perhaps considering whether the actions of their favorite *Star Trek* captain really conform to the ageless heroic mold.[1] But before tackling that question, we need to briefly examine a couple of the benchmark literary works which have helped shape our notion of the "hero" and see if Kirk really measures up to the literary notions of true heroism.

SHOW ME THE WAY TO GO HOME

Among the classics which portray the hero in action, two of the most important and instructive are the *Odyssey* (perhaps the first hero story in all of Western civilization) and *Beowulf* (the epic poem which marks the birth of "English" literature).

The *Odyssey* is the story of a Greek fellow named Odysseus, who after ten years of fighting the Trojan War spends the next ten years trying to get home. Widely credited to a Greek poet named Homer of the 9th or 8th century BC, the *Odyssey* recounts the story of the last several weeks of Odysseus' voyage home to Ithaca to reunite with his wife Penelope (who's been refusing all offers, reasonable and unreasonable, for twenty years) and his son Telemachus (whose own road trip to find his father occupies part of the larger narrative).

The *Odyssey* has been spellbinding readers (and, originally, listeners) for three millennia, largely because of the indefatigable main character, whose battles with all sorts of monsters, witches and even his own scheming, weak-willed crew mark him as incorruptible and quick-witted. Odysseus' heroism stems from his courage, of course — he's a noted warrior in Homer's companion volume, *The Iliad*, the story of the Trojan War — but his most heroic attribute is his cleverness. He frequently must create stratagems to win his freedom and continue his quest. If there is a unifying element in the various scenes that make up the *Odyssey*, it is Odysseus' craftiness. His ability to think his way out of trouble is his literary raison d'être. Later poets and playwrights sometimes used Odysseus as a model of not just intelligence but deceit and ruthlessness;[2] but in Homer, Odysseus uses his wits in the service of survival and for the greater good.

Beowulf gives us a slightly different kind of hero, one who would rather face death than lose a night's sleep worrying about that noise outside the cabin door. He is defined primarily by his physical prowess and his unflinching bravery. Whereas Odysseus finds himself the unwitting victim of the fates — and he devises clever stratagems to outwit his tormentors — Beowulf picks up the gauntlet that fate has thrown down and then slaps his foe right in the face.

The background, briefly: *Beowulf* is an epic poem written about 1000 AD by an unknown poet who was probably a scop (a medieval storyteller usually attached to a royal house). The story recounts the adventures of Beowulf, the strongest man alive, who brings a group of his fellow warriors with him from their home in Sweden to battle a vicious monster who's earned a reputation as the nastiest beast in Denmark (well earned, by the way — the beast, called Grendel, regularly stalks the local mead hall for a little late knight snack...). During their first meeting, Beowulf wrestles with Grendel while his comrades cower in fear — having just watched Grendel eat one of their drinking buddies. Beowulf rips Grendel's arm off at the shoulder, and the beast stalks away to die in his lair. Soon after, Grendel's mother comes to the mead hall and carries away a knight named Aeschere, a close friend of the king of the Danes. Beowulf tracks the beast to her lair (a blood-filled lake) and dives after her. He spends a day underwater, but finds her and, after one of the great battle scenes in all of literature, cuts off her head.

Beowulf returns to Sweden and becomes king, ruling for 50 years until he dies in hand-to-hand combat with a fire-breathing dragon. A young knight named Wiglaf assists Beowulf in his final battle, but the majority of his companions lose their nerve and avoid joining the fearsome fray. Their lack of courage condemns them to a life of shame and exile. Beowulf is revered as a great hero for future generations to venerate.

Throughout the epic, Beowulf is celebrated as a fierce fighter. True, he fights for the noblest of causes — the safety of his comrades, the sanctity of upholding an oath, a belief that God is on his side (though it's likely a pagan god) — but it is his battles that engage us, not his principles.

These two stories, different as they are, share many of the conventions of "heroic" literature still familiar today. From them we can enumerate some recognized qualities of the hero:

- Usually endowed with great physical or mental strength.
- Fearless, even in the most threatening situations.

- Acts decisively.
- Puts the safety and welfare of others before his own.
- Committed to a core set of values or beliefs that sustain him in battle.
- Leaves a legacy of improvement; changes the world for the better.

As our two examples show, there can of course be different "types" of heroes. Odysseus uses his intelligence as his weapon; Beowulf uses his sword. But both exhibit the heroic character traits enumerated above. In their individualized delineations, Odysseus and Beowulf can be said to represent two distinct types of the hero in literature, two approaches to living, which can be stated crudely as "man of thought" and "man of action." An excess of either (think of Hamlet — or his counterpart at the other end of the spectrum, Ahab) can lead to paralyzing psychological problems. And there are, of course, countless other "types" of heroes in literature, but generally, most of the great heroes in epic literature exhibit many of the qualities listed above.

So, to return to our question: is Captain Kirk — by the standards of classic literature — a hero? And if not, why do so many people *think* he's a hero?

THE CASEBOOK ON KIRK

If only Gene Roddenberry had originally referred to his proposed TV show as "Beowulf in Space" or "Odysseus in Space" (Arthur C. Clarke came a little closer), we'd have a quick and easy answer. Regrettably (for my purposes, anyway), Roddenberry famously referred to Star *Trek* as "Wagon Train to the stars." [3] That's not much help in answering our question, "Is Kirk a hero?" *Wagon Train* was a successful western television series which ran from 1958 to 1965 and featured a caravan of pioneers criss-crossing the plains as they interacted with hostile Indians, other settlers, colorful trappers and traders, etc.

Many critics and fans have written about Kirk as a "heroic" figure (the American Film Institute recently placed Kirk on its list of nominees for the "Top 50" movie heroes of all time),[4] but it is instructive to see what Roddenberry had in mind when he created the role. In *The Making of Star Trek,* Roddenberry's character sketch of the captain (originally called Robert T. April, and then Christopher Pike, and then finally James T. Kirk) is reprinted in full. Roddenberry's choice of words is intriguing at several points in the description, including this phrase: "A strong, complex personality, he is capable of action and decision which can verge on the heroic — and at the same time lives a continual battle with the self-doubt and the loneliness of command."[5]

Now that's interesting. Those words "can verge on the heroic" straddle both sides of our question, and the second part of the sentence adds an additional element of complexity to our "classic" hero. Odysseus and Beowulf were lots of things, but they never doubted themselves. Roddenberry spent a lot of time and ink fleshing out each of his characters — none more than his captain. He calls him a "Space Age Captain Horatio Hornblower," but also notes that "unlike most early explorers, he has an almost compulsive compassion for the rights and plights of others, alien as well as human."[6] Reading the early notes on the formation of April/Pike/Kirk, one would be hard pressed to plug him neatly into any of the literary types so common to classic literary adventure. Of course, even Roddenberry realized that the character on the page is frequently transfigured as stories wend their way through the creative process.

Perhaps the only way to get an answer to our question, "Is Kirk a hero?" is to see him at the end of the creative process (which, in television, means whatever made it into the broadcast episode), and judge for ourselves whether he acts in the mode of the hero we've outlined above. Let's examine Jim Kirk, as he first appeared, fully formed, in the *Star Trek* episode — and the pilot that sold the show — "Where No Man Has Gone Before." (The first pilot episode Roddenberry wrote, "The Cage," featured a different captain, Christopher Pike; the network rejected that pilot. It was Kirk's "Where No Man Has Gone Before" that sold the show.)

"WE'RE LEAVING THE GALAXY"

Before we even see Kirk in his debut, we hear him recording a Captain's log entry which immediately telegraphs the perils of the journey he and his crew are about to take.[7] "The impossible has happened," he announces, explaining that a piece of equipment from a space vessel that disappeared more than two centuries ago has been discovered by the *Enterprise*. Then, another seemingly "impossible" situation is introduced: Kirk is looking over a chessboard as Mr. Spock, the Vulcan science officer, tells him he's about to be checkmated. Kirk's response? He laughs, then makes a move that is (to quote the stunned Vulcan) "totally unexpected." Kirk wins the game.

Kirk is then informed the object from the lost space vessel is small enough to be brought on board — "*if you want to risk it.*" Kirk responds without hesitation: "Lock onto it."

In the first 90 seconds of this pilot episode, then, we've already gotten a taste of many of the qualities that would make Kirk so endearing to fans of the show: Cool under pressure (whether it's the threat of retrieving a piece of potentially dangerous space debris or the icy threats of Mr. Spock's irritating chess etiquette), decisive, good-humored and crafty. In fact, his besting of Mr. Spock will prove to be prescient. Kirk uses a last-minute stratagem to defeat a much stronger and over-confident enemy at the end of the episode — just as he defeated a much more logical chess opponent in this opening scene!

The episode revolves chiefly around the plight of a crew member, Lt. Gary Mitchell, a longtime friend of Kirk's who was mysteriously "zapped" by an electromagnetic charge when the *Enterprise* traveled through a force field at the edge of the known galaxy. Ever since getting jolted, Mitchell has developed supernatural mental and physical powers — as well as delusions of becoming Godlike.

The episode teeters back and forth between Kirk's feelings of friendship for Mitchell and his growing awareness that the supercharged Lieutenant poses a threat to the safety of the *Enterprise*. But when forced to choose between the welfare of his crew and his own unease over dispatching an old friend, he chooses his crew. He reluctantly agrees to strand Mitchell on a remote planet, and then when Mitchell breaks free of his forcefield-enclosed cell, Kirk goes after him alone, giving an order that if he doesn't return — or if Mitchell does — the remaining crew members must beam up to the *Enterprise* and then destroy the planet.

In the final face off, Kirk uses both psychology and physical force to battle Mitchell. Kirk is able to convince a female crewmember who was also "zapped" to use her powers to help subdue Mitchell, rather than join him as "God and Goddess" ruling their new planet. She agrees, and Mitchell is temporarily reduced to his former self. At which point, a good old-fashioned fistfight ensues between Kirk and Mitchell. Just when Kirk is about to clobber Mitchell with a rock, Mitchell regains his power and tosses Kirk off him. Mitchell stands before Kirk, radiant and vengeful, ready to annihilate him, when Kirk picks up a phaser rifle (which had proved useless against Mitchell moments earlier) and fires — not at Mitchell, but, cleverly, at a wall of rock behind Mitchell. The resulting avalanche buries Mitchell in the grave that he had fashioned for Kirk.

The final scene, after the bloodied and bruised Captain returns to the *Enterprise*, shows Kirk recording a "Captain's log" in which Mitchell is noted to have died in the service of the ship. "He didn't ask for what happened to him," Kirk explains to Spock.

KIRK: A HERO BY THE BOOK (MOSTLY)

On our scorecard of hero's virtues, Kirk would seem to have done pretty well: Though not endowed with superior physical strength, he nonetheless held his own during the fistfight with Mitchell (and would have won if Mitchell hadn't regained his super strength). If beating a Vulcan at chess can be considered proof of a superior intellect, Kirk must be given credit there as well. Throughout the episode he acted fearlessly — a trademark of all classic heroes — though not as decisively as a hero would (this was the necessary plot complication to keep Kirk from reaching an "easy" solution too early in the episode). Kirk frequently put the safety and welfare of others before his own — including his final log entry, when he "protected" Mitchell's reputation for posterity. He was committed to a core set of beliefs (at one time lecturing Mitchell on the need for Gods to show compassion), and the legacy of his adventure will be what it usually is on *Star Trek*: the advancement of knowledge, the further pushing of scientific boundaries for the benefit of future generations. Undoubtedly, his is a legacy of improvement.

And a tough act to follow. Captains Picard (*The Next Generation*), Janeway (*Voyager*) and Commander Sisko (*Deep Space Nine*) all differ from Kirk in many ways — yet each subsequent captain can lay claim to various heroic traits. Picard was deeply committed to a belief in rational problem solving and diplomacy, rather than brute contests of physical strength. That belief sustained him and often wrested glory from the jaws of defeat. Janeway acted decisively, even impulsively at times (perhaps that's a common difference between tea drinkers like Picard and coffee drinkers like Janeway?), and Sisko's fearlessness, his unflappability, was engagingly displayed whenever a hostile alien presence threatened his space station (dealing with the likes of Odo and Quark on a daily basis prepares one for any situation).

But the *Star Trek* captain who hews most closely to the "classical" hero of Western civilization and literature is James Tiberius Kirk, a man who, despite his humble Iowa upbringing, continues to go boldly (on TV, in film and countless *Star Trek* novels) where no man has gone before.

TWO

The Quest for Revenge

In the literary battle between forgiveness and revenge, the results are not very encouraging. In fact, it's been a rout. For every turned cheek, there are countless which got slapped. The urge to even the score has energized many narratives, dating back to Homer and the first revenge story, *The Iliad*. The reasons for this tendency seem clear enough. Where you have revenge, you have passion, anger, intense desire, pride... all the ingredients in the successful storyteller's recipe book. The greatest works of the greatest writers — Shakespeare, Milton, Melville — deal directly with our innate desire to even the score. Not coincidentally, the most memorable *Trek* episodes and movies also take revenge as their theme.

Revenge is an ancient theme, but the works which have done the most to establish the modern idea of revenge were written during the Renaissance, especially the drama from the late Elizabethan era. Shakespeare's *Hamlet* is probably the greatest of all revenge stories — and a pivotal work in numerous *Trek* episodes and movies. Understanding *Hamlet* is critical if one is to fully enjoy and be moved by several landmark *Trek* moments. Therefore, it's worth taking a brief trip back to Shakespeare's time to explore the revenge tragedy playbook which dramatists were working from, and to consider in what ways *Hamlet* is typical and in what ways it is unique.

Though now largely a literary footnote, the Roman writer Seneca did more to popularize the revenge play than any other writer did. His works — *The Trojan Women, The Mad Hercules, Oedipus* — are all adaptations of Greek playwrights' works. But it was those adaptations that taught many of the writers of Shakespeare's time how to construct a revenge play tragedy.[1] Seneca's plays were divided into five acts and featured soliloquies, as well as scenes of graphic violence and supernatural visitation.

Hamlet makes ample use of Senecan convention, though (as with all things Shakespeare) the source material gets absorbed and elevated almost beyond recognition. The tragedies of the Greeks, channeled through Seneca, were bloody — and not very subtle. Shakespeare's innovation was to take a fairly simple "You got *me* so now I have to get *you*" blueprint and cram in lots of ambiguity. That is, Shakespeare complicated the notion of "revenge," adding layers of moral complexity. Shakespeare doesn't really give you good guys to root for, or bad guys to root against. His heroes are flawed characters, filled with uncertainty. As a result, his revenge tragedies — with, again, *Hamlet* at the apex — morph into meditations on retribution (the Roman goddess of retribution, incidentally, was named "Nemesis") and moral justification. Hamlet, the character, agonizes over whether to commit murder — not because he's afraid to act or indecisive,[2] but rather because of the obvious contradiction of having to endorse murder in one instance while condemning it in another.

SPIRITS IN THE MATERIAL WORLD

For a play of such intellectual complexity, the plot of *Hamlet* is disarmingly simple. The prince of Denmark is brooding about the recent death of his father, the king. Hamlet's spirits don't get much of a lift, however, after Dad's ghost appears to him, delivering the news that he was murdered by his own brother, who is also the new husband (and king) of the widowed queen, Gertrude. Hamlet decides to check out the ghost's story through some psychological detective work. In the end, he concludes the ghost was right, but the new king is on to him, so they're now plotting to get each other. Hamlet uses his wits, but the king chooses poison. In the end, they both get it, along with anyone within earshot of those noisy canons that always seem to be firing around Elsinore Castle.

Hamlet's importance to the entire canon of *Trek* is paramount, and the many ways in which that particular play leeches into the episodes and movies (largely through snippets of dialogue from the play) need not be fully chronicled here.[3] But it is worth considering just why the play *Hamlet* was such a potent touchstone for the various *Trek* series writers. For all the critical ink which has been spilled trying to puzzle out its psychological sophistication, Shakespeare's most important play is really a roadmap for dealing with the choices we all must face: duty vs. desire, faith vs. certainty, life vs. "the undiscovered country" promised by death. *Hamlet* was the first real attempt in literature to explore the wrenching moral agony engendered by conscience. The desire for revenge poses the ultimate threat to one's moral code. It is sometimes easier to die for one's beliefs than to kill someone else to uphold those beliefs. Under the guise of a fairly straightforward "Did he do it?" whodunit, Hamlet the prince discovers the truth about himself while ostensibly solving the mystery at the heart of the play. But the real mystery to be solved is the mystery of human motivation, of what causes us to act, and whether those causes are worthy of action. Does the presence of anger — to the point of bloodthirstiness — indicate a proper response to a grievous deed (such as the murder of one's beloved father)? Or does such passion call into question our ability to reasonably conclude what is the right course of action? Hamlet's soliloquies could be said to comprise the first debates about *Trek*'s "prime directive."[4] "To be or not to be" is the question whose answer will govern the Federation's code of behavior. When is it appropriate to act? When is it not? Hamlet's contribution to the moral configuration of the *Trek* universe is as important as Zephram Cochrane's equations for warp speed.

THE PLAY'S THE THING

The original series episode "The Conscience of the King" — one of the many episodes from the various series to take its title from a line of *Hamlet*— is a perfect illustration of how the show appropriated and expanded the themes of Shakespeare's opus. To put the viewer in a Shakespearean frame of mind, the episode opens with a scene from one of the Bard's great tragedies being enacted on board the *Enterprise* by a troop of itinerant space age thespians. The scene is from *Macbeth*, and in what could have been simply a throwaway setup to establish mood, the writer opens with a play whose themes of ambition and bloodlust lead naturally into the plot of the episode — namely whether or not one of the actors of the troop is, in fact, a former mass-murdering war criminal. The aura of mystery created by the central question leads most fittingly into the recurrent allusions to *Hamlet*, whose central mystery also revolves around a possible act of murder.

The climactic scene of the episode takes place while the actors perform a scene from *Hamlet*, which acts like a palimpsest to the plot of the episode. Hamlet's father, a ghost from the past, speaks, while Captain Kirk tries to figure out if Karidian, the actor playing the ghost, is a ghost from his past, a brutal tyrant now masquerading as an aged, dignified actor. Lt. Riley, whose father may have been murdered by Karidian, delays (like Hamlet) over avenging his father because he's not sure if Karidian is guilty of the crime. Using *Hamlet*, the play, as a point of reference for the action unfolding on board the *Enterprise* reinforces all of the episode's main themes. Rather than simply trying to cram in lots of extra-credit-for-English-majors allusions to a classic work, the episode acquires a certain gravity, even a timelessness, by its cleverly echoed use of Shakespeare's play. The general story could have been told without the Shakespeare overlay — it is, in fact, a fairly overworked chestnut of many run-of-the-mill whodunits: can such a decent-seeming fellow *really* be guilty of murder? But as with Shakespeare's original handling of the material, the psychological complexities are expanded by a deepening of the basic mystery, and a further dramatic tension is wrested from the story by the recurrent motif of a "play within a play" just as in the original *Hamlet*. One can watch and enjoy the episode without ever having seen or read *Hamlet*, but for those who know the play, the way the characters morph in and out of their Hamlet-like counterparts provides an additional degree of enjoyment and understanding. *Hamlet* is one of the landmark works of Western literature — perhaps the single greatest literary achievement of the imaginative mind. Choosing to invoke its echoes is a bold decision, not least because of the certainty of coming up short against Shakespeare's greatest creation. One had better be sure the material can bear such critical comparisons. In this case, with the themes of war crimes and the need for retribution being the episode's chief concerns, the mirroring is apt. Shakespeare's play existed several centuries before the atrocities of modern war criminals became a blight on human history, but, as "Conscience of the King" proves, the search for justice and the thirst for revenge are timeless human preoccupations.

One thing the play *Hamlet* communicates is the driving need in the "moral individual" to be justified in one's quest for revenge, but many other literary works have given us characters who were not so troubled by whether they had "just cause." Sometimes characters lose sight of the original slight, and their hatred and bloodlust overwhelms them. The granddaddy of this character type is, without doubt, Captain Ahab, from Herman Melville's *Moby Dick*; and as we shall see, Ahab's maniacal quest has fueled some of the very best moments in the *Trek* canon.

A Madman's Wail

Melville's madman stands at the wheel of his ship, the *Pequod*, swearing vengeance on the creature that took his leg—and which has come to represent the presence of evil in his world. Much has been made of the symbolism of the White Whale—the pure energy of nature, the manifestation of beauty and power, primitive innocence, and countless other interpretations—but what the whale really represents is immaterial. It's what he represents *to Ahab* that is critical, and to a mind as ego-bloated and deluded as Ahab, the whale is simply the enemy, which must be destroyed at all cost. Whether the whale deserves Ahab's wrath is secondary. No rational thought has engendered Ahab's quest. His all-consuming passion for the whale's destruction has turned the creature into a totem of torment, a reminder to Ahab of his human frailty and a stinging rebuke to Ahab's delusions of omnipotence. Ahab seeks to destroy the whale not simply because of what he did to him—lots of other captains have had their bodies rearranged by the whale. Ahab has declared his war because the very idea of the whale's existence offends him.

Ahab often couches his verbal assaults on the whale in the phraseology of Christian soldiery (Melville, who knew his Bible well, takes Ahab's name from the biblical king who worshiped idols as if they were gods).[5] We get a taste of Ahab's all-consuming madness and his messianic delusions in passages such as this one, from the chapter titled

"The Candles," where Ahab thunders at his crew amid flashes of lightning, leading them in swearing oaths of allegiance during a demonic fire ceremony on the deck of the *Pequod* as they approach their encounter with the hated beast:

> The lightning flashes through my skull; mine eye-balls ache and ache; my whole beaten brain seems as beheaded, and rolling on some stunning ground. Oh, Oh! Yet blindfolded, yet will I talk to thee. Light though thou be, thou leapest out of darkness; but I am darkness leaping out of light, leaping out of thee! The javelins cease; open eyes; see, or not? There burn the flames! ... Here again with haughty agony, I read my sire. Leap! Leap up, and lick the sky! I leap with thee; I burn with thee; would fain be welded with thee; defyingly I worship thee![6]

In much of the *Star Trek* canon, one can often find echoes of a particular work of literature, but in the case of *Moby Dick*, the influence can be traced much more directly.[7] In fact, the one villain in the history of the *Star Trek* franchise who can be said to be cast in the same mold as Ahab has, we know, read *Moby Dick* himself, as we see the book on his shelf and hear him quote its passages. I'm speaking of course about Khan Noonien Soong, known simply as "Khan"— the most driven, egomaniacal and dangerous opponent ever faced down by a Federation captain. Khan was first seen in the popular original series episode "Space Seed," where we discover his Ahab-like taste for the demonic in his allusion to Milton's Satan in *Paradise Lost*—better to rule in hell than to serve in heaven. In *Star Trek II: The Wrath of Khan*, his anger at Kirk has simmered for twenty years, and his willingness to focus on his revenge — even at the cost of his crew, his son and his own life — establishes the parallel with Ahab (complete with quotations from *Moby Dick*, as when Khan, irritated by Kirk, intones "he tasks me!" just as Ahab does when explaining his driving need to annihilate the whale). Viewers who picked up on the frequent allusions to Melville's saga found a villain in Khan who was more metaphysically interesting than the run-of-the-mill cinematic black hat. The fact that Melville made Ahab a character who thought he was doing the right thing created the necessary moral ambiguity to make *Star Trek II* more than just an entertaining popcorn chomper. One can understand Khan's frustration at having been abandoned on a distant planet by Kirk and Company, and one can also sense his boiling animosity for the man responsible for his decades-long plight. Out of an emotional response not unlike that stew of pity and disdain one feels for Ahab, Khan emerges as someone who should be angry, but whose anger overrides his judgment and descends into monomania. Fans of *Moby Dick* knew, from the first glimpse of Melville's classic volume on Khan's desert-planet bookshelf, that this space Ahab would perish, leaving Kirk-Ishmael to tell the tale.

But Khan's hatred of James T. Kirk also partakes of another great literary tradition: the personal revenge fantasy. Following this template, someone who has been done wrong spends his days fantasizing about turning the tables on a personal enemy, even looking into his adversary's eyes as the enemy discovers the identity of his tormentor. Khan, unlike Ahab, wants to inflict pain on his tormentor (whereas Ahab simply wants to rid the world of his). Ahab has no desire to torment Moby Dick. When he gets his chance to kill the beast outright, he takes it. No psychological warfare is involved. But Khan is a different variety of villain, one who also draws upon the great wellspring of American Revenge Fantasy literature, which reached its apex in the work of Melville's contemporary, Edgar Allan Poe.

You Talkin' to Me?

One need look no further than Poe's "The Cask of Amontillado" to decode the literary paradigm for the "gotcha" template of revenge. An understanding of the role of personal animus in crafting a revenge story helps explain many a *Trek* villain — not only Khan but also the misunderstood antagonist at the center of *Star Trek X: Nemesis*, Shinzon, praetor of Romulus.

Many fans have derided Shinzon as "Khan Lite," but such a comparison is unfair. Whereas the pedigree for Khan's anger included biblical codes of justice and stretched from Milton to Melville to even Klingon proverbs, Shinzon exhibited a much more localized anger (dramatically justifiable, as Shinzon spent most of his life several thousand feet underground, in the dimly-lit world of Reman dilithium mines; one surmises his opportunity to peruse the classics was limited). And, as such, his quest for revenge is more personal and parochial — directed first against his former Romulan captors and then his current Federation nemesis, Captain Picard. While the movie may have failed to delineate fully the reasons for Shinzon's anger at Picard and his Federation counterparts, it does portray nicely his need to personalize his revenge — including the climactic face-off at the end where Shinzon waits to attack the *Enterprise* until he can look into the eyes of his nemesis. This is what revenge fantasy is all about, and it's why reading Poe is still such a chilling experience. Destroying an enemy is not enough. You have to leave your calling card so your enemy will know whom to thank. In Poe's "Amontillado," it is the character Fortunato who falls victim to the narrator's wrath. Admittedly, the revenge is disproportionate to the crime. Fortunato merely insulted the narrator's taste in wine, and for his sins he was walled up in an underground cavern. Psychotic behavior is also one of the earmarks of revenge fantasy, and the people seeking revenge have generally lost their grip on reality, as seems to be the case with Shinzon, who deteriorates before our eyes mentally as well as physically.

When Picard realizes that Shinzon won't strike out at the *Enterprise* until he can actually see Picard on his viewscreen because "he wants to look me in the eye,"[8] he is articulating a time-honored literary device in use from works as diverse as *The Count of Monte Cristo* to Mickey Spillane's Mike Hammer novels. And when Picard recognizes that fact (which he does, exclaiming "I've *got* him!"), the battle is won. Picard reverses the typical ending of the story because he recognizes the template, and, in the end, deprives Shinzon of his moment of triumph.

Star Trek has provided a pantheon of evil overachievers for four decades, many of whom have provided squirm-inducing thrills of singular horror. But the grim deeds of *Star Trek*'s villains have nothing on their literary predecessors.

THREE

Leaving Childhood Behind

Everyone grows up, but no two people view that experience the same way. It's perhaps ironic that so much of the mature prose from so many "classic" authors deals with the experience of childhood. The passage from youthful immaturity to the knowledge of the ways of the world has fascinated writers from Aesop to Zora Neale Hurston. Some of the most revered works in the English language — say, Blake's *Songs of Innocence and Experience*, or Wordsworth's *Prelude*—deal with the slippery psychology of childhood. Many of the canonized works of Western civilization testify to the preoccupation of the creative mind with those first few human years.

Perhaps not surprisingly, some of the most insightful and intriguing works that chart this psychic terrain are aimed at children themselves. Certain landmark works effectively hold up a mirror to the experience of childhood — its fears, joys, dreams and questions. Exploring the questions about childhood — Is it really a "golden time"? Do we ever truly graduate from childhood? What lessons from those years should we take into the adult world? — has generated a wealth of great reading. The very same questions Plato addressed and the same growth process charted by modern writers like James Joyce (all one needs to know about how a child sees the world can be gleaned from the first page of *A Portrait of the Artist as a Young Man*) have also been explored, thoughtfully and frequently, in *Star Trek*. This chapter will explore some classic works about childhood and their close connection to the world of *Trek*.

Many of the enduring literary works about "growing up" explore the notion of how difficult it is to leave childhood behind, from books which give us a glimpse of never-ending childhood (J.M. Barrie's *Peter Pan*) to those which question whether "childhood" even exists as a meaningful concept (William Golding's *Lord of the Flies*). And no discussion of "leaving childhood behind" can ignore the questions raised by "Pinocchio," a work that explores not only what it means to be a child but also what it means to be human. This is the question at the very heart of *Star Trek*.[1] Finally, there's Lewis Carroll's dreamy and bizarrely captivating *Alice in Wonderland*, a book which tells us much more about the *real* world children inhabit than the fanciful world of Wonderland.

Boys Will Be Boys

J.M. Barrie's 1904 classic, *Peter Pan*, is the ultimate ode to procrastination. The title character has come to represent the fabled "golden time" of childhood in his refusal to grow up. "Peter Pan" has become shorthand for prolonged immaturity, capturing the allure of a lifetime of play — and even lending the name to a psychological syndrome where an adult seeks to avoid responsibility and commitments of the grownup world.

The story is familiar: the boy Peter Pan has run away to Neverland, where he lives in the wild among fairies, his playmates "the lost boys," and the Darling children, whom he has enticed to leave their London home and join him for fun and games. Pan spends his days playing games and plotting against the evil Captain Hook. Eventually, the Darling children return home, but Wendy — the oldest daughter — promises Peter she'll return each spring.

The enduring popularity of *Peter Pan* — which has been made into a high-flying Broadway show and a much-beloved Disney film — is due, some critics suggest, to its portrayal of every adult's secret fantasy: to remain forever young. Pan's lost boys represent exactly that — the child who gets "lost" when youth gives way to maturity. Sure, they act a little wild, but that's their appeal. No rules, no bosses. Every day is Saturday; every hour brings another round of hide-and-seek. The only threat to the never-ending fun is Captain Hook, the nominal adult who's really only a part of the on-going game.

A half-century later, author William Golding turned the Pan story upside down. *Lord of the Flies* tells the story of a group of boys who are stranded on an island after their plane, which was fleeing atomic war in England, crashes. Right away, a reader can detect the Pan template's inversion. In *Peter Pan*, children learn to fly by thinking happy thoughts, and their flight takes them to magical places. In *Lord of the Flies*, the happy thought is "let's get out of here alive," and the idea of magically flying away to a better world crash lands on the terra firma of brutal reality.

Once on their island, the boys attempt to set up some type of leadership structure, but in-fighting, jealousy and violence mar their effort to deal with their increasingly adverse situation. The boys quarrel among themselves in their makeshift assemblies, held on the inlet of a lagoon (in *Peter Pan*, the lagoon is home to mermaids, frolicking in the surf and sunning themselves). Eventually, Golding's equivalent of the lost boys degenerate into scheming, murderous thugs, devoid of conscience and driven nearly insane in their brush with primitivism.

Two radically different views of childhood, two sets of children set free from the adult world, left to romp on their own and follow their own instincts. Can *Star Trek* be said to subscribe to either of these views? Well, the original series offered a classic episode that weighed in with a view of childhood which, remarkably, reconciled Barrie's utopia with Golding's dystopia in a masterfully clever, yet totally convincing, way.

CHILDHOOD'S END

The original series first-season episode "Miri" brings together the themes of an unsupervised group of lost boys (and girls) who engage in game playing, "rough housing" and juvenile indolence — with the occasional cruelty of Golding's flyboys — under the leadership of a Pan-like figure, a boy named Jahn. The children (called "onlies") find themselves alone after a disease has claimed the life of all adults on the planet. As if transplanted from Barrie's Neverland, the children have evolved lots of complex games and rituals, and have bonded in friendship and dependency. But these lost boys retain the edge of the dispossessed. Their attitude isn't "happy-go-lucky," largely because they've seen the tragedy of their peers who reach puberty (which in their world equals death; the disease which claimed the lives of all the adults on their world begins when childhood ends). Consequently, these children fear and distrust all adults they encounter, and they treat Kirk and company with hostility and brutality.

The episode is really impressive in its deft maneuvering between the dewy-eyed innocence of childhood (Kim Darby, who plays Miri, is affecting in her vulnerability and tragic sweetness) and the impulse toward violence, which is unleashed when the tight-knit community of "onlies" is threatened. It's as if the children in this episode have created a world that accepts the inevitability of death but have chosen to live as children anyway. Or, to return to our literary source material, it's the kind of story one would expect if Pan had visited Golding's island, or if the *Lord of the Flies* took place in Neverland. It's a complex portrayal that seems to suggest that although children *are* capable of extreme violence, they lack the capacity to truly hate. They react, but they don't despise. In *Star Trek*'s hybridization of these two stories, the message of both great works is refined. No one wants to leave the security of childhood, its plethora of joys and protection from the world of pain. But the violence and brutality of the adult world don't miraculously coalesce into being at puberty. They are there, as much a part of a child's world as the impulse to believe in fairies and flying pirate ships.

Keeping It Real

The story of Pinocchio, the wooden marionette who was granted the gift of life, is one of the most popular fantasy tales in the annals of children's literature around the world. As an icon, Pinocchio (and his nose, which grows with every lie he tells) is immediately recognizable. The interpretations that have accrued around Pinocchio are as numerous as the strings that animate a chorus of marionettes.

Pinocchio can be said to represent humanity before the fall: innocent, naïve, credulous. He is easy prey for the likes of fast-talking hucksters and duplicitous schemers. He represents belief in the perfection of the world. And his naïve wish to become "a real boy" rings hollow until he experiences firsthand the heartbreak and turmoil of humanity. But he *does* go through a learning process, and he does redeem himself. His reward is the gift of reality, not just existence.

The arc of Pinocchio's "life"—as an inanimate object created by an elder craftsman, his consciousness/activation, and his growing awareness of what it means to be human—must surely seem familiar to fans of *Trek*'s *The Next Generation* series. Commander Data, an android, is likened to Pinocchio in the series' pilot episode, "Encounter at Farpoint," after First Officer Will Riker visits the holodeck in search of the *Enterprise*'s new officer. What Riker finds both delights and disturbs him. Data's brutal honesty (in contrast to Pinocchio, Data is not conversant with the art of prevarication) disarms Riker. The android matter-of-factly states the case for his physical and intellectual superiority. At first, Riker is offended at this show of hubris, but his concerns about this "super being" are softened when Data admits that he would gladly sacrifice all of his advanced technology to become human.

"Nice to meet you, Pinocchio," Riker says.[2]

Throughout the seven-year run of *The Next Generation*, and in their films (*Star Trek VII* through *X*), Data had many "Pinocchio moments," times when his ignorance about the ways and whys of humanity made him sympathetic to viewers—but also got him into trouble. To discuss just one such moment, in the movie *Star Trek: Generations*, the seventh film in the franchise, there's a scene on an old-style British sailing frigate afloat in a holodeck-generated sea where everyone is laughing because Lt. Worf, who has just been promoted, has been dropped in the chilly water as a sort of initiation ritual. Wanting to contribute to the merriment, Data pushes the ship's doctor, Beverly Crusher, into the water—an act more cruel than comical. After being chastised for his behavior, Data flashes a puzzled look, which suggests he has no grasp of such a basic human concept as humor.

In the original *Pinocchio* story, written in 1883 by Collodi (the pen name of Carlo Lorenzi), Pinocchio's many missteps teach him right from wrong. His mechanical life is a learning curve en route to humanity. His sacrifice at the end of the story, his selfless rescue of the elderly Gepetto, earns him the prize of becoming "a real boy." So too Data, who in dozens of episodes and in the films moves closer to becoming "real." (Proof of his eventual "humanity" comes as his friends gather solemnly to mourn him after he sacrificed himself for Captain Picard at the end of *Star Trek: Nemesis*—just as Pinocchio put his own life in peril for Gepetto.)

So *Pinocchio* can be read on several levels, from the simplest children's story to a metaphor for salvation through sacrifice. In almost all interpretations of the story, Pinocchio can be said to represent a symbol of possibility, of movement from "controlled" to "controller," from a state of dormancy to an awakening. Pinocchio's strings, Data's programming: necessary connections to the physical world. But as Collodi, or Gene Roddenberry, knew, the important connections are the ones you can't see.

Lewis Carroll (actually, Charles Lutwidge Dodgson) also came to distrust the world he saw[3]—so he created a character, Alice, who saw through the eyes of a child, and he transmitted her vision in a perplexing and captivating narrative of childlike wonder.

Go Ask Alice

Alice in Wonderland, it can be argued, is one of the most influential texts of the *Star Trek* universe. Its premise serves as a template for many *Trek* adventures: a character is uprooted from his or her "normal" world, transported to a weird, unfamiliar landscape, and forced to cope with strange customs and bizarre, often threatening, creatures. Alice's adventures *are* the voyages of the Starship *Enterprise*, transposed. But the overriding similarities beg some larger, troubling questions: Does the world exist independent of our perception, or do we create our own reality? *Alice in Wonderland* is the apparent product of a dream—ephemeral, unreal. But how does the residue of that memory impact our lives? (*The Next Generation* explored this very question in the best episode of its seven-year run, "The Inner Light," discussed elsewhere in this book.) Other questions: what role do our own insecurities play in trying to determine if someone poses a real threat? Alice finds lots of menacing characters in her dream world, but are they really threatening? Or is Alice seeing the world through a skewed filter? How do we know what to be afraid of? Which fears should be faced and which should one flee from? Is someone's gigantism just a product of one's own diminished sense of self? Do all children find the adult world frightening? In what ways do we all — even adults — cling to childhood? And on and on, the questions could continue.

As I said, there are many *Trek* episodes where "Alice" themes come into play. The most obvious to longtime *Trek* fans is probably the original series episode "Shore Leave," in which Dr. McCoy not only watches a giant white rabbit race off to keep "a very important date," but also meets Alice herself. But perhaps the most interesting use of Lewis Carroll's opus is in the *Deep Space Nine* episode "Move Along Home."

Deep Space Nine lends itself more easily to Alice-based interpretations than any of the other *Trek* series because the parade of characters who pass through Commander Sisko's station usually do so after tumbling through a "wormhole" — the space-age equivalent of Alice's rabbit hole. Plus, as a port of call (rather than on a single, specific Federation starship, which is where the other series take place), lots of odd creatures from different worlds naturally bump into each other, often causing the kind of confusion Alice found in her Wonderland when she tried to get directions — or even a straight answer.

In the episode "Move Along Home," a group of formerly-unknown aliens from the Gamma Quadrant arrive at Deep Space Nine and force Quark, the proprietor of a crooked gaming establishment, to play a strange game in which Federation crew members become human pieces being moved around some weird, virtual-reality labyrinth. This strange race of game-playing aliens uses oblique, threatening language which suggests the game is one of life-and-death, creating an atmosphere of anxiety among the already-shaky Quark and his saloon mates. And the crew members grope along a shifting landscape, filled with Wonderland-type traps, fearing for their own safety and seeking answers to the riddle of their location.

This uneasy alliance of game/reality creates some real dramatic tension until the end of the episode, when the whole exercise is revealed to be merely a diversion for this strange race of masochistic visitors. There were never any real stakes, and the crew is returned a bit shaken but intact, just as Alice awoke from her Wonderland journey. Yet the experience of mutual confusion and terror has brought the crew closer together, and in Quark's genuine distress over the crew's fate, he exhibits a vulnerability and honesty which make his character more sympathetic.

Shaking off the psychic residue of a mind-altering dream is not easy. Both Alice and her many heirs in the *Star Trek* world implicitly endorse a belief that things that happen to one in a heightened state of consciousness can help guide one's life during more "normal" times. Every experience teaches a lesson, and in the case of *Star Trek* and some of the classic works of literature which look at the difficult journey from childhood to maturity, it's often a lesson that leaves one sadder but wiser. As Alice says in the final paragraph of her account of her Wonderland experience:

> Lastly, she pictured to herself how this same little sister of hers would, in the after-time, be herself a grown woman; and how she would keep, through all her ripe years, the simple and loving heart of her childhood: and how she would gather about her other little children, and make their eyes bright and eager with many a strange tale, perhaps even with the dream of Wonderland of long ago. And how she would feel with all their simple sorrows, and find a pleasure in all their simple joys, remembering her own child-life, and the happy summer days.[4]

FOUR

The Pain of Love

Here's a precious irony: the one character in the history of television who most exemplifies logic, detachment, and emotional control is also the one who suffers near-fatal bouts of lust, enduring pains during a mating cycle which must be satiated — or else. Among the many enigmatic characters *Trek* has presented over the years — and even the minor personages usually have complex, richly drawn selves — no one comes near the beloved status of the icy Vulcan science officer Mr. Spock, played with an almost felonious understatement by the estimable actor-director Leonard Nimoy. For many fans of the original series, Spock *is Star Trek*, and there is plenty of anecdotal evidence to suggest that Spock's elusive appeal helped keep the show alive. (Indeed, Spock's fan mail was such that the actor needed to hire a private secretary during the show's original run just to handle the volume.[1]) But Spock is interesting to viewers because he is inescapably contradictory, a set of unresolved tensions. The contradiction is apparent when one considers that everybody loves Spock as a character, but no one in his or her right mind would choose to live *as* Spock. He's a curiosity — no more so than in the arena of love.

To understand the delicate and dangerous idea of Spock as a romantic partner, one must venture into the world of Vulcan physiognomy. *Star Trek* has presented several Vulcans, and they all give us humans pause. What must it be like to live as a being divorced from those elemental aspects of humanity which the greatest artists celebrate in poetry, prose, music and painting? There is something in the human propensity for overstatement that makes "the pain of love" a rather quaint and wry expression. But for Vulcans, it's dead on.

Before exploring the consequences of unrequited Vulcan amour, it's worth revisiting some timeless statements from classic literature about the pain of love. As shall become clear from a consideration of some famous fictional manifestos of attraction, the idea of love as a sensation that can cause great pain has been appropriated by *Star Trek*—with a few subtle twists on the work of Shakespeare, Edna St. Vincent Millay, and Vladimir Nabokov.

WHEREFORE ART THOU?

Any writer in the last 400 years who has weighed in on the plights and delights of romantic love has probably paused to consider how what he or she wanted to say differs from the Ur-text of romantic angst, the most famous statement of love's agony, Shakespeare's *Romeo and Juliet*. The Elizabethan-era romantic tragedy is as well known today — better known, in fact — as when it first mesmerized audiences at London's Globe Theater. A lot has changed in 400 years, but apparently the invidious sting of adolescent love remains constant. Romeo and Juliet are not just a fictional couple who long for each other against the wishes of their families. Their names have become bywords for the pain of thwarted passion.

The timeworn story predates Shakespeare by as much as Shakespeare predates *Star Trek*. Two lovers who happen to be children of feuding families find their romance prohibited by inflexible, unreasonable parents. But being in love, being young, and being characters in a drama requiring a compelling plot, they find a way to carry on their love in secret. Flush in the throes of new love, they feel every sensation at a heightened level: joy, lust, rage, more lust. They desire each other deeply enough to counter their families' prohibitions on seeing each other, and risk banishment and even death to continue their romance. Nothing will come between them, they vow. What drives them to be together is beyond their control, no longer rational, transposed into an extension of the natural world:

> JULIET: 'Tis almost morning; I would have thee gone,
>   And yet no further than a wanton's bird,
>   Who lets it hop a little from her hand,
>   Like a poor prisoner in his twisted gyves,
>   And with a silken thread plucks it back again,
>   So loving-jealous of his liberty.
> ROMEO: I would I were thy bird.
> JULIET: Sweet, so would I,
>   Yet I should kill thee with much cherishing [II, ii].[2]

Romeo and Juliet get so swept up in their mutual desire that they become blind to what awaits them — though their creator, Shakespeare, frequently hints that their ending will be unhappy (tipping his hand even in the prologue to the play, calling the lovers "star crossed"). They are so smitten with each other that they seem powerless to prevent their own foolish and dangerous behavior. It is this idea of a force driving them, something beyond their conscious control, that becomes important in the *Trek* template of love.

In *Romeo and Juliet*, romantic desire cannot be denied — even if it means death. In *Star Trek*, that notion is preserved in the concept of *pon farr*, the name given to the Vulcan mating cycle, which impels every adult Vulcan to satisfy an intense mating drive every seven years. Failure to act on the feelings of *pon farr*—which is really a periodic neurochemical disruption in the brain — can be fatal. This "blood fever" has been the subject of several *Star Trek* episodes, providing a rare glimpse into what most Vulcans spend their waking hours avoiding: passion. (Spock, it should be pointed out — actually, he points it out many times to Dr. McCoy and others — is only *half*-Vulcan; he had a human mother.) Beyond an intriguing plot device, the concept of *pon farr* has given *Trek*'s writers a chance to explore those urges which provide psychic locomotion, those feelings and drives which make us do the things we do. If Spock, after all, can't control his mating drives, what chance does the womanizing James T. Kirk have of curbing his libidinous desires — even in the cold climes of outer space?

That's one of *Trek*'s signature strengths, raising questions under the guise of its intergalactic ethos which really impact us here and now. Are biochemical urges to be acted upon? Ignored? Treated pharmacologically? Indulged? Shakespeare gave us a young couple that seemed powerless to resist their mutual attraction, and he laid the blame for their destruction at their families' feet. *Star Trek* gives us Vulcans, at the apex of their mating cycle, similarly powerless to resist — but instead of being able to point to an outside culprit, *Trek* makes the very urge the culprit itself. We can't blame Spock, or his fellow Vulcans, for acting on urges which are both destructive and a part of their neurology. What *Trek* has done is graft post–Freudian awareness of sexual drives onto the timeless fascination of human attraction to give us a rich hybrid of human desire, which both honors a literary tradition but takes it into the modern era.

The first examination of *pon farr* occurred in the original series episode "Amok Time." The episode begins with a discussion between McCoy and Kirk about some increasingly strange behavior on the part of Spock. Kirk theorizes that Spock may just be in one of his "contemplative phases." But just then, in the middle of their conversation, Spock has an outburst, throwing his lunch tray in the hallway, raising his voice at Kirk and demanding to be taken to his home planet of Vulcan. There is a sense of urgency in his words that certainly seems un–Spock-like.

Kirk presses Spock for his reasons for wanting a leave. Spock reluctantly offers the equivocal answer that "I need rest — on Vulcan." Kirk consents, but then receives orders to alter course to accommodate a changing timetable for a previously scheduled diplomatic mission. Spock secretly countermands those orders; and while Kirk tries to make sense of this mutinous behavior, he learns from McCoy that Spock must get to Vulcan — or die.

Leonard Nimoy's performance in the episode rises above the sometimes-melodramatic script, infusing the onset of *pon farr* with genuine pathos and just the right touch of modesty. Spock seems almost in as much pain admitting that he's suffering from *pon farr* as from the actual symptoms themselves. Kirk tries to console Spock, telling him there's nothing to be ashamed of, that it happens "to the birds and bees." Nimoy delivers a string of broken lines with searing sincerity: "The birds and bees are not Vulcans, Captain. If they were, if any creature as proudly logical as us... to have our logic ripped from us as this time does to us... humans have no conception... it strips our minds from us, brings a madness which rips away our veneer of civilization. It is the *pon farr*, the time of mating."[3]

There's the rub. Spock hates what's happening to him, but he is powerless to resist. He cannot seek solace in even his shipboard comrades, for they are incapable of understanding his pain, and it shames the Vulcan in the mere telling. The fact that Spock shares this information with Kirk is another sign of their unusually deep connection, and it adds a further ironic twist to the ending, when Spock is required to vanquish the foe of his mate's choosing — and she chooses Kirk.

There's a touch here of Romeo and Juliet in space: lovers facing death, fighting for the right to conjoin. There are sword fights, cultural traditions that must be acknowledged, authority figures who are inflexible, and rule breakers who will assist the lovers (Friar Lawrence, James T. Kirk). But *Trek*, being *Trek*, adds a few twists to the already problematic situation. "Amok Time" goes beyond a simplistic morality play by introducing elements of Spock's mutinous behavior and putting his friendship with Kirk in lethal jeopardy. The episode unearths rivalries as well as affections (Spock loves Kirk, but Spock must kill him), history opposed to the future (the *pon farr* rituals stretch back to the beginning of time on Vulcan), and humanity's values versus those of "alien" cultures. It's a rich stew of overlapping fidelities, a Gordian knot of connections almost too deeply embedded to untie.

THANK HEAVEN FOR LITTLE GIRLS

The mix of insatiable desire, undeniable longing, guilt and divided loyalties which underlie "Amok Time" are present in explosive amounts in one of the great literary texts of the twentieth century, *Lolita*, which comes about as close as literature gets to showing the human equivalent of *pon farr*. In fact, we get the pain of *pon farr* in the very first line of the narrative: "Lolita, light of my life, fire of my loins." Vladimir Nabokov's lust-fueled protagonist, Humbert Humbert, may not share Mr. Spock's integrity (he is, after all, a rapist, child molester, kidnapper and murderer), but the scenes in which Nabokov shares the pain of Humbert's unfulfilled urges read like excerpts from the Vulcan book of mating cycles. Nabokov peppers his text with such *pon farr*-like phrases as "the hidden tumor of an unspeakable passion," the "throb of the longest ecstasy man or monster had ever known," and, plainly but powerfully, "never have I experienced such agony."[4] These are all variations on the "fire of my loins" theme, and they — and hundreds of other direct references throughout 1955's international best seller—testify to the power (at times, and in some human subjects) of the pain of love. *Lolita* predated *Trek* by a decade, but the psychological complexity and sexual frankness of Humbert Humbert—a European sophisticate, a letch, a glib raconteur, a liar, a scholar—must have appealed to Gene Roddenberry, a writer who consciously explored the many personas of the human personality. As Roddenberry once explained,

> I love this world. I love its people. And when I present myself to this world, then that's who I am—outside. Inside, I am a great many things. I'm not just one person. As you are not. But that's what makes us creators. That's what makes us able to meet and to experience so many people as they are. And to enter into experiences we couldn't otherwise have. If we were not multidimensional, we could never be writers.... But humans have a great need to define themselves. I don't. I don't like to define myself, because as soon as I do, I realize that I have put imitations on how others perceive me.[5]

As Humbert Humbert puts it, "I feel my slippery self eluding me, gliding into deeper and darker waters...."

People, then, are more than they appear. They harbor buried desires, unspoken regrets, even hidden lives. And when the hidden thing is a past love, sometimes you get poetry—a way of remembering, of working through the pain of love's loss:

> What lips my lips have kissed, and where, and why,
> I have forgotten, and what arms have lain
> Under my head till morning: but the rain
> Is full of ghosts tonight, that tap and sigh
> Upon the glass and listen for reply,
> And in my heart there stirs a quiet pain
> For unremembered lads that not again
> Will turn to me at midnight with a cry.
> Thus in the winter stands the lonely tree,
> Nor knows what birds have vanished one by one,
> Yet knows its boughs more silent than before:
> I cannot say what loves have come and gone,
> I only know that summer sang in me
> A little while, that in me sings no more.[6]

Edna St. Vincent Millay's famous sonnet in praise of love come and gone captures a side of desire which is perhaps more common—

and certainly more congenial — than the harsh, physical pains of love previously discussed. Millay's ode, a potent testament to the omnipresence of all those whom one has ever loved, is also a fitting template for an episode of the original series which many fans consider the best single hour of *Trek*, "City on the Edge of Forever." If Spock and his Vulcan brethren must deal with wrenching physical pain stemming from desire, then Kirk must have his turn as representative human lover — until he, too, loses what he loves. In Millay's world, and in Kirk's, the rain is always full of ghosts. One of those ghosts is named Edith Keeler.

WHAT'S DONE *CAN* BE UNDONE

"City on the Edge of Forever" hits many of the marks which define *Star Trek*: there is a compelling science fiction story (penned by no less an eminent sci-fi scribe than Harlan Ellison), time travel, social commentary and a taut timeframe in which the mission must be accomplished. Plus, the fate of humanity also hangs in the balance. Typical *Trek*.

But the episode also gives us the most powerful and painful romantic relationship fans of *Trek* would ever experience in the show's history, and it is this romantic angle that elevates the episode to greatness. Kirk, womanizer without peer, not only experiences gut-level affection but also must give it up, willingly sacrificing his heart's desire and allowing this deeply-affecting woman to meet an untimely death while he looks on impotently. It is powerful stuff.

Here's the plot, briefly: McCoy, in a fit of delirium because of an accidental overdose of an experimental drug, beams down to a planet which the *Enterprise* had come to investigate. Kirk and the rest of the crew beam down to find McCoy, and also a large, living machine called the "Guardian of Forever," a kind of gigantic TV screen showing images of Earth's past. McCoy leaps through the portal like screen, Kirk and Spock follow. They all end up in New York City, around the time of the Great Depression. Kirk meets a social worker named Edith Keeler, who runs a soup kitchen and homeless shelter. While those two are walking around New York, falling in love, Spock discovers how to graft 1930's technology onto his tri-corder, and in doing so, he discovers that because of the *Enterprise* crew's presence in the past, there are now *two* possible timelines for Edith Keeler: She will either launch a highly successful pacifist campaign that delays U.S. entry into WWII (allowing the Nazis to triumph and obviously altering human history), or she will die in a traffic accident and the more familiar timeline will occur.

In the episode's climactic scene, McCoy is about to save Edith from an oncoming car, but Kirk restrains him. Kirk's pain is manifest in his body language, and he exudes a deep sense of regret. There's little doubt that this is James T. Kirk's toughest command decision (interestingly, in the original draft, Kirk freezes at the scene and it's Spock who must keep McCoy from acting).[6] This is a difficult plot point to pull off convincingly because most rational people would, one presumes, also choose as Kirk does, given the stakes of his decision, so that limits the potential dramatic tension. The episode has to create such a heightened sense of affection between the two romantic leads that they might be expected to act irrationally. Just as Romeo and Juliet acted irrationally, and Humbert Humbert certainly acted irrationally, why not Kirk and Edith Keeler? After all, love does funny things to a person.

Yet it is Edna St. Vincent Millay's view of love which predominates, a rational but also regretful perspective. Millay's poem provides the necessary distance to revisit lost loves, in all their pain and glory, with a wry sense of remembrance. When she laments that summer "will sing in me no more," such a matter-of-fact assessment seems disarming, but also accurate. Each lost love takes its toll, each relationship nibbles away at something irreplaceable. When Kirk returns to the *Enterprise*, he will be hundreds of years removed from Keeler's time, from their shared past. And Kirk will have lots of relationships after this one, of course, but the depth of his love — and sacrifice — ensure that the memory of their New York encounter will become one of the friendly ghosts that haunts him throughout his career.

"And in my heart there stirs a quiet pain," Millay wrote. So love hurts. At least on board the *Enterprise*. *Star Trek* seldom sank to the depths of simplistic television romanticizing. *Star Trek*, in each of its series, gave us painful partings, difficult relationships, heart-wrenching choices and a comet's tail worth of regret. Love, on this *Trek*, was always highly prized — and highly priced. But there is some comfort, one supposes, that even in the scientifically advanced twenty-fourth century, no one seems to have figured out love's complexities. The Starship *Enterprise* may have been on a five-year mission, but the journey to find love appears to be timeless.

FIVE

The Way of the West

The scene is one of the most familiar in imaginative literature: a man alone, walking purposefully down some dusty street, solemn and resolved, towards a waiting foe or posse arrayed menacingly in black, partly eclipsed in shadow. Outnumbered and out of time, our hero strides to his spot nonetheless, turning to face off with the dark contingent twenty paces away. Throw in, if you wish, the furrowed countenances of the townspeople, peeking through blinds and peering around cisterns. And, for some additional last minute drama, a whore with a heart of gold who rushes between the two sides, pleading for an end to the senseless cycle of killing, until the barber, or the saloon keeper — or both — drag her back to safety and clear the street for the inevitable showdown.

This picture owes its clarity, its mutability and its permanence in the mental landscape to the conventions first established by the literary genre known as the "Western," a vein of writing which constitutes, in the words of one critic, "America's contribution to world culture."[1] There's no question that the benchmarks of the western have become standard global fare — largely through the vehicle of film. From the classic western movies of John Ford to the delightfully weird, spare "spaghetti westerns" by Italian filmmaker Sergio Leone, the whole culture of the cowboy has thrived for more than a century. But it owes its existence — and its colorful, codified format — to literature. Critics and fans of the world of the Old West can trace many of its trail-hardened features to a handful of works that emerged in the late nineteenth and early twentieth century. From these works, American readers—and artists, photographers, writers, singers, dramatists and screenwriters— disseminated a vision of the Old West that became as well worn as the Old Chisholm Trail. Though much of the early literature of the American West was comprised of throwaway pulp and cheap romanticizing, some work of enduring literary value emerged from the dust of this authorial trailblazing. Those benchmark works which have bequeathed to us the sights and sounds of a long-extinct frontier featured a rich combination of historical detail, American idealism, and even—if the critics are to be believed—a pedigree that stretches back to the celebrated tales of Medieval chivalry.

The most important of these works was written by a man who was dispatched to Wyoming after a mental breakdown in 1885. It was hoped he would regain his health on the open frontier. He recovered his wits, and uncovered a culture he deemed worthy of the very best writers of his generation. His name was Owen Wister, and his novel, *The Virginian,* remains one of the best-selling Westerns every published.

WRITE 'EM, COWBOY

A Harvard-graduated composer and, eventually, a lawyer, Owen Wister seems at first blush an unlikely candidate for literature's most passionate chronicler of the cowboy. But that's what he was, and in a series of short stories and books leading up to *The Virginian* (which was published in 1902), Wister laid down the tracks for the train of authors waiting to depart for the great, undiscovered fictional frontier.[2] Wister's education and training made him, in fact, the perfect person to meld the "sophistication" of the East (he was educated at private schools throughout Europe and was close friends with Henry James) to the rough-and-ready character of the cowpuncher (he was also friends with Theodore Roosevelt, the dedicatee of *The Virginian*). Wister saw the cowboy as somehow representative of the American ideal of freedom, while linking us to the storied, romantic past of our European forbears. As he put it in *The Virginian*'s prefatory "To the Reader," the cowboy "will be here among us always, invisible, waiting his chance to live and play as he would like. His wild kind has been among us always, since the beginning: a young man with his temptations, a hero without wings."³

It would perhaps be too easy to point out that James T. Kirk is a hero *with* wings, and at the risk of stretching the metaphor beyond logic, it is worth remembering that *Star Trek* creator Gene Roddenberry envisioned the show to be "*Wagon Train*" in space, and that the western ideal profoundly resonated with Roddenberry. To understand the original five-year mission of the *Enterprise*, and to fully appreciate much of what followed in the various series over the past four decades, it's worthwhile to consider *Star Trek* in light of the fiction of the frontier in general and Wister's work in particular. Many of the conventions of the western were first adumbrated in *The Virginian*—conventions that were not lost on *Star Trek*'s scriptwriters.

THE MAN WITH NO NAME

Primarily, *The Virginian* established the idea of the cowboy as hero. The Virginian himself is an otherwise-nameless figure who represents what we now think of as the Western hero: laconic, no-nonsense, fearless, efficient with a gun or an axe. It is from *The Virginian* that we also get a description of the frontier town, those anonymous facades comprised of (usually) a saloon, a hotel, a sheriff's office, a stable, a blacksmith and a railroad station. And, perhaps most importantly, it is from this work that the idea of the American romance with the wide-open spaces of the West found its widest and most popular expression since *Huckleberry Finn*. Here's a passage of vintage Wister (which, we shall see, profoundly informs the entire concept of *Star Trek*):

> At noon, when for a while I had thrown off my long oilskin coat, merely the sight of the newspaper half crowded into my pocket had been a displeasing reminder of the railway, and cities, and affairs. But for its possible help to build fires, it would have come no farther with me. The great levels around me lay cooled and freed of dust by the wet weather, and full of sweet airs. Far in front the foot-hills rose through the rain, indefinite and mystic. I wanted no speech with anyone, nor to be near human beings at all. I was steeped in a reverie as of the primal earth; even thoughts themselves had almost ceased motion. To lie down with wild animals, with elk and deer, would have made my waking dream

complete; and since such dream could not be, the cattle around the deserted buildings, mere dots across separating space, were my proper companions for the evening.[4]

That's Wister's vision, and his mantra: wide-open space, "mystic and indefinite," with brave cowboys boldly going where no man has gone before. Though Wister's cowboy is a man more at home living among the elk than swapping stories at the Elk's lodge, he's no rube. Perhaps Wister's greatest contribution to the western mythos of the cowboy — and the one of the greatest importance to *Star Trek* — is the moral code he gives his hero. The Virginian is a man who tries to avoid violence whenever possible. He seeks to solve problems, even when provoked — through a sort of frontier diplomacy. The very first scene in the book provides a glimpse of *The Virginian*'s alternative approach to problem solving. While a group of tenderfoot cowboys brusquely tries to lasso an uncooperative horse — racing at it, chasing it around a pen, flinging their ropes wildly in its direction — the Virginian simply walks nonchalantly around the horse and then, after winning its confidence, flicks his wrist, and the rope is firmly around the horse's neck. In another scene ripe for conflict, the Virginian uses his wits to convince a high-strung, somewhat obnoxious traveling salesman to surrender his bed for the night, rather than confront the man in a public showdown over who ought to get the bed.

The most important display of the Virginian's violence-as-a-last-resort posture comes on the day before his wedding, when Trampas, our hero's sworn enemy, tells the Virginian to get out of town by nightfall or else he's gonna come looking for him. "I don't want trouble with you," the Virginian tells him, to little effect. Later, as he explains the ticklish position he's in to his fiancée — who tries, of course, to talk him out of keeping the appointment — Wister's protagonist explains the vintage "a man's gotta do what a man's gotta do" code of conduct:

> "I am goin' my own course," he broke in. "Can't yu' see how it must be about a man? It's not for their benefit, friends or enemies, that I have got this thing to do.... Don't I owe my own honesty something better than this?"[5]

The gun battle proves anti-climactic. The whiskey-besotted Trampas fires but only grazes the Virginian, who fires back twice, then mutters to no one in particular, "I expect that's all." And he walks away.

The allure of the Western has proved irresistible to *Star Trek*'s creative brain trust. Its most significant use of the cowboy motif can be found in the original series episode "Spectre of a Gun," and in the most recent series, *Enterprise*, in the episode "North Star." In both episodes, one finds the basic template undisturbed. Yet each example offers a glimpse into the way *Star Trek* has cleverly appropriated some established themes and made them very much their own.

EVERYTHING IS OK

In "Spectre of a Gun," Kirk and his crew find themselves transported by a mysterious race called the Melkotians to a planet that is barren, except for a ramshackle Old West–style town. They soon discover, much to their dismay, that they've been cast as the ill-fated Clanton gang in the seminal battle of western legend, "the Gunfight at the OK Corral." This most famous of all historical shootouts occurred in the aptly-named town of Tombstone, Arizona, on October 26, 1881, with the Earp brothers (Virgil Earp was the putative marshal, assisted by brothers Wyatt and Morgan) brandishing sidearms against Ike Clanton and his largely-disreputable cohorts.

Simply putting the *Star Trek* characters in the conventional western genre would have been sufficient to create some amusement and interest in how Kirk and Co. would perform as cowboys. After all, Kirk has often been referred to as a space cowboy by many fans and critics. But placing them in this particular historical moment heightens the dramatic tension because we know what happened to the Clantons. The Earps, assisted by the famously consumptive Doc Holliday, filled most of the Clanton gang with fatal doses of lead. If Kirk, Spock, and McCoy are the Clantons, aren't they doomed to suffer the same fate? The episode hews closely to the conventions of the western (a blustering but cowardly sheriff, bad guys daring you to reach for yer shootin' iron, whiskey-soaked villains terrorizing the town folk, innocent maidens planning weddings as the undertaker fashions pine boxes, lots of closeups of the clock ticking toward the fateful five o'clock hour...). The only way for the Clantons to triumph in this re-encounter is to somehow change the rules of the conflict. This allows *Star Trek* to do what it does best: take a historically-accurate no-win situation and apply the enlightened thinking of the twenty-fourth century — offering an implied lesson in how much better a conflict *could* have been handled.

Employing a typically bold Roddenberry-esque historical twist, the space-age Clantons use the power of their mind — and its ability to create a new reality — to change the seemingly-inevitable ending. The crew discovers — in the genre-dictated nick of time — that the only threat posed by the re-enactors of the legendary western feud is if Kirk and his comrades *believe* themselves to be in danger. Spock convinces the crew to imagine the bullets simply passing through them with no effect. If we don't think the bullets can hurt us, they agree to conclude, then they can't. And, of course, they don't.

Thus, through Kirk, Spock and McCoy's determination to avoid repeating the famous, violent denouement (with Kirk at one point screaming at the sheriff that he won't kill the Earps, even though he's being goaded into the battle by the sheriff himself), they re-write the bloody ending to the famous face-off. Such a resolution to the conflict takes the impulse toward non-violence embedded in westerns such as *The Virginian* and infuses it with a zen-like humanism (reminiscent of the Buddha's ability to turn arrows fired in wrath into flowers). And it should be remembered that, for all his talk of avoidance of conflict, in the end the Virginian faces his opponent and shoots him dead. At the end of "Spectre of a Gun," Kirk is offered the same chance. After Wyatt Earp empties both his guns into Kirk, the captain takes out his gun, holds it in front of him, ponders for a moment his position, and then drops it.

The final scene of the episode has Kirk being contacted on the bridge of the *Enterprise* by the Melkotians, asking him why he didn't shoot Earp. Kirk explains that such violence, though common in 1881, is no longer the way of his people, the human race. He and his crew are promptly invited to the Melkotian planet to establish friendly relations. James Kirk has lived up to his reputation as a space cowboy, but the code of the Old West acquired some striking new twists.

THE NORTH STAR

Star Trek has recycled the frontier motif in various ways over the past four decades, but perhaps the episode which serves as the most fitting legacy to the ideas which informed "The Spectre of the Gun" is the *Enterprise* episode "North Star." It establishes its debt to the genre's conventions quickly. The opening scene features a torch-bearing posse galloping through town, followed by the requisite exchange of scowls and insults at the local "hanging tree"—soon to be the site of another lynching. The camera's choreography is ripped from the catalog of western images, with the moment of actual hanging filmed from the obligatory ankle angle. But lest the reader expect a by-the-numbers Western tale, *Enterprise* delivers an engaging episode built on some unexpected, un-genre-like, twists.

"North Star" evolves from high-style Western to cultural parable. The premise is this: Captain Archer and his crew come across a mysterious planet, which resembles in every way an "Old West" town. Baffled by this anachronism, they investigate and discover that the planet's original inhabitants, called skagorans, abducted 6,000 humans from Western towns of the American plains in the nineteenth century—to use as slaves. Soon after their arrival, however, the humans staged an uprising, overthrew their oppressors, and established a civilization they knew best: the "Old West."

When the *Enterprise* comes upon them, the former oppressors now constitute the slave-like underclass (they're called "skaggs").[6] Archer must decide whether to 1) assist a small group of humans who are secretly trying to improve the life of these skaggs (but risk prison, or death, if discovered); 2) allow the human majority to continue oppressing the skaggs; 3) inform the humans about what life is like on earth today (they have no concept of "earth" life, being three centuries removed and subsisting on various creation legends), and arrange for their return to earth; or 4) simply get back in his ship and fly away.

Such a dilemma puts into play lots of potentially-conflicting threads: the United Federation of Planets' general prohibition on getting involved in other planets' disputes; Archer and his crew's belief in the equality and dignity of all species; the evils of slavery; the need for punishment of evil-doers; and the highly subjective nature of justice. The skaggs committed horrific acts of enslavement and cultural genocide... is it "just" to turn the tables and have them live the life they sentenced their human captors to? And how long a term of punishment is long enough?

The episode, which provides no easy solutions, ends on a note of uncertain optimism. Archer lands a shuttlepod on Main Street. He solicits a commitment from one of the human community's most respected leaders — the town sheriff, no less — that he will try to bring about a change in the ways the humans treat the skagorans. Archer promises that once his current space mission (chasing an alien race called the Xindi) is completed, he'll return — though he tells them it could be years.

At the end of the episode, the new series pays homage to the original series, the historic gunfight at OK corral, and the dramatic demands of the story with an old-fashioned shootout (this time with phasers!) between the humans (who are distrustful of Archer and his alien-appearing comrades, whom they believe are skagoran collaborators trying to re-conquer the planet) and the crew of the *Enterprise*.

"North Star" explores the issues which have made *Star Trek* such a popular and enduring entertainment. Slightly less sanguine than "The Spectre of a Gun," the episode suggests that merely making it to the twenty-third century is not insurance against the evils which have plagued humanity for centuries: hostility, mistrust, a thirst for revenge. (Apparently, you can take humanity out of the frontier, but the reverse is much more difficult.) Archer warns the sheriff that his people will have to get over their vindictive and petty jealousies if they are ever to return to Earth, but a renegade schoolteacher tells him she doesn't think they'll ever be ready. Archer acknowledges that social progress on Earth has been a long, slow process. The episode ends with the *Enterprise* returning to space to continue their battle with the Xindi, a time-traveling species (from the twenty-ninth century) who are hostile, vindictive and bloodthirsty. So much for a future of universal peace.

SIX

Time Traveling

If Gene Roddenberry is the father of *Star Trek*, then H.G. Wells should be thought of as the mildly eccentric uncle in the *Trek* family tree. It was Wells who first popularized a concept that *Trek* has used dozens of times — the idea of traveling through time, just as one can travel through space. Wells also seems like a fitting progenitor for much of the spirit of *Star Trek*, providing through his fiction a vision of the future which contains lots of cautionary tales for our own time. And, just as the original series drew directly from groundbreaking scientific achievements of its day (and, conversely, influencing many people to consider careers in science and space exploration),[1] Wells drew ideas for his fiction from the science of *his* day. In fact, Wells was a trained scientist who studied zoology at England's Royal College of Science and wrote a biology textbook long before he began his science fiction career.

Wells might not be considered one of literature's great eminences — with his works often labeled, somewhat derisively, "popular," rather than profound — but he looms hugely over the landscape of certain strains of science fiction (though he called his works "scientific romances," as the term "science fiction" had not yet been coined). And his breakthrough work, 1895's *The Time Machine*, is one of those pieces of imaginative literature that has attained an almost mythic status due to a confluence of events. In Wells' case, it was his ability to synthesize the public's growing interest in time travel (which was fueling the imagination of a young scientist named Albert Einstein, who would make his own breakthrough a decade after Wells), the growth of popular, serialized stories of the "fantastic" and the near-obsessive preoccupation among the growing middle-class with issues of economic security and the relationship of employer to employee. *The Time Machine* pulls all those levers.

Because it's almost impossible to discuss *Star Trek* without discussing time travel, and because it's similarly prohibitive to discuss time travel without discussing Wells, it's worth looking more closely at *The Time Machine* to see what ideas that book bequeathed to *Trek*, and how those ideas have been handled over the forty years of that franchise's evolution.

SAY WHEN

If one could travel back in time to the early nineteenth century, one would discover that time travel stories were, even then, wildly popular. Early American writers such as Washington Irving and, later in the century, Mark Twain were satisfying the desire for fiction which played with the notions of moving both forward ("Rip Van Winkle") and backward (*A Connecticut Yankee in King Arthur's Court*) in time. The time travel story was well established before H.G. Wells began playing with the form, but he took time travel to a different place, imbuing it with sociological depth and wrapping it in the patina of science.

Among the many approaches and themes which Wells puts forward in *The Time Machine*, the most useful, and arguably most substantive, ideas—from a *Trek*ker's standpoint—include the following: (1) traveling through time can be discussed as a scientific possibility, not merely as a speculative amusement; (2) accounts of time travel will be received skeptically by one's contemporaries; (3) the earth's ecology is headed towards dissolution, with many species—and humanity itself—facing certain extinction (though the process is much too slow for any single generation to notice); and (4) social problems can be thought of almost like their own species—that is, they either evolve over time, increasing in magnitude and severity, or they become extinct. It all depends on the social climate.

Wells begins his tale earnestly, seeking to embed the subsequent fantastical account of the narrative in the realm of respected scientific fact. The story is begun by a narrator named Hillyer, one of several professional men who regularly gather at the home of a man who is known throughout the story simply as the "Time Traveler." Meeting as usual one night for dinner, brandy and cigars, the host reveals to the group that he has discovered the principles of time travel. They are of course skeptical, but he piques their curiosity with his sincerity and then tries to establish a foundation of rationalism, appealing to his listeners' credulity through the language of science:

> "Clearly," the Time Traveler proceeded, "any body must have extension in *four* directions: it must have Length, Breadth, Thickness and — Duration. But through a natural infirmity of the flesh, which I will explain to you in a moment, we incline to overlook this fact. There are really four dimensions, three of which we call the three planes of space, and a fourth, Time. There is, however, a tendency to draw an unreal distinction between the former three dimensions and the latter, because it happens that our consciousness moves intermittently in one direction along the latter from the beginning to the end of our lives."[2]

As the novel unfolds, the group is held spellbound by the story the time traveler tells of his increasingly bizarre and unbelievable trip from the year 1895 to 802,701. He recounts his time among a civilization made up of two races. One is a gentle, frail race, living in apparent harmony with nature and free from ambition almost to the point of lethargy. They are called the Eloi, and in their vegetarianism and docility they seem almost utopic. The other race is called the Morlocks, an underground-dwelling race of troglodytes who literally feed off of their quieter, surface-dwelling cousins, staging nighttime raids to satisfy their cannibalistic longings. (Some critics read this as Wells's indictment of capitalism, with wealthy-but-grubby captains of commerce feeding off the lifeblood of their exploited workers.)

Much of the narrative involves the Time Traveler's life for a week among the Eloi (including a relationship with a childlike Eloi female named Weena), and his fending off attacks from the savage and glutinous Morlocks, who steal and hide his time machine. Eventually, the traveler recovers his device (a sort of high-tech sleigh) and escapes from this nightmarish dystopia, racing forward even further in time to witness the planet Earth millions of years in the future, as the sun begins to die out and the lifeless oceans bathe beaches filled with the last remnants of life: huge, ugly, primordial crab-like creatures crawling toward extinction. Another ride in his time machine, "in great strides of a thousand years or more," and even the crabs have disappeared:

> "I looked about me to see if any traces of animal life remained. A certain indefinable apprehension still kept me in the saddle of the machine. But I saw nothing moving, in earth or sky or sea. The green slime on the rocks alone testified that life was not extinct."[3]

The traveler then escapes back to his own time, with the scraps of his horrifying journey still clinging to his memory. His recounting of the tale, however, meets with a not-unexpected skepticism. As one of his assembled listeners, a newspaper editor, remarks after hearing the traveler's account, "What a pity it is you're not a writer of stories!"

Despite having begun his tale by invoking the scientific possibility of time travel, the traveler's guests are to be forgiven their skepticism because the story is so outlandish and the implications so extreme. Like many of the more than two dozen *Trek* episodes that have dealt with time travel, Wells isn't as interested in exploring the "how" of time travel as he is exploring how humanity evolves through time. This too was Gene Roddenberry's prime concern (but in this, the two creative geniuses often part company, with Wells generally envisioning a bleak, increasingly hostile world while Roddenberry finds great hope in the likely advancement of the human species).

A look at one of *Star Trek*'s most popular films — as well as one of its most effective treatments of time travel — should help illuminate the connections between Wells' treatment of time travel and that of *Trek*.

TANKS FOR THE MEMORIES

In *Star Trek IV: The Voyage Home*, Kirk and his crew must travel back in time to retrieve a couple of humpback whales — which, we are told, are extinct in the twenty-third century. Their trip is occasioned by a probe, which is wreaking havoc on Earth, seeking the song of any humpback whale but finding only silence in return. Unless this intergalactic pager picks up a whale call, Planet Earth will be destroyed. So, the *Enterprise* crew — in a "borrowed" Klingon vessel (their own ship was destroyed in *Star Trek III*) — heads back to late twentieth century Earth to find a pair of whales to answer the distress call.

The film doesn't dwell at length on the scientific aspects of time travel, but there is, of course, the requisite "technobabble" for which *Star Trek* has always been known. The dialogue smacks of scientific-sounding justification for attempting time travel. Kirk orders Spock to "Start your computations" for time travel, suggesting — as Wells did in *The Time Machine* — that there is a mathematical rationale for leapfrogging across time. Dr. McCoy reiterates the idea behind time travel for the viewer who may still be a bit foggy about how it's supposed to work — adding a touch of his trademark gallows humor: "Slingshot around the sun, pick up enough speed, and you're in time warp. If not, you're fried."[4] Kirk then sends a message to Starfleet headquarters: "We are going to attempt time travel." The implicit message of the scenes where the plan is hatched, agreed upon, and explained, is that time travel is indeed possible. (Whether or not scientists today believe that time travel is possible has been the subject of many books and articles, and, though interesting, not really my focus here.[5])

After some intense rattling on the bridge of the Klingon ship, blinding light flashes, bolts coming loose and some dazzling, sunburst-style special effects, the crew discovers they've made it to San Francisco, circa 1986.

So, the science was dependable. They traveled through time. But just as Wells' traveler had difficulty finding anyone who believed him, Kirk is unable to convince the resident marine biologist at the city's Cetacean Institute — home to a couple of crowd-pleasing humpback whales — that he is really from the future, and that he means no harm to the whales. She thinks, of course, that he is crazy. And, after Spock takes a swim with the institute's whales in their captivity tank, she has her doubts about him as well.

Most of the crew's San Francisco adventure is played for laughs, but there's a very serious undertone to both the movie and the mission of the movie's heroes: extinction is a very real possibility. In *The Time Machine*, the traveler discovers that the sun, which sustains life on earth, is burning out, and that as it is extinguished, so too will be the life it sustains. The scene in which he stands on the beach which once teemed with all manner of life and surveys a moribund world, with the lone surviving life form lumbering sadly back into the stagnant water, is affecting. *Star Trek IV* borrows a page from Wells, but pastes it in a contemporary chapter, showing how mankind's own greed and near-sightedness can lead to the destruction not only of a single species (the whales) but also of the entire planet. When Spock declaims to the marine biologist that hunting a species to extinction is not logical, she retorts: "Whoever said human beings were logical?"

The Time Machine also suggests that greed and competition for precious resources will lead to a destructive split in mankind: the Elois and the Morlocks. Or, to put it in contemporary economic vernacular: the haves and the have-nots. Wells sees society's problems following the path of social Darwinism, an idea which was gaining currency in his time. That is, left to their own evolutionary energy, greed, malice, competitiveness and envy will evolve just as surely as the living creatures of the planet. Gene Roddenberry articulates the same view but from the reverse angle. His view of the world seems to suggest that social problems are at their worst now, and if we don't act to fix them — immediately — we will be affected by them long after we've learned to rise above them. The savage hunting of the whale in the twentieth century, driven by greed, will destroy us, even though one day greed may be a thing of the past (in *Star Trek IV* we are reminded again that future earth inhabitants have no need for money).

Kirk and his crew make it back to their own time, just in time to free their humpback passengers and save the world. The scene where the whales are released is one of pure joy, with both cetaceans and humans splashing around in the sea, the "voyage home" now complete.

As time travel fantasies go, *Star Trek IV* is both satisfying and simple. Few questions were raised about the impact "going back" in time would have on the future, about whether such an undertaking would violate the already established timeline of human history. Such questions have led to almost paralyzing paradoxes in the literature of time travel. But *Star Trek* has often squarely confronted these puzzles, from the wrenching original series episode "City on the Edge of Forever" (in which Kirk must allow the death of a woman he loves to occur in order to restore the timeline of human history) to the Hugo-nominated *Deep Space Nine* episode "The Visitor" (where Jake Sisko tries to breach the boundaries of time and space to save his father from a fatal accident). No episode demonstrates such complexity better than "All Good

Things...," the series finale for *The Next Generation* and a sort of time capsule itself for all of *Trek*'s time-traveling tropes. But for all its paradoxes, even "All Good Things...." draws from Wells' 100-year-old antecedent.

THE END OF AN ERA

Captain Jean-Luc Picard spent a good part of the seven-year run of *The Next Generation* series being thrown about in time. He's been transported back to the time of Robin Hood, nineteenth-century San Francisco, and the Jazz Age. He's met his own ship, the *Enterprise*, from two decades earlier, he's grown old and had grandchildren in a civilization that died a thousand years before he was born, and he's even met himself, only hours apart from his own reality. In the world of Time, Jean-Luc gets around. But nothing quite prepared him — what could?— for the final encounter with the time-toying deity known as "Q" and the flinging about through time that Picard endures in the final *The Next Generation* episode, "All Good Things...."

Slipping back and forth between the present, seven years in the past, and 25 years in the future, Picard must try to maintain some sense of continuity — or at least sanity — as he puzzles out what's happening to him. Though science plays no direct role in explaining Picard's time traveling (it's all due to the impish Q), there is a good deal of science behind the solution to Picard's dilemma, for the only thing that seems to connect all three of Picard's different "presents" is the presence of some sort of a spatial anomaly in a part of space known as the Neutral Zone. Picard tries to assure his crews in the various dimensions about what's happening to him, but they are skeptical of his time travel story; they respect him, of course, but quite naturally think his behavior is odd, and they are beginning to doubt his rationality and his fitness to serve as captain. Eventually, Picard discovers that the anomaly — a tear in the fabric of space and time — is bigger in the past than in the present. "Q" confirms this is true by taking Picard all the way back to the time when life was to have formed on Earth and showing him how the anomaly has now disrupted that process, preventing life from ever forming on the planet. And to make matters worse (if something could be said to be worse than the wholesale elimination of life as we know it), "Q" tells the captain that he and the *Enterprise* crew are responsible for creating the anomaly in the first place and sending it backward in time.

The scene where "Q" and Picard survey the bubbling, primordial ooze from which earthly life was supposed to have sprung is rich in Wells-like lament for the now-lifeless planet, and the traveler's dialogue could have been lifted right from *The Time Machine* and given to Captain Picard:

> The darkness grew apace; a cold wind began to blow in freshening gusts from the east.... From the edge of the sea came a ripple and whisper. Beyond these lifeless sounds the world was silent. Silent? It would be hard to convey the stillness of it. All the sounds of man, the bleating of sheep, the cries of birds, the hum of insects, the stir that makes the background of our lives — all that was over.[6]

So Wells' lament for the demise of Earth became the keynote theme for *The Next Generation*'s series finale. But just as the Time Traveler was able to make it back to his Victorian drawing room, safe and relatively sound, so too does Picard figure out how to reverse the anomaly and restore the natural order of human history. And, in another fitting nod to H.G. Wells, just as the Time Traveler returned to meet his regular group of friends, and to relate the tale of his travels among intimates, Picard — for the first time in the series' history — joins the officer's weekly poker game on board the ship, ending the series by uttering a line (as he's dealing cards) which surely must have crossed H.G. Wells' mind sometime during the conception of his masterpiece: "The Sky's the Limit."[7]

So Wells' clanky time sleigh is supplanted by Roddenberry's sleek, time-warping *Enterprise*, but the psychological landscape they visit is much the same. The future contains things which would — should — shock us, and if you could take such a trip today, no one would believe your report of the radical changes which await us in the future. The critical difference between their visions is that Wells delineates for humanity a grim, inescapable destiny, whereas for Roddenberry, the best is always yet to come.

SEVEN

The Ravages of War

From one very unoriginal idea — "War is Hell" — have come some of the best and most original *Star Trek* episodes and films in the franchise's history. This is one of those themes that seemed to have affected *Trek* creator Gene Roddenberry deeply and at a personal level.[1] Fans and critics of the show have frequently debated whether *Trek* was "political" in its intentions, but there can be no doubt that an antiwar message of peace and universal respect for all sentient beings lies at the heart of *Star Trek*. From the original series to the latest incarnations, *Trek* has never shied away from its pacifist proclamations. This may seem an odd statement for a show in which so many space battles — not to mention phaser blasts and photon torpedoes — were featured. But if the crew of the Starship *Enterprise* had a way to solve a problem peacefully, they almost always chose to do so. Warlike races were often marked by a ferocity of demeanor that made it easy to anticipate who would be the unsolicited aggressor and who would be the resistor. Even James T. Kirk, space cowboy and cosmic provocateur, held his fire a surprising number of times. Kirk's ship was a vessel of peace, as was Picard's, Janeway's and Archer's.

The horror of war, of course, has been more than a plot device for *Star Trek*. It's been the cultural backdrop of the series, from the original voyage — which was launched amid the rising unease about the Vietnam conflict — to the prequel *Enterprise*, which featured an entire season which seemed framed by the September 11, 2001, terrorist attacks.[2] If war is hell, then the message of *Trek* is that one day humanity will have the good sense to avoid it. The bad news is, by the time peace becomes pervasive on this planet, we'll be out in the planetary hinterlands, flying around in worlds where warfare is often the space age lingua franca.

What's a peace-loving race of warp-speeding humanoids to do?

Well, that's the question faced by Kirk, et al., and their answers over four decades have provided a clear and morally consistent response to universal aggression. So clear, in fact, that many of *Trek*'s attitudes about warfare and humanity can be traced to some of the most important and lasting works in literature, from classical epics to modern-day examinations of war in our time. On the one hand, it's somehow quite comforting to discover that the crafters of human narratives have been preaching peace for several millennia. On the other hand, it can be disconcerting to consider how frequently that message has been disregarded. The best *Trek* episodes help us come to grips with both responses. Of course, the same can be said about the works that have paved the way for *Trek*'s world-war-weary blueprint. Among the many important war-related narratives, special attention is due to the classical epic *The Aeneid* — a war story steeped in an irony which seems more modern than aged — and a work considered by many to be the best anti-war novel ever written, *All Quiet on the Western Front*.

So, set a course for ancient Rome, program your universal translator for Latin, and get ready for a wild ride.

WHEN IN ROME

For most modern readers, the "epic" form has lost its appeal. Often seen as dense, complex, rigidly governed, and lengthy, the epic has certainly fallen out of favor as the genre of choice for readers — or writers. At the time Virgil was writing, however, the epic was a career-maker. Any Roman scribe worth his salt was trying to incorporate contemporary events and political figures into 12-book romans à clef. Virgil (Publius Vergilius Maro, to be precise), born about 70 BCE, was not only a great poet, but a writer with a mission: to glorify the rule of Caesar Augustus, pay tribute to the rich mythic culture surrounding the founding of Rome, and to celebrate the virtue of peace — even if he often appropriated the high epic style of Homer's war poem, the *Iliad*. Though the *Aeneid* is one of the great nationalistic epics in literature, Virgil never descends into mindless patriotism. His work endorses the enduring values of decency, justice and humanity — though, as in *Star Trek*, peace sometimes has to be hastened by the drawing of a sword (or a phaser).

The Aeneid, which occupied the last decade of Virgil's life, reveals the poet's distaste for the bloody strife which threatened to upset the urbanity of his Augustan world. The poem regularly lunges toward peace, only to see those pacifistic longings upended by schemers from both this world and the world of the Roman gods, as in this passage, where the Fury Allecto brags about how she has stirred up strife between the Trojans and their hosts, the Laurentines:

> "Lo, discord is ripened at thy desire into baleful war: bid them now mix in amity and join alliance! Insomuch as I have stained the Trojans with Ausonian blood, this likewise will I add, if I have the assurance of thy will. With my rumors I will sweep the bordering towns into war, and kindle their spirit with furious desire for battle, that from all quarters help may come; I will sow the land with arms."
>
> The Juno answering: "Terror and harm is wrought abundantly. The springs of war are unsealed: they fight sword in hand; fresh blood stains the weapons that chance first supplied."[3]

So, sometimes even the gods have it in for you, whether it's Allecto tormenting Aeneas, Apollo humiliating Kirk, the Q tweaking Picard or Janeway, or the Pah Wraiths wreaking havoc on *Deep Space Nine*.

It might seem odd to classify *The Aeneid* as a poem of peace when Virgil presents such an unflinching and vivid picture of battle ("She hurled her torch at him, and pierced his breast with the lurid smoking brand..."[4]). But *The Aeneid* makes clear how wasteful and destructive are the wages of war. The epic affirms, at last, the values of peace — between neighbors, between rulers and subjects, and between countries. As the poet states during a climactic scene in the penultimate book of his epic, "In war is no safety."[5] That idea, as we'll see, has informed many of *Trek*'s finest hours.

Keeping Quiet

Virgil's antiwar message often emerges from between the lines of his epic, but for many writers, the antiwar message is the text, not the subtext. Such is the case with the German writer Erich Maria Remarque, author of the gold standard of antiwar novels, 1928's *All Quiet on the Western Front*. A searing indictment of the mindset which sees war as noble, the book provides an irony-tinged march through trench warfare, providing the reader with an armchair view of the gaping chasm between the youthful warriors who are sent into battle and the aged, ossified "patriots" who champion war.

The book's first chapter shatters any notions about the wisdom of the elder generation in their ready desire to send their younger comrades out to die for god and country. The narrator, 20-year-old Paul Baumer, reflects on the misplaced trust he and his peers placed on their high school teachers, who urged them all to enlist with vigor:

> For us lads of eighteen they ought to have been mediators and guides to the world of maturity, the world of work, of duty, of culture, of progress — to the future. We often made fun of them and played jokes on them, but in our hearts we trusted them. The idea of authority, which they represented, was associated in our minds with a greater insight and a more humane wisdom. But the first death we saw shattered this belief. We had to recognize that our generation was more to be trusted than theirs. They surpassed us only in phrases and cleverness. The first bombardment showed us our mistake, and under it the world as they had taught it to us broke in pieces.[6]

That idea of a "broken" world rules the narrative. War breaks everything, everyone. As with *The Aeneid*, warfare makes the "higher pursuits"—literature, music, even the cultivation of loving relationships—impossible. Remarque was an avowed pacifist who hoped to bring about a change in the way mankind viewed war. Conflicts on the battlefield not only lead to death of the body, they lead to death of the spirit, a dissociation of the human soul from all that is worthwhile: " The summer of 1918 is the most bloody and the most terrible. The days stand like angels in blue and gold, incomprehensible, above the ring of annihilation."[7] The tone never softens, Remarque never lets up. The brief, final page in which the death of the narrator is revealed, is one of the most pointed exits in the history of modern literature:

He fell in October 1918, on a day that was so quiet and still on the whole front, that the army report confined itself to the single sentence: All Quiet on the Western Front. He had fallen forward and lay on the earth as though sleeping. Turning him over, one saw that he could not have suffered long; his face had an expression of calm, as though almost glad the end had come.[8]

Both *The Aeneid* and *All Quiet on the Western Front* articulate a clear-eyed disdain for the ravages of war. Both promulgate the view that war moves us further from those ideals which ought to sustain us— peace, love, beauty, culture — and both place a large part of the blame for warfare on meddlers and malcontents who think war serves some useful function (usually to advance their own narrow aims). War creates psychic damage — scarring the combatants — and leaves a technological trail of terror for future generations to deal with. Gene Roddenberry's opus re-articulates many of those same themes, which can be seen in the original series episode "A Taste of Armageddon," through *Voyager*'s taut "Dreadnought" and *Deep Space Nine*'s morally complex "The Cardassians." Finally, there is *Star Trek VI: The Undiscovered Country*, in which long-held notions of personal enmity and nationalistic prejudice are revealed, challenged and ultimately overcome.

Not to Everyone's Taste

Gene Roddenberry might have been an idealist, but he was no naive, dewy-eyed pacifist. In the original series episode "A Taste of Armageddon," *Trek* revealed a highly nuanced and pragmatic view of humanity's frequent, destructive embrace of warfare. The episode has a lot to say about our society's warlike impulses. At one point, after being challenged by the highly intelligent, rather chilly planetary leader Anan 7, Kirk is forced to admit to mankind's murderous instincts (as Captain Picard would be, twenty years later, in *The Next Generation*'s pilot episode, "Encounter at Farpoint"). But Kirk rises above simplistic moralizing, stinging his interrogator with his deceptively sophisticated response to the charge that murderousness is a part of humanity's makeup, that all people are killers at heart: "We can admit that we're killers," Kirk says. "But we're not going to kill *today*."[9] In other words, just because we occasionally feel the urge to strike out, that urge can be controlled.

Kirk's foe in this episode is the head of a society which believes it has found a use for war (in contradistinction to Virgil's command that there is no use for war); namely, that war can be sanitized to the point that attacks are only simulated — but the casualties are real. Anan 7 explains that after hundreds of years of conflict with a neighboring planet, the two sides agreed to spare their civilizations the usual wages of war: cities destroyed, culture annihilated. These two worlds use computers to fight their wars, but the citizens must agree to be casualties in these "simulated" battles. A computer strike might wipe out a city on a map. The expected number of casualties must march into vaporizing machines.

"We have a high consciousness of duty,"[10] says one of the subjects, heading to the vaporizer. It is precisely such mindless adherence to duty that is blasted to bits in Remarque's *All Quiet on the Western Front*. When Anan 7 tells Kirk that although millions of people die, "our civilization lives,"[11] one can't help but recall those scenes where the elder schoolmasters gleefully urge their young students to give their lives for the good of their country.

THE DREAD OF WAR

What you sow, you must reap, and when you sow the seeds of war, you will reap a legacy of sorrow. As both *Trek* and world history will attest, the inescapable wages of warfare are often paid by generations far removed from the original conflict. Land mines planted during the Viet Nam war, for example, continue to maim scores of innocent victims even to this day. What you sow, you must reap.

That sentiment dates back to the Bible, and finds expression in many of the classic works which deal with warfare, including *The Aeneid* (where the effects of the Trojan War lasted for decades on its combatants — and centuries for human history) and *All Quiet on the Western Front* (where we see the first vivid effects of "shell shock" on the surviving soldiers and their families).

In the twenty-fourth century, the same rules apply: what you sow, you must reap. In the *Star Trek: Voyager* episode "Dreadnought," that inescapable consequence is powerfully illustrated. The episode features a super-weapon that had, at one time, a different destination in a different part of space. But when you unleash the tools of destruction, there's no calling them back.

The drama revolves around a missile sent, once-upon-a-time, to destroy a Cardassian munitions dump. The episode's sense of irony derives from the fact that it was B'Elana Torres, a member of Voyager's crew, who originally programmed the missile to destroy its target. Now, she and the rest of the Starship Voyager are trying to keep the missile from destroying a planet in the Delta Quadrant, where it has inexplicably arrived, and wiping out its two million inhabitants — even if it means intercepting the missile and blowing themselves into space dust.

Because Torres knows the missile personally, so to speak, she actually beams aboard this huge, hurtling projectile, and tries to reprogram it. But the missile thinks it's an enemy deception (yes, it *thinks*... and like the computer Hal in *2001: A Space Odyssey*, defies the wishes of its human progenitor), and refuses to be reprogrammed.

When Captain Janeway informs the leader of Rakosa — the world now targeted for destruction — that his planet faces annihilation and that he'd better mobilize his planet's defenses, he tells her, pointedly, "We're not a warlike race — we haven't devoted our resources to building weapons, like yours."[12]

The moral is clear: those cultures which unleash war pose threats not only to their own world but also to worlds far beyond their own. And, as Remarque makes clear in *All Quiet on the Western Front*, when a society spends its time and money developing war technology, it loses the chance to develop the "higher" human callings which earmark a civilization. It's a message that *Trek* viewers have seen in the franchise's regular emphasis on diplomatic solutions over military conflict, in honest brokering over deceit, in building rather than tearing down. In "Dreadnought," the very business of Voyager's peaceable sojourn through the galaxy is compromised by former guerillas — who are now sowing what they reaped in their previous life as space warriors.

As explosive as any war's technological legacy is the psychological aftermath of battle. The true cost of war has little to do with machines or resources, but rather with people. In *Deep Space Nine*'s "The Cardassians," we're confronted with one of the uglier prices of warfare: the impact on children.

This multilayered episode is held together by a central plot involving a Cardassian boy who was separated from his real father for years after Cardassia withdrew from Bajor after years of battling the Bajoran guerillas. The boy became one of the many war orphans who were not only abandoned but also shunned by the Bajoran population. But when he is reunited with his father on the space station Deep Space Nine, the boy shuns *him*, calling him a savage and a criminal. He tells his father he could never live as a Cardassian, and he returns to the protection of his adoptive Bajoran family.

The episode provides a searing overview of how race-based wars can engender feelings of self-loathing and racial prejudice. The Cardassian boy had been raised on stories of Cardassian savagery, and, marinated in the stew of hatred for his own people, he came to identify with his "enemy," the Bajorans. But in that bonding, *Trek* implicitly and subtly honors the idea which pervades so much war-related literature: people are the same everywhere. A Cardassian Boy *can* love his Bajoran parents — why not? Throughout works like *The Aeneid* and *All Quiet on the Western Front* runs the thought that wars are not only wasteful, they are built on the most arbitrary of rationales. As one of the war-weary recruits in *All Quiet on the Western Front* tells his jingoistic sergeant during a debate about the rightness of the war:

> But just you consider, almost all of us are simple folk. And in France, too, the majority of men are laborers, workmen, or poor clerks. Now just why would a French blacksmith or a French shoemaker want to attack us? No, it is merely the rulers. I had never seen a Frenchman before I came here, and it will be just the same with the majority of Frenchmen as regards us. They weren't asked about it any more than we were.[13]

ONCE A WARRIOR?

The final voyage of the entire original crew — and the last to be supervised by Gene Roddenberry — sends our space heroes out in true *Star Trek* fashion: as universal peacemakers. *Star Trek VI: The Undiscovered Country*, involves Kirk and Company in their most difficult quest — to achieve peace with the Klingon empire. The movie features all the things fans of the franchise have come to expect from big-screen *Trek*, such as rousing space battles, Kirk-Spock-McCoy banter, and the drama of brinkmanship. But *Star Trek VI* also gives us something quite new, a Kirk who must come face to face with his own hatred and distrust of the Klingon race to complete his mission. In this final quest of Kirk's *Enterprise*, he really does explore undiscovered country (although the phrase, lifted from Hamlet's most famous soliloquy, refers to the kingdom of death, not the future of the Federation). And he bravely faces the new world he helped bring about, the world of cooperation, not confrontation.

Star Trek VI encapsulates many of the ideas about war and peace loosely incorporated into the *Trek* world over its first 25 years (the movie came out concurrently with Paramount's yearlong celebration of *Star Trek*'s twenty-fifth anniversary, as well as the serendipitous collapse of the Soviet Union and the end of the cold war).[14] Aeneas didn't let the carnage of the Trojan War dissuade him from trying to establish an eternal city of peace. Erich Maria Remarque took his trench warfare experience and turned it into the twentieth century's most profound plea for peace. It's too early to predict whether Gene Roddenberry's cultural creation will endure for centuries to come, but his message of eventual universal brotherhood remains, for many, a necessary balm to humanity's self-inflicted war wounds.

EIGHT

Return to the Sea

Human beings have always been attracted to vast bodies of water. The sea has exerted an almost primal pull on people. You can see it along any seashore, with little kids mimicking white-winged gulls, or elder members of our race wistfully eyeing whitecaps. The ocean — vast, deep and ageless — speaks to humanity on a special frequency. Some explanations have been put forward to explain this attraction: the rhythm of the waves mirrors the human breathing cycle, forcing one to relax, calming a hyperactive population. Or, life came from the sea, inspiring in all of humanity an implicit recognition of our home, making people feel nostalgia of a sort. But nobody can say for sure.

The strong connection between humans and the watery parts of the world have inspired sublime creative works such as Melville's *Moby Dick*, Claude Debussy's musical tone poem "La Mer," or Brueghel's famous painting "The Fall of Icarus." And yes, *Star Trek* has also made use of the motif of mankind's desire to return to the sea. In fact, in what could be termed *Trek*'s quieter moments, the sea has often surfaced as a potent symbol of the franchise's very essence: the desire to see what lies beyond, the challenge of traversing the seemingly infinite, the plunge into the unknown.

In the *Trek* universe, the influence of the sea manifests itself in many ways. First, there is the established and oft-cited evidence which demonstrates how series creator Gene Roddenberry modeled his space hero–captain on the fictional sea hero–captain Horatio Hornblower, the protagonist of a wildly successful series of naval potboilers.[1] Then there are the many references and allusions in various episodes and movies about the allure of the sea. And of course, there are the creatures of the sea — specifically whales — who serve in *Trek* as metaphorical "stand-ins" for the human race, and whose treatment by humans in the late twentieth century can be said to determine our fate in the twenty-third century.

Time, perhaps, for a plunge into the drink. Humanity's desire to return to the sea can't solely explain, of course, the popularity of *Trek*, but a deeper look into the lore of the sea might yield some hints about the treasures to be discovered in deep space. The best place to begin is with the good Captain himself, that brave and intrepid explorer millions of people have grown to love as he embarked on his adventures into the unknown. This captain, however, received his commission five centuries before James T. Kirk was ever born.

BLOWING YOUR OWN HORN

Even if Gene Roddenberry hadn't tipped *Trek* fans off to the fact that his captain was based on Horatio Hornblower, readers of C.S. Forrester's eleven-book sea adventures would have probably noticed the connection. There are not only those traits which the two leaders share — battle-hardened bravery, casual attitude toward their own death, reverence for the sea and sky — but also some very specific connections sprinkled throughout the canon. *Trek* has always had a reverence for naval protocol, and from Spock's funeral to the change of command on the bridge of Picard's *Enterprise*, naval procedures have always been observed. In fact, the line for which Jean Luc Picard is best known — "Make it so!" — was written in tribute to Hornblower, who often issued the same command to his first officer.[2]

In the book *The Making of Star Trek*, Roddenberry's original outline for the series is reprinted, and includes this description of his prospective captain:

> PRINCIPAL CHARACTER: *Robert T. April*. The "Skipper," about thirty-four, Academy graduate, rank of Captain. Clearly the leading man and

central character. This role, built about an unusual combination of colorful strengths and flaws, is designated for an actor of top repute and ability. A shorthand sketch of Robert April might be: "A space-age Captain Horatio Hornblower," constantly on trial with himself, lean and capable both mentally and physically.[3]

Readers unfamiliar with C.S. Forrester's captain will recognize a lot of Roddenberry's "principal character" when they encounter Horatio Hornblower, even as a callow midshipman in the first book of the series, when Hornblower is still finding his sea legs. His first-chapter face-off with a bullying fellow sailor named Simpson in *Mr. Midshipman Hornblower* reminds one of Kirk's pokerfaced bluff in the first season episode "The Corbomite Maneuver." Here's a taste of Hornblower, a new draftee in the service of a Captain Masters, after Hornblower has just challenged the older, meaner and more experienced Midshipman Simpson to a duel. The captain sizes him up:

> Masters looked at Hornblower as he dismissed him even more keenly than he had done when Hornblower first came on board. He was looking for signs of weakness or wavering — indeed, he was looking for any signs of human feeling at all — but he could detect none. Hornblower had reached a decision, he had weighed all the pros and cons.[4]

But Hornblower is no Spock, despite the apparent absence of human feelings. Hornblower can't sleep the night before the duel, he's almost sick to his stomach on the way to the duel, and at the critical moment, just before the face-off, Hornblower's humanity finally emerges: "It was in that second that he decided he could not kill Simpson even if it were in his power, and he went on lifting his pistol, forcing himself to look to see that it was pressed against the point of Simpson's shoulder. A slight wound would suffice."[5]

Many of the personality traits embedded in that passage — the projection of power amid internal questioning, sacrificing to uphold one's principles, ingenuity despite a rigid militaristic code governing one's actions — would continue to define both Hornblower and Kirk for the duration of their fictional lives. Such "borrowings" were not inadvertent. No less a *Trek* icon than novelist and screenwriter Nicholas Meyer, who directed *The Wrath of Khan* and is credited by many fans for "saving" the franchise, had this to say about the Hornblower-*Trek* connection:

I related to [*Star Trek II*] when I began to think of it as the adventure of Captain Horatio Hornblower in outer space. Once I got that, I thought, OK, this is about the Navy, this is about gunboat diplomacy — and I grew up loving those books, so I redesigned the uniforms, or caused them to be redesigned, and made them more militaristic, whether you call them Navy, or whether you call them the Coast Guard. This more or less characterizes all the spinoffs since.[6]

Horatio Hornblower, then, was an important influence on Roddenberry, and his seafaring yearnings became one of the leitmotifs of the franchise. But Roddenberry appropriated more than just Hornblower's commitment to exploration and his idea of sacrifice for the good of Mother England. He also borrowed C.S. Forrester's celebration of the sea as a place where one could find one's self, a testing ground for the mettle of a man's character. And he drew on the lore — and lure — of the sea in the popular imagination, a tradition which celebrates the ocean as a place of mystery and ultimate freedom.

DEPTH CHARGES

Many of the greatest writers in Western Civilization have rhapsodized about the sea and its effect on the human psyche. Shakespeare, Melville, Milton, Woolf, Emerson, Lord Byron and Yeats have all famously intoned about the magic and mystery of the deep. Homer started it all with his *Odyssey*— a simple sea story, really — and since that time, countless creative writers have turned seaward, inky quill (or laptop) in hand, trying to capture the rhythm of the waves and the song of the sirens. Almost every literary anthology will include, by accident or design, lots of poems in praise of the "wine dark sea." One of the greatest and most enduring odes to the sea — and mankind's ache to return to it — was written by an unknown author in a tongue no longer spoken. Yet its beauty, power and nuance make it a paragon of the genre.

"The Seafarer" is an anonymous, 112-line lyric, written in the highly alliterative style of eighth-century Old English. Fortunately for contemporary readers, most of whom were never forced to learn this archaic precursor of modern English, a number of good translations are readily available. Although scholars argue over the origins and intentions of the poem — or whether it was written by a single poet or a score of scribes over a number of centuries — the work inarguably evokes how strongly the sea speaks to people. And it's also a surprisingly nuanced lyric (as opposed to the often blunt-edged moralizing of much Old English poetry) which acknowledges the hardship of life at sea (with all its attendant danger) while still praising the depths to the heights.

Here are a few lines from this influential archaic ode:

> The groves take on their blossoms; the towns grow fair,
> The meadows beautiful; the world revives;
> All things urge on the hearts of the eager-minded
> To the journey, the hearts of men who bethink them
> To depart far over the flood-ways.
> Yet the cuckoo sings a warning with its mournful notes,
> The guardian of the summer bodes forth sorrow
> Bitter in its breast-hoard. No man can know,
> Who dwells in comfort, what they endure
> Who lay their paths of exile far and wide!
> So now my thoughts go roaming;
> My spirit is with the sea-flood
> Beyond the home of the whale; it hovers afar
> Over the expanses of the world; it returns to me
> Greedy and yearning. The solitary flier cries out;
> It drives me irresistibly on the whale-road....[7]

The combination of the grandeur of diction, largeness of theme and elemental simplicity of subject might help explain why the poem inspired such latter-day Romantics as William Wordsworth and Walt Whitman. Boiled down to its bare bones, the poem is an argument that mankind simply cannot resist the tug of the ocean, despite its risks and hardships. Life on shore is placid, the world's towns merely "fair." But life on the sea puts one in touch with some electric currents of thought, elevating the soul: "My spirit is with the sea-flood," our anonymous author/mariner declares. "It drives me irresistibly on the whale road."[8]

Trek has often traded on that longing, equating the exploration of the stars with the traversing of the high seas. Some of the most explicit links between sea and space exploration can be found in the fifth *Star Trek* film, *The Final Frontier,* which can boast, among its other themes, the idea of the sea as a magnet, pulling humanity to its undiscovered depths.

WATER, WATER EVERYWHERE

There's a deftly played little scene in *Star Trek V: The Final Frontier* that speaks volumes about the franchise's debt to the literature of the sea. The scene occurs as Kirk, Spock and McCoy are being shuttled to the *Enterprise* after being abruptly recalled from a wilderness vacation, thoughts of rock-climbing still very much in their minds (as are the strains of the campfire song they sang right before sleeping, the nonsensical but nautical "Row Row Row Your Boat"). As they lay eyes on the *Enterprise*, wondrously alight against the expansive night sky, Kirk says simply, "All I ask is a tall ship and a star to steer her by." McCoy, thinking he recognizes the quote, says "Melville." Spock corrects him: "John Masefield."[9] What's interesting about this brief moment is what this scene implies, as well as what it actually delivers. Explicitly, the sea-space link is established by Captain Kirk, who connects the voyages of tall, three-masted schooners with his mission to explore the stars. He appropriates the nautical idiom as if it were the natural way for a starship captain to express himself. A ship on the sea, guided only by the stars, is really just another way to think of the *Enterprise*.

Implicitly, and perhaps more important, is the embedded suggestion that in the twenty-third century, Melville and Masefield, who both wrote about the sea, would still be commonly known. Melville wrote *Moby Dick* in 1851, and yet Dr. McCoy thinks immediately of Melville when he hears a famous sea-related quote. To realize that the works of Melville and Masefield retain a currency and commonality five centuries after composition is to validate the importance of the sea narrative as a linchpin of literary culture. And it suggests something about how each future age appropriates tales of sea exploration and grafts them onto their own adventures. The link between ancient days aboard wooden ships and warp-driven spaceship exploration is further cemented during a later scene in the movie when the very purpose for *Star Trek*, its reigning spirit and very motto ("To boldly go where no man has gone before"), is seen inscribed on a bronze plaque mounted on an old wooden steering wheel from the deck of a tall-masted ship which is now on the *Enterprise*'s observation deck.

One final, fun link between the literature of the sea and *Star Trek V* can be found by comparing the grander, overall theme of the film to the final line of "The Seafarer," which sums up the previous 111 lines of the poem. The movie revolves around a character named Sybok, who takes control of the *Enterprise* so that he can find Sha Ka Ree, the Vulcan equivalent of Heaven, he explains to the ship's crew, the place "from which creation sprang." So the purpose of exploration isn't really to chart stars and meet other alien races. The purpose is to return to the source of life, Sha-Ka-Ree, heaven.

Here's the last line of "The Seafarer": "Let us strive to reach our heavenly home."[10]

SOUNDINGS

If humanity's centuries-long ride atop the waves in search of new lands and new adventures has inspired visions of the future, then the wondrous and wild creatures underneath all that water can be seen as a link to our primal past. Nowhere has that point been made with more grace and potency than in *Star Trek IV: The Voyage Home*, a film beloved perhaps as much for its ecological message as for its usual mix of space operatics. The movie is not very subtle in its message: if the whales disappear, we'll disappear. But the movie also finds great joy, humor and pathos in the way it untangles the interconnected web of life on the third planet from the sun. And it makes great use of one of the great poems in the English language, a work about whales that is almost as sprawling and grandiose as the mammoth mammals themselves.

The movie's central premise is that whales have become extinct on earth by the twenty-third century. Unfortunately for earth, a probe sent by a whale-based civilization has been trying to make contact with its long lost (lost for good, it would seem) brothers of the sea. With no whales to respond, the probe is wreaking havoc with the world's oceans, causing tidal floods and waves of destruction, which threaten to wipe out humanity. Kirk and his crew do the only thing they can think of which will stop the ravaging: they return to the past, rescue a couple of whales, and deposit them in the future, where they can answer the call and turn off the tumult.

It plays as implausibly as it sounds, but it's great fun to watch and it's carried out with lots of heart. One of the finest moments of the movie takes place when the whales have just been beamed aboard the

Enterprise, booked for the return trip to the twenty-third century. Kirk stares into the tank, watching these gentle giants lolling safely aboard the *Enterprise*: "They say the sea is cold, but the sea contains the hottest blood of all."[11] It's the perfect line for the occasion, delivered by the Captain with the right mix of awe and affection, and it comes from the perfect poem about the turbulence and beauty of the whales.

Kirk was quoting D.H. Lawrence's poem "Whales Weep Not!" a celebration of the life force teeming beneath the sea. The poem is perfect in the context of the movie because it implicitly argues that humans need to move from seeing these creatures as merely beastly, as swimming storehouses of oil or blubber, to creatures like ourselves, seeking love in the depths, companionship in the dark. And because it celebrates, to be frank, whale procreation, it reinforces the theme of extinction vs. propagation that propels the movie. It is the perfect poem to be in Jim Kirk's mind at that moment.

Star Trek IV: The Voyage Home is a film which also dares to dream of the end — the end of whales, and the end of humanity, both bound to each other's fate. And like its successor, *Star Trek V: The Final Frontier*— and like Lawrence in his poem — it finds a spiritual component in the pacific world beneath the surface.

Star Trek IV gives us a payoff scene with the whales being released, frolicking in the water, as the crew of the *Enterprise* jumps playfully into the sea along with their cargo, exultant and revived by the plunge into the deep. Humanity is saved, whales are saved, the day has been saved, once again, by the *Enterprise* crew. But the lesson has been learned: human life may not have originally crawled out of the sea, but our lives depend upon it now, depend upon the thriving of sea creatures. The movie leaves viewers, in the words of D. H. Lawrence, "eyes wide open in the waters of the beginning and the end."[12]

NINE

Failure to Communicate

In many *Star Trek* episodes and movies there's a scene where the captain orders that a message be sent "in all languages and all frequencies" to some alien vessel or planet. That's always a telling moment for fans who read *Trek* between the lines. *Star Trek*'s creators seem to hold out faith that if humans ever *do* meet an alien race, it will merely be linguistic differences that need to be overcome.

And in fact, *Trek*'s otherworldly encounters usually do go well. Once that handy little device known as the "universal translator" is employed and communication becomes possible, some measure of understanding generally follows. The show places an immense amount of implicit faith in the ability of the communicative act to overcome vast differences of culture. It's perhaps an extension of franchise honcho Gene Roddenberry's belief in the inevitable improvement of humanity through contact and conversation with alien worlds. It's as if *Star Trek* equates progress with communication. Talk to me and I'll *understand* you. I may not agree with you, but the process of dialogue will create a bond. It's a hopeful premise, and one that has certainly not always been borne out here on Earth.

As a creative construct, writers have been using the "failure to communicate = conflict" formula since the beginning of literature. The frustrations and misunderstandings that arise when two people, or two countries, are unable to communicate have added lots of dramatic tension to many stories. In fact, some stories have been built entirely on that premise, so it's useful to consider the ways in which *Trek* has appropriated this idea. As I hope to show, the trunk of this literary device has also produced some intriguing branches, for the failure to communicate has not only shown up in stories about human communication, but also about the difficulty of communicating with animal, and mechanical, beings. As *Trek* has clearly drawn on these traditions as well, it's worth looking at their literary exemplars.

The best place to begin a discussion of the confusion of cacophonous conversation is at the source that claims credit for that confusion, a story from the Old Testament, which seeks to explain why humans speak so many languages and how our linguistic labyrinth became so complex.

BABEL ON, BABYLON

Although it has become more familiar as a metaphor for misunderstanding than as an actual structure, there was, according to legend, a real "Tower of Babel"—or so a fundamentalist reading of the Bible would suggest (many contemporary archeologists, however, remain unconvinced).[1] In the first book of the Old Testament, when the origin of the world is still being laid out in religious terms, there's a story about how God got angry with a group of people living near what would be later known as the City of Babylon, and how he did something to them which created unprecedented confusion. Here's the account, from Genesis, Chapter 11:

> Now the whole Earth used the same language and the same words. And it came about as they journeyed east, that they found a plain in the land of Shinar and settled there. And they said to one another, "Come let us make bricks and burn them thoroughly." And they used brick for stone, and they used tar for mortar. And they said, "Come, let us build for ourselves a city, and a tower whose top will reach into heaven, and let us make for ourselves a name; lest we be scattered abroad over the face of the whole Earth. And the Lord came down to see the city and the tower which the sons of men had built. And the Lord said, "Behold, they are one people, and they all have the same language. And this is what they began to do, and now nothing which they propose to do will be impossible for them." "Come, let US go down and there confuse their

language, that they may not understand one another's speech." So the Lord scattered them abroad from there over the face of the whole Earth; and they stopped building the city. Therefore its name was called Babel, because there the Lord confused the language of the whole Earth [Verses 1–9].²

As with every other part of the Bible, there are lots of conflicting and competing claims among theologians about the meaning of this passage, or what it was about the tower that so angered God. (Most religious scholars conclude that He was upset either at his creations trying to reach heaven on their own, and hence seeking to supplant God, or that he was fearful the impressive tower would serve as a magnet for humanity and keep them from spreading across the globe and populating the rest of the planet, which he had bade them do a few chapters earlier.) Fortunately, Trekkers need not concern themselves with the theological dimensions of that debate. What is important, however, is the realization that the bedrock text of the Judeo-Christian society establishes the failure to communicate as a threat to social order and an impediment to progress. All other variations on the "failure to communicate" theme are merely changes in degree, not kind. The central idea remains intact and powerful: despite human intellect, and even innate goodness, without the ability to communicate, we live in a Babylon which prevents understanding and promotes parochial self-interest.

Of course, the opposite is also true: *if* we can find a way to understand another, if communication can be achieved, then détente will follow and conflicts can be eradicated. Not to put too fine a point on it: if failure to communicate engenders chaos, conflict, and isolation, the *ability* to communicate should result in harmony.

Star Trek has dealt with the ramifications of the failure to communicate — and its potentially lethal consequences — in several episodes. A good place to start the discussion of *Trek*'s exploration of this theme is *The Next Generation* episode "Darmok," in which Jean Luc Picard and his crew must solve a puzzling linguistic riddle. The premise of the episode draws directly from the Tower of Babel story: different races, using speech codes which share the same lexicon of words but which signify different meanings, are thrown together in a tense situation. The inability to understand each other ratchets up the tension.

The plot involves the *Enterprise* trying to establish diplomatic relations with the "Children of Tama," a peaceful race whose language is comprised of snippets of descriptive phrases like "Darmok and Gilard at Tinagra" and "When the Walls Fell."³ The Children of Tama, or "Tamarians," continue to repeat such phrases when the *Enterprise* encounters them in space, and while the crew tries to understand what it all might mean, Captain Picard is suddenly beamed off the bridge and onto a grassy landscape — where he faces the leader of the Tamarians, who is now brandishing a knife.

The Tamarian leader offers Picard a knife, but Picard refuses to take up the implied challenge to fight. As the *Enterprise* struggles to retrieve their captain (the Tamarians have jammed the *Enterprise*'s communications and beaming frequency), Picard and the Tamarian leader spend the night huddling around separate campfires, wary, trying in vain to understand each other.

Meanwhile, back on the *Enterprise*, tension mounts as the crew struggles with how to save the captain and how to deal with the incomprehensible Children of Tama who have fired warning shots at a shuttle craft sent to rescue Picard. As Commander Data and Counselor Troi attempt to decipher the Tamarian language, they express their frustration at their failure to communicate. As Troi notes, "All our technology and experience, our universal translator, our years in space, contact with more alien cultures than I can even remember, and we still can't even say hello to these people. A single word can lead to tragedy. One word misspoken, or misunderstood, and that can happen here, Data, if we fail."⁴

Ultimately, Picard and the Tamarian are forced to set aside their linguistic differences to fight off a cloaked, lethal creature that is viciously attacking them. As the Tamarian captain tries to hold off the incursions of this mysterious creature, Picard begins to understand that he is uttering phrases which describe past events in the Tamarian culture, snippets of description from mythic battles which have come to be used to describe everything in Tamarian culture.

"That's how you communicate. By citing example!"⁵ Picard concludes excitedly. But just then, the electromagnetic beast attacks the Tamarian captain, and Picard, who tries to rush to his aid, is immobilized by the *Enterprise*'s latest attempt to beam him up to the ship. When the failed beaming attempt finally releases Picard, the Tamarian has been fatally wounded.

In their final moments together, before the Tamarian expires, Picard gets the wounded man to share more Tamarian myths, and as he talks, he fully comprehends the centrality of Tamarian myth to their language. Picard also learns that the Tamarian had himself and Picard beamed down to the planet together so that they might fight off the enemy together — because in Tamarian myth, such a battle took place among two warriors, and afterward, they formed a bond of lasting friendship. The Children of Tama were hoping that such a side-by-side battle, Picard with their leader, against the beast, would lead to a lasting friendship between the Children of Tama and the Federation.

Once Picard is returned, the Tamarian ship and the *Enterprise* stand down from their red-alert battle status, and the episode ends hinting that such an alliance between the two races is likely now that their Tower of Babel has led to a summit of understanding.

Bridging the communication gap between two races that, though different, are able to communicate through words and gestures, can be a daunting prospect. But how does one communicate with a life form that uses no words and has no recognizable features? Can such a link be established? And what if it's not? What are the consequences of continued misunderstanding? These are the questions at the heart of an episode that is always near the top of the various surveys of "all-time favorite" *Star Trek* episodes: the original series' "The Devil in the Dark."[6]

Serpents

It's easy to see why the episode is so popular. It's a mysterious, frightening and genuinely moving story. All of *Trek*'s strengths come to the fore in this episode, from the captain's heroism and commitment to moral behavior in space, to Spock's icy logic and his ability to "mind meld" with a separate entity, and McCoy's benevolent cynicism. The episode features a seemingly vicious alien — with a real twist. There are the famous "red-shirted" federation victims — the semi-anonymous supporting actors whose fate is sealed during an episode's costume call — the greedy, shortsighted human profiteers, plus a generous dollop of science, philosophy, and spirituality. At its core, "The Devil in the Dark" is built on the tensions generated from an inability to communicate with an animal-like life form, and as such it draws on a small but significant literary tradition in which encounters between humans and beasts have been delineated. A superb example of this type of literature is D.H. Lawrence's poem "The Snake,"[7] a work that is anthologized in some literature textbooks but worthy of a much wider audience.

"The Snake" is a poem with a message, namely that human beings who react viscerally out of disgust to non-human creatures — in this case, a snake — not only dishonor themselves but miss a critical chance to achieve some sort of connection with a fellow planet dweller. Lawrence's poem tells the story of a British ambassador living in Sicily who steps out in his robe one hot summer morning to fill his water jug. And he sees a snake drinking at his trough, and must wait for this invader to leave:

> A snake came to my water trough,
> On a hot, hot day, and I in pyjamas for the heat,
> To drink there.
>
> In the deep, strange-scented shade of the great dark carob-tree,
> I came down the steps with my pitcher
> And must wait, must stand and wait, for there he was at the
>   trough before me.[8]

Just in these few lines we get some of the important themes exploited in "The Devil in the Dark." The snake is there just to drink, to satisfy a biological imperative. The man is impatient, indignant even, as he waits for this scaly interloper to finish and go. As the man watches the snake, he is both attracted and repulsed (the battle of those two impulses also provides the tension in "The Devil in the Dark"):

> And voices in me said, If you were a man
> You would take a stick and break him now, and finish him
>   off.
>
> But I must confess how I liked him,
> How glad I was he had come like a guest in quiet, to drink at
>   my water trough
> And depart peaceful, pacified, and thankless,
> Into the burning bowels of the earth.[9]

And like Kirk, who encounters his mysterious creature deep in the earth, Lawrence teeters between fear and respect:

> And truly I was afraid, I was most afraid,
> But even so, honoured still more
> That he should seek my hospitality
> From out the dark door of the secret earth.[10]

So this slithery interloper takes a long drink, then turns to depart the way he came, through a hole in a retaining wall. As this marvel of nature slithers away, the man's education, breeding and culture overcome his awe, and he hurls a stick at the snake, startling the creature. Lawrence's account of the scene is more beautiful and moving than it ought to be, a poetic indictment of man's knee-jerk response to the unfamiliar:

> I think it did not hit him,
> But suddenly that part of him that was left behind convulsed in undignified haste,
> Writhed like lightning, and was gone
> Into the black hole, the earth-lipped fissure in the wall-front,
> at which, in the intense still noon, I stared with fascination.
>
> And immediately I regretted it.
> I though how paltry, how vulgar, what a mean act!
> I despised myself and the voices of my accursed human education.
>
> And I thought of the albatross,
> And I wished he would come back, my snake.

The poem ends with the lament of what's been lost in such a vulgar and mean-spirited attempt at first contact:

> And so, I missed my chance with one of the lords
> Of life.
> And I have something to expiate:
> A pettiness.[11]

What Lawrence eulogizes in "The Snake" is mankind's failure of imagination. The typical response to the unfamiliar is all-too-familiar to Lawrence, and many other writers who have staged cross-species contact with an aim towards exposing humanity's baser instincts.[12] But those fears are largely dispelled by the magisterial "Devil in the Dark," which in essence rewrites "The Snake" to provide a more virtuous and satisfying ending.

Nine. Failure to Communicate

MINER INCURSIONS

The episode revolves around the actions of an alien creature, an ottoman-sized blob of rubber cement that has killed a number of miners on the planet Janus VI. The supervisor of the mining operation requests the *Enterprise*'s assistance in tracking down the creature and destroying it so that the mine can continue to operate, producing rich deposits of Pergium, a valuable mineral.

As the crew investigates the killings, they discover that a valuable piece of equipment needed for life support in the mines has been hidden by the same creature killing the miners. Spock concludes that the creature, which tunnels through rock, is highly intelligent; and after it is located and wounded, Kirk asks Spock to mind-meld with it. This is the heart of the episode, for in what would pass as a "breakthrough" moment in any psychotherapist's office, the creature speaks through Spock in a teary and tragic monologue, revealing the real reason it has killed the miners.

The blob-like entity, known as a "Horta," communicates to Spock that buried within the rock that is being mined are thousands of its eggs — its children, essentially. The beast pleads with its human excavators to stop the destructive practice. By the end of the mind meld, Spock has been reduced to a quivering blob himself, and the miners, who were indignant that Kirk didn't blast the creature into chalk dust when he had the chance, are now dumbstruck at the notion that this rock creature was simply exercising motherly love.

Once communication has been established, a compromise is quickly, and satisfactorily, reached. The Horta's thousands of remaining eggs will hatch, unmolested by the machinery of the miners. Once hatched, the little Hortas will themselves assist the miners in extracting the pergium. Despite the pragmatic, even mercantile, nature of the arrangement, everybody gets what he or she needs. A new race of Horta will be born and the Federation will continue to get its valuable mineral.

"The Devil in the Dark" is an object lesson in the value of cross-species communication. Revisiting the squandered opportunity of Lawrence's "The Snake," humans (well, Jim Kirk — hey, that's a start) in the twenty-third century seize the opportunity to bridge the communication gap between humans and non-humans. The heroic and compassionate acts of Kirk, Spock, and even Dr. McCoy (who heals the Horta's wounds with a cement-like mixture, though only after famously protesting that "I'm a doctor, not a bricklayer!"[13]) take humanity — and our animal brethren — to the brink of a truly brave new world.

TEN

Staying Sane in an Insane World

Insanity wears lots of different masks. People talk about the insanity of war, or of the nuclear arms race, or of a deranged killer going on a rampage. There is the image of the crazy, Norman Bates–type lunatic, locked in an insane asylum, filled with screaming and delusional patients. Scenes of riots at soccer stadiums, or in urban areas during civic conflagrations, are often described as "insane." Even the media is not above terming a really bad traffic snarl during rush hour as "an insane amount of traffic."

While it may be difficult to define precisely what "insanity" is, most people would consider it to be at the extreme opposite end of what constitutes, for them, "normal" behavior. But what happens when one's normal, balanced, "sane" world is suddenly supplanted by a world where the insane has *become* the norm? This turning of tables — the "normal" is now replaced with the "insane" — has whetted the appetites of many creative artists, from Rod Serling (whose popular television show *The Twilight Zone* operated weekly on just such a premise) to Franz Kafka, who lent his very name to this type of inversion, which we now call "Kafka-esque." And not surprisingly, *Star Trek* has explored this shadowy area as well, placing its "heroes" in situations where the normal world is a chimera and the new rules of the game can seem insane. And what do thoughtful, moral and highly civilized people do when placed in "insane" situations?

Star Trek answers that question many times, and in many "insane" scenarios, often drawing on literary works which have explored the balance between the normal and the insane in some particularly pressurized environments. This body of literature can be roughly divided between those works which give us an external world of insanity, with all of the expected results when normal social controls are suspended, and internal words of insanity, where the cause of turmoil and disjunctiveness is generated from within. The specific literary treatments worth looking at here include a harrowing narrative about the insanity of prison, with its often ruthless tormenters, deliberate violations of human dignity and capricious exercise of punishments, and a recounting of the insanity caused by depression and the many counterproductive treatments for mental illness, such as forced withdrawal from "normal" society, which only lead to greater depression and paranoia. The classic authors who have charted the course through these labyrinths, Edgar Allan Poe and Charlotte Perkins Gilman, have much to say to today's reader, and to the avid *Star Trek* fan, about how to behave when the walls of normalcy come crumbling down.

CELLING YOUR SOUL

The idea of incarceration has always frightened and mesmerized people. With its deprivations — physical and mental — and its sense of being so utterly "different" from normal society, average people have always looked with fear and awe on the prospect of being "locked up." High-profile trials of celebrities who face possible prison sentences regularly capture the popular imagination as increasingly large numbers of television viewers follow trial coverage on the major news networks and cable television channels now dedicated solely to criminal justice. There have been many books, movies and television series about life behind bars, and interest in this sub-genre of prison-related material remains unabated.[1] Sociologists and psychologists continue to debate the underlying cause of this widespread interest and its impact on society at large. And writers keep turning to the idea, re-dressing plots involving some "average" person being thrown suddenly into the insane

Ten. Staying Sane in an Insane World

underworld of violence and terror that is prison life. The grimmest and most spine-tingling account of someone who emerges on the wrong side of the freedom/incarceration divide is Edgar Allan Poe's disturbing, widely anthologized short story "The Pit and the Pendulum," which captures perfectly the difficulty of staying sane in an insane environment.

Poe's nameless narrator begins the tale by recounting the sentencing that placed him in his cold and stony prison. Right out of the gate, we get the mental combustion of a man trying to reconcile the highly sane and civilized protocol of jurisprudence with the ghastly and horrific manner of its delivery and the grimness of the verdict:

> I saw the lips of the black-robed judges. They appeared to me white—whiter than the sheet upon which I trace these words—and thin even to grotesqueness; thin, with the intensity of their expression of firmness—of immovable resolution—of stern contempt of human torture. I saw that the decrees of what to me was Fate, were still issuing from those lips. I saw them writhe with a deadly locution. I saw them fashion the syllables of my name; and I shuddered because no sound succeeded. I saw, too, for a few moments of delirious horror, the soft and nearly imperceptible waving of the sable draperies which enwrapped the walls of the apartment. And then my vision fell upon the seven tall candles upon the table.[2]

There's a patina of dignity and ritual behind this surreal and unjust affair. The narrator has been sentenced to death by a tribunal of the Spanish Inquisition, and his punishment is as insane as the very body which bloodily terrorized European "heretics." He's placed in darkness, in a cell with an unprotected pit deviously fashioned in the center of the cell (which he accidentally discovers but avoids), and subjected to all sorts of gruesome torture — not with the immediate aim of killing him so much as amusing his captors and breaking his spirit: "I could no longer doubt the doom prepared for me by monkish ingenuity in torture. My cognizance of the pit had become known to the inquisitorial agents,"[3] who then proceed to do lots of other insanity-inducing things, like tie him down and unfurl a slow, sharpened knife blade on a pendulum, cover him with rats, heat up his cell walls to a white-hot intensity, that sort of thing.

Poe's tale makes for thoroughly unpleasant reading. Significantly, however, Poe's narrator keeps his wits and is able to survive until a last-second rescuer appears, literally as the narrator is falling into the pit ("An outstretched arm caught my own as I fell, fainting, into the abyss."[4]). Throughout the tale, the victim tries to remain as calm and collected as necessary to overcome the torment and tricks of his insanity-inducing captivity. As one Poe critic, noting the insanity of the situation, has summed it up, "The young man in 'The Pit and the Pendulum' was able to maintain his sanity by the power of his will to escape the swinging knife-blade just long enough to be fortuitously rescued from a private psychic world which every moment threatened him with insanity and annihilation."[5]

Trumped-up charges, a nightmarish, surreal trial, a brutal and cruel subterranean prison, lots of schemes to harm or even kill a prisoner, a valiant attempt to keep one's wits amid the madness, and a daring, last-second rescue. If *Star Trek* fans feel they've seen that blueprint played out somewhere in the *Trek* universe, they're right. It was just that mix of elements — along with *Trek*'s trademark optimistic turn — that provided the dramatic oomph in *Star Trek VI: The Undiscovered Country*.

JUSTICE IS MINE

Because the movie had so many rich sub-themes, fans and critics could easily overlook the film's debt to stories of prison life and its many horrors. And even though many of the movie's prison scenes were leavened with *Trek*'s trademark good humor, there are some interesting parallels between works such as Poe's "The Pit and the Pendulum" and *Star Trek VI*.

The plot of *Star Trek VI* involves the pursuit of something formerly unthinkable in the *Trek* universe: peace between the Federation and the Klingons. Kirk is chosen to be the Federation's ambassador in the initial stages of outreach to the Klingon Empire, a position he reluctantly accepts. His reticence is understandable. Not only has he been fighting the Klingons for most of his Federation career, but also the Klingons are responsible for the death of Kirk's only son, David (which took place on the Genesis Planet in *Star Trek III*). He feels powerless to refuse the mission, but he admits in a private captain's diary entry that he'll never trust the Klingons.

Ten. Staying Sane in an Insane World

After an exceedingly awkward dinner in the Klingon Chancellor's honor aboard the *Enterprise*, an apparent "mishap" occurs, and the Klingon ship is fired upon. The chancellor suffers fatal wounds. Kirk and his crew, it turns out, had nothing to do with it (a group of Federation-Klingon conspirators were responsible), but Kirk is arrested and, along with McCoy, found guilty in a trial right out of a Poe story. Surreal lighting, murmuring in decipherable tongues, a hooded "chief justice" presiding in a curtained opera-box wielding an iron ball as a gavel... it's all very bizarre.

And it becomes more so. Despite any concrete evidence against them, Kirk and McCoy are sentenced to life in prison and sent to an arctic-type penal colony, where attempts to escape are met with near-instant freezing, and attempts to merely survive don't fare much better (with a battery of hostile aliens hovering around, waiting to knife, strangle or pummel you for their own advancement — or simple amusement). As soon as Kirk arrives, a hulking, big foot–like creature begins pulverizing the captain, as the guards look on with wry bemusement.

There is plotting among the inmates, betrayal, violence, thievery and a pervasive air of deep desperation. One can only imagine how quickly sanity would dissipate in such an environment. Of course, Kirk is unflappable, sizing up the prospects for escape and formulating a plan while romancing a shape-shifting fellow inmate who turns out to be as conniving as she is curvaceous. She pretends to assist them in a daring aboveground escape while actually leading them into a trap set by prison officials — who would then be able to say they killed these "Federation criminals" while trying to escape. But the wily captain has been monitored the whole time by Mr. Spock, who was waiting for the two captives to get far enough away from the prison that a prohibitive force field would no longer prevent them from being beamed aboard the *Enterprise*. As the prison guards close in on the captain and McCoy — taking aim at them, with fingers on the triggers, creating maximum suspense — Spock has them beamed out of there. Just in the nick of time.

The insane world of the prison never engulfed Kirk, and as a result of his ability to stay sane, to keep his head while many of those around him were literally losing theirs, he triumphed. The scenes of the Klingon penal colony are among the darkest and most disorienting in the *Trek* universe, and the threat of annihilation — from without *and* within — was ever present. A less balanced mind would have had no chance of coping with the horrors and hardships of Klingon "justice."

Trek has never been afraid to explore the dark corners of the human condition, to try to illuminate the hidden anxieties and baser instincts in the deep recesses of mankind's collective mind. Human beings, *Trek* acknowledges, can often create horrific circumstances which upset the balance of even the most balanced mind — think of the torture devices of the Inquisition, or the Nazi concentration camps. Insanity, under those circumstances, can sometimes seem like the only logical consequence.

But what about when everything appears to be just fine? It doesn't take a Klingon prison to induce insanity — although that might make for an effective starting point. For some people, insanity is something that is generated from their own mind, not imposed on them by the external world. The most chilling and effective exploration of how one's mind can become the agent of one's own deterioration was written by a woman who had some experience with this sort of thing. In a work that has been called a "harrowing journey...into insanity,"[6] one finds all the elements of a crackup-in-progress, dressed in the genteel garments of Victorian storytelling. The tale is "The Yellow Wallpaper" by Charlotte Perkins Gilman, and this famous short story not only provides a glimpse behind the ornate curtain of "normalcy," it also provided *Star Trek* with a blueprint for some of its best episodes.

IF THESE WALLS COULD TALK

Charlotte Perkins Gilman had a roller-coaster life, filled with the highs of motherhood, marriage and fame, and the lows of motherhood, marriage and fame. The fulcrum of her teeter-totter life was a debilitating bout of depression, ultimately leading to an emotional collapse shortly after the birth of her daughter in 1885. Gilman sought the assistance of a prominent doctor, who treated her in a way that was commonly administered for all "hysterics" in the 1880s: complete bed rest and total avoidance of any "intellectual stimulation." The result? Gilman said she went from being depressed to the brink of "utter mental ruin."[7] Unfortunately for her, it led to an uncomfortable public divorce and her agreement to give up her daughter to her husband and new wife. Fortunately for posterity, it led to the short story "The Yellow Wallpaper."

The story captures in remarkably insightful pre–Freudian psychological complexity the steady erosion of one woman's grasp on reality. Based on her own experience in near-total social isolation, the story recounts how a woman tries to recover from depression in a stately, isolated country house (which the story slyly suggests has always doubled as mental institution, with its barred windows and beds bolted to the floor), attended only by her physician-husband and a nursemaid for her baby. Well, there *are* other characters — if you count the mysterious, ghostlike women who are trapped in the wallpaper and eventually begin appearing to the narrator.

The story can be — has been — read in lots of different ways, from a feminist railing against the constraints of marriage and domesticity to an amalgam of gothic horror and Henry James–style psychological tale. It can also be read as a blueprint for a mind groping wildly to discover what is "real," and trying desperately to cling to those scraps of reality until what's real and what's hallucinogenic merge disquietly (the exact premise, incidentally, of *The Next Generation*'s classic episode "Frame of Mind," which will be considered below).

The narrator seems to be going insane right before the reader's eyes, and the drama of the story comes, in part, from the tension between the actual erosion of her mental state and the sedate and reasonable tone of the language describing it (a motif J.D. Salinger would later appropriate for his famous tale of creeping insanity, *The Catcher in the Rye*). Discussing her desire to return to normalcy, the depressed narrator states matter-of-factly that "I must use my will and self-control and not let my silly fancies run away with me." But she can't, because the wallpaper distracts her: "It slaps you in the face, knocks you down, and tramples upon you. It is like a bad dream." As she slips deeper and deeper into her inexorable insanity, she understands why the wallpaper moves, and relates it, again, in the most reasonable diction: "I really have discovered something at last. Through watching so much at night, I have finally found out. The front pattern *does* move — and no wonder! The woman behind shakes it!"[8]

By the end of the story, the woman is wildly clawing at the wallpaper, though "it sticks horribly," and trying to get at the spirits who live in the wallpaper, "All those strangled heads and bulbous eyes."[9]

The story ends with the narrator locking her husband out of the room and slithering about the floor like a lizard. Her stifling environment and her misconceived treatment have pushed her over the edge, turning her depression into a form of insanity that has divorced her completely from reality.

Modern pharmacology and a more progressive view of depressive psychosis would surely rewrite the end of the story, but the motif remains creatively powerful: a mind seeking to connect with reality, trying to remember and recapture the sane world, slipping inexorably into the realm of the insane. As alluded to above, *The Next Generation* episode "Frame of Mind" also shares the idea of a mind slipping in and out of sanity, seeking desperately to rearrange the scraps of normalcy in a world spinning out of control. It is perhaps the most harrowing episode *Star Trek* ever produced.

The Play's the Thing

Though the journeys have been entertaining, there's always been a good deal of danger to be faced in the unexplored regions of deep space. Not all alien races are committed to peaceable relations with the representatives of the Federation, and it is on a mission into hostile alien territory that Commander William Riker has his "Yellow Wallpaper" moment.

Sent to rescue Federation hostages on the planet Tilonus IV, Riker is captured himself, and while his captors drug him so they can transfer the contents of Riker's mind into their databanks, the commander imagines himself in a play that he really *was* rehearsing on board the *Enterprise* shortly before the rescue mission, and then in an insane asylum on Tilonus IV, being experimented on by menacing doctors, and then back on the *Enterprise* performing the play, and then back at the asylum, ad nauseum. The competing delusions create an unstable mental environment, leading to his near total collapse.

Just as the narrator of "The Yellow Wallpaper" began to see faces in the design of the paper as her crack-up progressed, so too does Riker continue to have delusions of seeing Tilonians when he thinks he's aboard the *Enterprise*, and the *Enterprise* crew members when he thinks he's on Tilonus. He comes to distrust what he thinks is real, whether it is a trickle of blood from his temple or a visit from an away team sent to rescue him.

The teleplay is relentless in toying with Riker's sanity, allowing him to become convinced of the "reality" of his Tilonian world, and then having him back on board the *Enterprise*, performing a play about a man who thinks he is going insane, and then sending him, in his mind, back to Tilonus, where the lab he's in approximates the set of the play. It's weird, wild and perfectly scripted to create a truly harrowing sense of dislocation, with the always-steely William T. Riker now reduced to debilitating tremors of uncertainty. As we learn at the end of the episode, it was only Riker's memories of the play that helped keep him sane, and as the Tilonians drained more and more of Riker's neural energy from him, subconsciously he began clinging more and more to his most recent memories as a hedge against insanity. As Charlotte Perkins Gilman's heroine slid into insanity amid the "comforts" of home, so too does Riker begin to slide down the slope of madness amid the faces and places which he's always identified with "home": namely, the *Enterprise* and its crew.

Fortunately for Riker's sanity, the drug he was given begins to wear off, he regains for a brief moment full consciousness of his surroundings as he overhears the Tilonians talking about his neural transfer, and he's held onto enough of his wits to know what's happening. He signals the *Enterprise* crew for an emergency beam-out, and returns to the *Enterprise*, wonderfully familiar but oddly unsettling as well. Riker is shaky but he'll recover, his bout with the insane world of hallucination and delusion over (but, like his warmest memories which helped preserve his sanity, also now a part of him).

ELEVEN

Mismatched Pairs

There are some couples who probably ought not stay together. That rather glib observation has been enough to fuel some of the greatest narratives in imaginative literature, from chronicles of couples whose conflicts spilled over into society (consider the Trojan War) to lightly comic examinations of human incompatibility (think *The Odd Couple*). The appeal of this idea to the creators of *Star Trek* is, upon reflection, pretty clear. Stories which delineate the difficulty of overcoming fundamental differences in character or culture are what *Star Trek* is all about.

Not unexpectedly, *Trek* has explored lots of such mismatches: between individuals, alien cultures, even between human and machine. The *Enterprise* crew might profess to follow the "Prime Directive" — a standing Federation policy dictating noninterference in the development of another culture — but there's no policy which can keep these strong-willed space explorers from falling for the fellow beings they encounter on their travels.

In many stories about these doomed pairings, the matches that turn out to be the worst appear, at their inception, to be among the best. The dramatic appeal of these mismatched pairs often derives from our desire to believe that "love conquers all." The landmark literary works which have explored the nature of relationships force us to question the very notion of "compatibility," and what can cause a "good" relationship to end not only badly, but sometimes in despair — or even death.

A multitude of literary works offers a window into the turbulent world of mismatched pairs. Sometimes the reader is left rooting for the relationship. Other times we're left simply waiting for it to implode. Can love really overcome different expectations, different belief systems, even different species? A brief look at three classic works will shed some light on *Star Trek*'s subsequent spinning of this theme: Henrik Ibsen's *A Doll's House,* Shakespeare's *Othello,* and the timeless tale *Beauty and the Beast*. And though *Star Trek*'s mismatched pairs seldom rise to the level of Elizabethan tragedy, we'll see that *Trek* seems to have learned a few lessons from these earlier tales of problematic relationships. *Trek*'s view of relationships often challenges the very notion of what constitutes a "mismatch," and how one should act when faced with obstacles that have doomed other couples.

HELLO DOLLY

It's hard to say which usually turns out worse: relationships where we try to fool each other, or relationships where we try to fool ourselves. In Ibsen's *A Doll's House*, one doesn't have to choose, because the playwright provides plenty of both. Although *A Doll's House* has been claimed by a variety of competing academic camps (naturalists, modernists, Marxists, feminists, and various others), Ibsen's main idea seems fairly clear and discernible from the text. *A Doll's House* is the story of a marriage that never should have happened. There was a house, children, and all the Victorian-era amenities, but Nora, the protagonist, was never really loved by her husband Torvald — any more than a doll is loved by a child. The tragedy at the heart of the play is not the failed relationship, but the failure to discover until much too late that there never really *was* a relationship.

The plot amplifies many of Ibsen's preoccupying social concerns,[1] but it is easily recapitulated. A woman named Nora Helmer is married to a midlevel bank administrator named Torvald. Nora has kept a secret for many years: she forged her father's signature on an I.O.U. to get money for a trip to restore her husband's health, and now that her husband is about to be promoted, a disgruntled, incompetent underling at Torvald's bank is preparing to reveal the secret (thus ruining her reputation) unless Nora can get her husband to change his mind about firing him. Nora deludes herself that even if the secret is revealed, her husband will insulate her from the shame attached to this indiscretion by claiming that he, not Nora, committed the forgery.

But when Torvald finds out, he acts petulantly, blaming his wife for ruining them both and chastising her like a child for her rash, indefensible act (even though it was done to preserve Torvald's fragile health). He stomps and fumes and tells Nora how ignorant and self-absorbed she's been. Torvald then receives news that the disgruntled employee has decided *not* to make the news public, and Torvald, greatly relieved, tells his wife he'll forgive her, and they can forget the whole thing ever happened.

Except Nora can't forget. At the critical moment of her married life, she discovered her husband doesn't really love her — he was only concerned about his reputation and future. His failure to stand up to the blackmailer and to support his wife emotionally reveals their weak and worthless relationship. Nora, who leaves her husband (whom she calls a "stranger") as the play ends, vows to start her adult life, to stop living like a doll in a doll's house. Nora slams the door. The curtain falls.

Lots of lesser writers have picked up that theme, the "who have I been living with all these years?" motif, but it finds its most crafty and compelling expression in Ibsen. The Norwegian playwright had a gift for dramatically synthesizing people's complicity in their own psychological destruction. The genius of the play's construction is manifest when considered retroactively. That is, everything Torvald *isn't* has been obvious to us from the start — and should have been obvious to Nora, but she allowed herself to be deluded. She's a victim of her own baseless fantasizing as much as she's been victimized by Torvald's spinelessness.

This couple thought they knew each other, but they only knew what they hoped lay at the core of their relationship, not what was really there: an empty space, an emotional vacuum.

But at least this couple lived to tell the tale. In Shakespeare's *Othello*, the couple discovers how wrong they were for each other as they die tragically in one of the most famous murder-suicides in all of literature.

Lots of critics have weighed in on *Othello*, but so much has been written and said about the racial tension (he's black, she's white) and Iago's crafty duplicity that few readers have probably ever thought about how Othello and his wife, Desdemona, really didn't have much of a relationship to begin with. She fell for him because she used to eavesdrop on his stories of martial bravery and she was attracted to his physical prowess. He fell for her because she took pity on him for all the travails he endured in battle. The very qualities they prized in each other (his brutality, her vulnerability) led indirectly to their undoing. When Othello kills Desdemona in a fit of jealous rage, he is exhibiting that tendency that made him such a fierce warrior: passionate, unrestrained violence directed towards those he feels have wronged him.

The green-eyed monster, jealousy, is usually held up as the responsible culprit in the crime, but it can be argued that this pair was mortally mismatched from the start. As a model of what happens when two people who don't really know each other very well have their first fight, it's pretty extreme. Yet, as with Nora and Torvald, the end result may be tragic but it shouldn't really come as a surprise.

In Ibsen and in Shakespeare, we get a template for ill-fated relationships. In *Trek*, as we shall see, characters just as ill-suited for each other are often brought together, but they often give evidence of having learned a lesson from such morality tales. One of the most popular and beloved tales of love between unlikelies is *Beauty and the Beast*, a tale dating back to medieval times but generally attributed to Madame Gabrielle de Villeneuve, around 1740.

Popularized for a generation of readers by Walt Disney, and better known to many through the movie version or the long-running Broadway play, *Beauty and the Beast* tells the story of a virtuous young woman named Belle who ends up as the captive of a fierce creature who was once a handsome young prince but now — because of his arrogance and lack of compassion — has been turned into a beast. He is fated to remain a hideous creature until he learns what it really means to love and be loved.

His lovely prisoner is, of course, repulsed by him — at least at first. This, too, is a timeless motif, appearing in various incarnations from Hugo's *Hunchback of Notre Dame* to Edward Rostand's *Cyrano DeBergerac*. Such an initial recoiling paves the way for the usually inevitable reconsideration and the deeper "second look" into the soul of the scorned and deformed would-be suitor. The message of such narratives is that the "real" person is buried beneath the facade, and that to judge someone by outer appearances is superficial. And in fact, Beauty learns to look past the Beast's outer self to see the nobility within. Once she loves him for who he truly is, he is restored to his former, physically attractive self.

Should physical characteristics be a factor in one's determination about who to love? *Trek* has addressed that question in many of its episodes and films. One of the most potent explorations has involved the tender infatuations of young Wesley Crusher, who found himself drawn to a visitor on the *Enterprise* whose youth and beauty were but one aspect of her character.

FEELING HORNY. AND SCALY.

In *The Next Generation* episode "The Dauphin," Wesley gets his first taste of attraction as his adolescent heart is won by a winsome royal visitor named Salia (played by actress Jamie Hubbard, who convincingly conveyed genuine adolescent passion even though she was 10 years older than Wil Wheaton, who played 16-year-old Wesley Crusher).[2] Though she's under the strict supervision of a mother-figure chaperone stern enough to scare away even the bravest male suitor, Wesley persists in his desire to get to know her better. And just when he's seen enough to shift his teenaged hormones into overdrive, he gets an additional piece of information about this paragon of young female loveliness. She's a fierce, grossly unattractive beast.

Actually, she's a shape shifter whose primary incarnation is as a large, scaly monster. But who said love is perfect? Well, that's Wesley and Salia's dilemma. The princess represents a race of people who are "allasomorphs," or shape-shifters. (Interestingly, in medieval literature, shape shifters were a commonplace in "heroic" narratives, often attempting to dissuade a hero from achieving his goal; Satan, incidentally, is perhaps the most famous shape-shifter in literature.)

After Wesley witnesses Salia's transformation into a grotesque (to him) creature, he storms out of her quarters feeling betrayed. This is that moment of discovery which can either lead to personal growth (as with Nora, in *A Doll's House*) or gnawing, self-destructive anger (Othello's unfortunate course of action). Wesley treads both paths, first exhorting in bitterness his sense of having been deceived. His anger overwhelms him — until he confronts her, and she apologizes but explains why she felt she couldn't give him the whole story. He realizes they could never be together (a Nora Torvald moment) because they are, to understate the case, different people. Yet their mutual recognition of what they have achieved — a genuine, abiding affection even though they have seen the beastly side of each other (Salia, the physical; Wesley, the emotional) — leads to what could be called their "*Beauty and the Beast*" détente. They recognize their mutual imperfections, but they accept them, and in doing so they honor the impulse which allows love to bloom across chasms of culture and breeding. What might appear at first blush to be a throwaway "puppy love" episode with some sci-fi special effects thrown in for the hardcore *Trek*ker (the scenes where the princess and her chaperone shift into monsters is rather cheesy but effective because it's so jarring in the context of the up-to-then rather "sweet" episode) is really a thoughtful synthesis of a variety of strains of the "mismatched pairs" theme.

Trek has always found perceptive, even brave, ways to illustrate the obstacles couples must overcome (remember, Kirk and Uhura gave national television viewers American TV's first interracial kiss).[3] But perhaps surprisingly, *Trek*'s best and most humane exploration of "love across the divide" was provided by a machine, the EMH ("Emergency Medical Hologram") known quasi-affectionately to the crew (and fans) of *Voyager* simply as "The Doctor."

DANCING IN THE DARK

Trek has never been above moralizing. Lots of episodes are built around metaphors that advance *Trek*'s usually progressive social notions. But the very best, most effective and moving episodes from the *Star Trek* canon tend to "sneak in" their message, often asking the viewer to make the necessary mental connections between plot and moral. One of the best examples, and one of the most powerful *Trek* episodes of any of the various series, is the second-season *Voyager* episode "Lifesigns."

The episode is a beautiful example of how *Trek* takes a theme such as mismatched pairs and peels away layer after layer of the myth to reveal some implicit truths about the human condition. "Lifesigns" moves from a story simply about mismatches — the Doctor and his Vidiian patient, Denara; Tom Paris and his commander, Chakotay — through a series of concentric circles to include mismatches between holographic reality and physical reality (mind vs. body), and, ultimately, the inescapable mismatch between the joy of life and the pain of death. And rather than merely illustrate these ambiguities, *Trek* presumes to solve these existential dilemmas.

The story starts in classic *Trek* fashion, with a distress signal from an unidentified vessel being received by the crew. It turns out the vessel contains an escapee from a world ravaged by a disease (called "the phage") which has spread through the Delta Quadrant. The leprosy-like condition has affected the occupant of the shuttle now in distress. She is beamed to Voyager's sickbay, where the doctor — a holographic projection who seems lifelike in every way — is able to preserve the victim's cognitive function in a computer memory bank. He then uses a holographic replicator to recreate her physical form — an attractive Vidiian female.

In a stirring scene early in the episode, the now-restored holograph stands over her physical, disease ravaged body — an inversion of the *Beauty and the Beast* motif where someone attractive is turned into a beast. Here the woman, Denara Pel, can't believe how beautiful and youthful she has become. The two incarnations of her being form a kind of mismatched pair of their own, but the remaining plot revolves around the Doctor's slow and unsteadying slide into love for Denara that explores the mismatch idea further.

Counterpointed against the growing bond between the Doctor and Denara is the further dissolution of the bond between Voyager bridge officers Paris and Chakotay — a conflict which becomes almost archetypal, with Paris representing the creative, spontaneous, renegade mentality, and Chakotay playing his role of the regimented, by-the-book autocrat. This relationship, like the Doctor and Denara's, appears plagued by insurmountable difficulties. (The fact that the breach is not repaired by the episode's end — in fact, the conflict erupts into violence — helps create a context of dramatic tension for the drama simultaneously playing out with the Doctor's relationship.)

As the Doctor spends more time with his "patient," he notices how distracted and unfocused he is becoming. He attributes this to a program malfunction, until his assistant, Kes, points out that these "malfunctions" began shortly after Denara beamed aboard. The doctor says he doesn't like what's happening to him, yet he admits these feelings possess an undeniable appeal. He chooses an awkward public moment to declare his affections for Denara, and, put very much on the spot, she rebuffs him. The Doctor is confused, Denara is embarrassed and the whole relationship seems shaky and perhaps doomed to failure. This is the moment when one might expect a mutual break-up, an acknowledgement that there are too many obstacles in their path: the Doctor simply does not know how to love. Add to this the fact that Denara's holographic state cannot be maintained much longer because she needs to return to her physical body before her program begins degrading, and the complications preventing a romantic connection seem overwhelming.

Denara even goes so far as to administer a lethal dose of a drug to her phage-affected body — a twist on the Desdemona murder scene; this time, the Doctor intervenes, convincing Denara that she must remain alive, even in her plagued state, because that would give them two more weeks to be together before Voyager returned her to her home world, where she could live for months, maybe years.

"Be with me as long as you can," the Doctor pleads with her.[4] This is an extraordinary admission by the normally reserved and emotionless Doctor. She consents, and the final scene of the episode is powerful: the diseased Denara emerges from the shadows, reaches out to the Doctor, and he activates a new "dancing" program that he's downloaded so they could share a dance together.

The message of the episode is both simple and immense: we all face death and decay, and the only real response is to find someone you love — and then dance. *Trek* implicitly suggests that the *quality* of time, not the quantity, define one's life. We are all members of mismatched pairs — there is no perfect relationship. Human life itself is not well matched for those worlds we might encounter: the worlds of time, of pain, of consciousness, of death. Othello and Desdemona were doomed, but no more so than any other two people trying to get through life with a little dignity and a little joy. *Star Trek*'s message, if one can be distilled through such episodes, is that jealousy, despair, anger and confusion aren't necessarily markers of doom. They are the products of a fundamental mismatch between a world that's perfect and the world we live in. In *Trek*'s worldview, emotional turmoil isn't just an unpleasant sensation. It can also be a lifesign.

TWELVE

Reinventing the Self

Consider this question: who are you?

OK, it seems a rather obvious question. You are, well, you. That is, you have a name, a personality, an identity in the eyes of the world. You are yourself.

However, the very idea of "self" is one of the most problematic and complex concepts in psychology, philosophy, even literature. Some scholars and writers have gone so far as to question whether or not the "self" actually exists. Assuming, however, that there is a discreet, identifiable aspect of every person which we can call the self, let's pose an even more intriguing question: can a person reinvent himself or herself, changing his or her personality, remaking the "essence" of self?

If these were merely questions in a Psych 101 textbook, thinking about such matters would be an academic exercise — and none too entertaining. But the questions of self — what it is, how it's constructed, etc. — have been the launching pad for some great novels, plays and films. Writers in every age have taken these questions and wrapped them in a variety of plot devices, such as giving characters amnesia, or having someone don a disguise and pretend to be another "self." One of the most compelling spins on this theme is the idea of the "reinvented self," in which a character sets out to remake his own identity, to change something at the fundamental level of personality. Viewed through the prism of a reinvented self, the question "Who are you?" no longer seems quite so simple.

This conundrum of whether or not one can become a different or "better" self—and just what the price is of that change—has been chewed over in lots of different works of classic literature. A rough division can be found between those narratives (often non-fiction) which relate a "reinvention" of the self which turns out happily, and ones where the attempt to change results in a glitch in the psychic hard-wiring. And, as always, *Star Trek* borrows freely from both traditions, as we shall see after a brief discussion of two seminal works exploring the concept of reinventing the self: Booker T. Washington's *Up from Slavery*, which elucidates themes both universal and typically American, and George Bernard Shaw's *Pygmalion*, a drama which uses humor to hide the pain of reinvention. Both of these works take as their working premise the idea that the "self" can be reinvented—but always with profound consequences.

Mastering the Circumstances

The outline of Booker T. Washington's life is perhaps familiar to most people.[1] Born into slavery in the decade before the American Civil War in Virginia, he and his mother were the property of a planter named James Burroughs (the identity of Booker's white father remains uncertain). When he was nine, the war ended and his mother took him and his three siblings to West Virginia, where Booker's mother reunited with her husband, who worked in the salt mines. Booker worked for three years in the salt and coal mines of West Virginia—all the while sustaining his dream of getting an education. (He had been able, clandestinely, to acquire a fundamental level of literacy.)

When he began working as the houseboy for a mine owner's wife, Mrs. Viola Ruffner, his fortunes began to change. Apparently impressed by his demeanor, she provided him a more formal education and helped get him into the Hampton Institute, an industrial vocational school for Blacks and Native Americans near Norfolk. Washington made an impression on the faculty, graduated with honors in 1875, and returned to teach there shortly after graduating. In 1881, Washington was chosen to supervise the founding of a new school for black teachers, known ever since as the Tuskegee Institute.

The autobiography, *Up from Slavery* deals largely with Washington's attempts to establish and maintain Tuskegee as a prominent, black-run institution while trying to promote his own philosophy of black education and raise his profile as a national black leader. Washington's emphasis on self-improvement and the acquisition of "practical" skills often put him at odds with other black leaders who were more militant and more political in their message. To some, Washington seemed to endorse the idea that blacks had to prove they could be economically productive citizens before they were entitled to the full rights promised to all in the Declaration of Independence. He dedicated his career to helping develop institutions and programs to give blacks the education and skills he felt were required for equal footing in society.

Washington's almost-conciliatory tone, even when addressing the wretchedness of slavery, has been hard for many of his readers to accept. For instance, writing about his unknown but presumably privileged white father, Washington notes, "He was simply another unfortunate victim of the institution, which the Nation unhappily had engrafted upon it at the time."[2] This stance put him at odds with the other great black orator and activist at the time, Frederick Douglass, whose delineation of the evils of slavery was less genteel, informed by personal indignation and a broader sociological view.[3]

Washington's narrative was one of the most popular books of the early nineteenth century, and its echoes can be heard in the religious, political and imaginative literature of the time. Its emphasis on black empowerment and self-improvement, and the focus on the acquisition of economically-viable skills, helped carve the contours of the debate which continues to this day regarding the rights, and responsibilities, of the American "underclass."

And for fans of *Star Trek*, Booker T. Washington's life and work provide an illuminating corollary to the life and work of a deeply misunderstood character, Shinzon of Remus, the villain of the tenth *Star Trek* film and a character drawn from the depths of the American descent into slavery and civil war.

Finding a Way Out

Coincidence seekers can find a lot to connect Shinzon to Booker T. Washington. Both never knew their fathers, both were slaves, both worked in the mines, both had a civil war change the course of their lives, both worked tirelessly to acquire skills, knowledge and positions of influence. Both were deeply mistrusted by members of their own race, and by opposing races. The intellectual parlor game of finding similarities could continue far beyond this short list. But it's the non-coincidental connections, which are interesting and helpful in appreciating Shinzon's problematic existence. Both force one to confront the question: how does one overcome oppression? Intriguingly, they answer the same way: reinvent yourself.

Shinzon is the product of Romulan plotting. He's a clone of Jean Luc Picard, developed from a skin cell or hair follicle from the venerable Federation captain. As a human in the Romulan world, he's really sort of a non-person — especially after the plot to replace Picard with Shinzon is shelved (after a Romulan civil war) and Shinzon is exiled to the Romulan dilithium mines. In his status as a non–Romulan (he's from Remus, not Romulus), Shinzon approximates the position of the slave in the American nineteenth century. He is a bottom-of-the-ladder laborer, victimized by his "masters," treated as an animal and accorded no respect or standing. Glimpsed briefly in the tenth film, *Star Trek: Nemesis*, the spooky depths of the dilithium mines offer one of the most despairing landscapes ever captured in the *Trek* world. Now consider Booker T. Washington's assessment of his surroundings in *Up from Slavery*: "My life had its beginning in the midst of the most miserable, desolate, and discouraging surroundings."[4]

Shinzon, like Washington, spent his waking hours plotting a way out of his misery, forging a plan, which revolves around reconstituting the self. But while Washington vowed to master his circumstances through education (he reads Benjamin Franklin and Frederick Douglas's, among others, and ingratiates himself to "sponsors" who are in a position to help him along on his quest for empowerment), Shinzon channels all his anger and energy into fomenting a Reman uprising, including assassinating powerful Romulans, building weapons and seizing control of the empire. As a result of Washington's efforts, he became a college president and noted orator and thinker. Shinzon became "praetor," or leader, of the Romulan empire.

So, some similarities, some differences. Yet Washington's success was due to his commitment to reinvent himself, to dismantle his slave self and build in its place a formidable personality noted for its intellect and drive. So too Shinzon, who found in the depths of the mines a new self, an obsessive outcast who embraced ruthlessness and climbed his way, literally and figuratively, to the top of his society. Their answers to the question "Who are you?" attest to the malleability of the self: I am whatever I choose to be.

But what happens when someone's "chosen" self is at odds with his "natural" self? Can someone simply set aside all that they are in the quest to become someone new? For that psychological riddle, we must turn to another literary tradition, exemplified by George Bernard Shaw's *Pygmalion*.

WHEN FAIR IS FOUL

The central question at the center of Shaw's *Pygmalion*—probably more widely known in its musical recreation, the much-beloved *My Fair Lady*—is a real puzzler: when we seek to acquire the language and culture of a "higher" class of people, are we doing something noble or are we making fools of ourselves? Are efforts at personal enhancement to be applauded—or derided? Put another way, do attempts to improve our nature move us closer to, or further from, our real selves?

A host of novelists and playwrights have voted in favor of the latter, tapping a rich vein of comedy in humanity's quest to better itself. Usually, these stories end with some forlorn schlub making a fool of himself at a country club, art gallery, or some other highfalutin' affair. Inevitably, the deluded self-improver concludes that he or she shouldn't aspire to be like someone else, ultimately finding contentment in the comforts of one's lowly station. From Popeye's decidedly anti-intellectual "I am what I am" to King Lear's realization that man is simply a "poor, bared, fork'd animal,"[5] some efforts at self-improvement are by nature more ridicule than radical.

That brings me back to *Pygmalion*, a play aimed at making us feel both pity for the poor self-improver and humor at the folly of self-improvement. This formula infuses *Trek* deeply, from the efforts by non-humans (e.g. Spock, or Data) to emulate human behavior, to the sad and endearing quests by human characters to become "better" people (think of shy, bumbling crewman Reg Barkley from *The Next Generation*, courageous only in the confines of his Holodeck fantasy programs).

Twelve. Reinventing the Self

In Shaw's play, Eliza Doolittle becomes the subject of a vast re-education campaign, orchestrated by a pompous linguistics professor named Henry Higgins. Joined in his efforts by a fellow professor and language expert, Colonel Pickering, Higgins sets out to turn Eliza from a low-class, uneducated flower-selling vowel masher into a lady of refinement. The humor is often predictable, as in the scene when Eliza reverts to her brash, unschooled self at a fancy gala during her first "try-out" as a lady. Yet there is genuine pathos as Eliza begins to discern how different her life will be if she actually succeeds, and how differently her former gutter-dwellers will treat her once she acquires some culture. For example, when Colonel Pickering encourages Eliza to "slang back" at Higgins, who has just insulted her with some mild, street-wise swearing ("I'll see you damned first," he bellows), she retorts:

> I can't. I could have done it once; but now I can't go back to it. Last night, when I was wandering about, a girl spoke to me; and I tried to get back into the old way with her; but it was no use. You told me, you know, that when a child is brought to a foreign country, it picks up the language in a few weeks, and forgets its own. Well, I am a child in your country. I have forgotten my own language, and can speak nothing but yours. That's the real break off with the corner of Tottenham Court Road [the corner where she used to peddle "flars"].[6]

There are two profoundly important psychological conditions being analyzed by Shaw in *Pygmalion*, and both bear close consideration by *Trek* fans. On the one hand, we all want to improve ourselves, and we are willing to cast off our former lives for the prospect of ending up on the right side of the societal divide. On the other hand, we often end up regretting having forsaken our "true selves" in our quest for improvement. *Pygmalion*, which is most often read as a commentary on the relationship between language and social status, is also about our ambivalence about self-improvement. Shaw's work comes down firmly on the side of comedy, but with undertones of regret for what gets sacrificed in the bargain.

Eliza Doolittle, slum-dwelling flower girl, deserved a better life, and at the end of the play she seems ready to handle her new, improved state. But what of characters who seek to improve themselves, only to discover their efforts were pointless, their quest for greatness doomed from the start? Shaw raises these issues, but he leaves it for others to explore. Would it truly profit someone to gain the world but lose his own soul? If we're talking about profit and *Trek*, we must be talking about the Ferengi.

Quark's Quirks

Although they made their initial appearance in *The Next Generation* series, it wasn't until the series *Deep Space Nine* that the opportunistic alien race with the outsized ears and the even more outsized appetite for profit came into their own. Brought into the *Trek* world merely to function as a "new" kind of villain,[7] the Fernegis ultimately acquired a far richer psychology than early viewers of *The Next Generation* would ever have suspected. Brought to life by a host of gifted actors (who faced the challenge of communicating genuine emotion while encumbered by a lumpy latex head piece, ridiculously outsized ears and Wolfman-like fangs), the Ferengi teetered constantly between their nature as opportunistic space trash trolling the universe for a quick buck, and creatures with a unique culture and a highly codified set of rules governing their behavior (known as the "Rules of Acquisition").

The Ferengi (the singular is the same as the plural) named Quark, who runs a lounge on the Deep Space Nine station, is as slimy as he is lovable. Quark shares his race's proclivity for turning a profit, but underneath that Ferengi headpiece just might lurk a thinking, feeling creature. The Ferengi function in *Star Trek* kind of like surrogate nerds: funny looking, awkward beings who act dopey but who harbor a secret longing to be taken seriously.

In one of the best of the *Deep Space Nine* episodes, the double-dealing Quark gets his shot at respectability. Like Eliza Doolittle he accepts the challenge. But unlike her, he discovers it was a cruel joke and that he was apparently destined to be just another big-eared profiteer living low on the space food chain.

The episode is "The Nagus," and like *Pygmalion*, it teeters between humor and tragedy. Quark receives a visit from the Grand Nagus — a sort of emperor of the Ferengi people. Quark becomes convinced the Nagus is there to buy out his bar — at less than fair market value. Quark offers his typical backhanded hospitality — offering the Nagus the very best accommodations: his *brother's* room. It turns out that the Nagus says he is there to anoint the slippery Quark as his successor. As he is giving the newly elevated Quark advice on how to deal with his "subjects," the Grand Nagus keels over and dies. Quark is now fully acknowledged as the Nagus. At first disbelieving, Quark gradually warms to the idea, assuming power and learning to enjoy the fawning, toady-like behavior of the other Ferengis toward whomever is the Nagus. He makes people kiss his scepter in the time-honored tradition of prostrating one's self before the Nagus. He demands visitors make an appointment before they come to see him. But we also watch Quark wrestle with the real issues that come with leadership — how to delegate, whom to trust, etc. — and we watch this formerly foppish con artist begin to reimagine himself as a powerful presence (including an homage to Marlon Brando's "Godfather").[8]

Dramatic tension is generated by challenges to Quark's authority and plots against his life, while Quark takes steps to consolidate his power among his fellow scheming Ferengi. It's great fun to watch all of this unfold, but also it's easy to overlook how Quark's reinvention results in the same kind of split experienced by Eliza Doolittle: a sense of separation from one's former life, a feeling of being something of a fraud in your new incarnation, while at the same time savoring your new social power and hoping you will learn to become more comfortable in your new identity. The humor in this episode comes from watching Quark exercise his power over his former friends and cohorts, assuming an air of total unquestioned superiority. The pathos comes from Quark's sense of isolation, loneliness, and even paranoia.

In the end, Quark learns that the old Nagus whom he replaced has not really died — that it was a test of how the other Ferengis would react to the transition to a new leader. Mostly, they don't react well, so the old Nagus reclaims his title and the Ferengi world returns to its former order. Quark is left with the hope that one day, perhaps, his chance will come again. He is disappointed, of course. His new "self" was aborted when the old Nagus was resurrected. His reinvention is left in suspended animation, but the implication is that underneath his self-serving, sarcastic, opportunistic self, Quark just might have what it takes to be the Nagus — adding a further complication to our initial question "Who are you?" In Quark's case, the proper answer is: it depends when you ask me.

New Worlds, New Selves

Star Trek has always been about reinvention, from the original series' first season episode "What Are Little Girls Made Of?" (where a scientist has replaced his wife with an attractive female drone) to the third-season *Enterprise* episode "Similitude" (where a clone of a member of the crew was grown to maturity in a laboratory, with the same DNA but a different personality). All these variations on the theme of reinvention testify to Gene Roddenberry's vision of humanity as a species capable of growth and change. The mandate of the Starship *Enterprise* when she first sailed across television screens in 1966 was to explore "strange new worlds." In its explorations of the mutability of the "self," that mission has been accomplished.

THIRTEEN

Vampirism

If one were to visit the official *Star Trek* website (www.startrek.com), one could do a search in the online archives of all of the "aliens"—friendly, hostile, omnipotent, annoying—which have provided so many dramatic sparks over four decades of *Trek*. Dozens of different weird creatures are listed, each with a thorough discussion of home planets and distinguishing characteristics. Blue skin, catatonic states of semi-consciousness, telepathy—every manner of spaced-out specialness is represented in the litany of extraterrestrials.

But type in the search term "vampire" and nothing comes up.

Technically, this is correct, but also quite misleading, for among the many celebrated "monsters" which existed in fiction before the incarnation of *Trek*, the vampire has played a major role in the creation of many important *Trek* aliens. Think of the vampire and what comes to mind? A zombie-like creature, thirsty for blood, rising from its dark lair and seeking out the living. A creature of the night, mysterious, mesmerizing, hypnotic. A shape-shifting predator, a charming but lethal companion, a dark knight on a dark night.

As shall become clear, the legacy of the vampire—both in literature and the popular imagination—has directly informed the creation of many of *Trek*'s aliens. And though Count Dracula himself—surely the best-known exemplar of the vampire motif—might not have ever beamed aboard the *Enterprise*, his dark, disturbed kin found ways to infiltrate Gene Roddenberry's cosmos and vex the future of humanity.

The vampire has one of the richest and weirdest pedigrees in the history of the supernatural. Linked to real-life places, people and events, the vampire can boast — in a way such fiends as the werewolf, Frankenstein's Monster, and little green men from Mars can't — of a basis in fact. But it has also engaged the literary imaginations of some of the best writers in the pantheon of literature, from Lord Byron to Edgar Allan Poe, from H.P. Lovecraft to Charles Baudelaire. The twofold path of provenance followed by this prince of darkness — reality and fantasy — has made vampirism an unusually fruitful source of stories. You can make up vampire stories, or simply retell some long-believed legends. At some point, fact and fiction meld. One is left with stories which testify to the presence of vampires, or which attribute their qualities to other evil beings, or which romanticize certain vampiric traits.

The literary works which are most responsible for establishing the idea of vampires in our minds also have a lot to say to the average *Trek* fan. Much of what took place in the dark dens of Transylvania, or the Gothic castles of England, has found its way into the world of *Star Trek*.

I'M DRAINED

No one author can claim to have "invented" the vampire myth — though a surprisingly small number of titles have established most of the traits modern readers would consider vampiric. To understand vampirism fully, though, one must look back before cinema, before printed books, even before the written word, to the time when folk beliefs emerged as a means of helping people understand the world around them.

Though anthropologists have not been able to locate the precise origin of vampiric creatures, they have found similar beliefs in a wide variety of cultures across time and around the globe. Many Greek myths tell of trips back and forth from the world of the dead to the world of the living. Many world religions have myths that involve slaying and rebirth, or the drinking of blood, or of human sacrifices. Pre-Christian Europe was awash in tales of spirit beings, shape-shifting fiends and reanimated beings, or zombies — myths common to places as far flung as South America, Mongolia and the Slavic Hinterlands.[1]

Most of these folkloric creatures fall under the category of "revenants," a term which denotes a being that has returned from death in the form of a ghost, zombie or vampire. These revenants, or reanimated beings, almost always exhibit an obsession for the flesh of the living, they act in a hypnotic state, and they also exhibit superhuman strength. Revenants not only help us understand the development of the vampire myth but they also provide the blueprint for one of *Star Trek*'s most reviled and popular alien villains: the Borg.

I'VE GOT YOU UNDER MY SKIN

When you think about it, the Borg really *are* just high-tech vampires. The threat they pose to humanity is the same as the threat posed by the undead cult of Count Dracula: when they appear before you, they overwhelm you ("resistance is futile"), penetrate your flesh (with elongated metal fingernails), suck out your "essence" and turn you into one of them: a drone which now does the bidding of the darker forces of nature. The Borg "sleep" in regenerative pods, unconscious until they receive the signal which wakes the collective; vampires sleep in coffins, unconscious until the sun sets and they are awakened by the rising of the moon. They even dress the same: dark colored outfits over pallid skin.

One suspects the similarities aren't accidental, for the Borg are intended to do what vampires have always done in the human psyche: unsettle us with their bizarre and threatening manner, posing a threat which is immune to reasoned discussion, rational negotiation or even fighting back. Vampires are a force of nature, or anti-nature, members of the army of the undead. (What fear could they have, after all, of being killed if they're dead already?) The same thing applies to the Borg, a race of "assimilated" cultures who have died as their former selves and been reborn as Borg — altered humanoids who have been implanted with cybernetic devices.

And just as vampires are shrouded in mystery, so too the Borg. Here's some of what is known about these undead soldiers of the galaxy:[2] Each member of the Borg "collective" is linked through a subspace network, commanded by a Borg "queen" and traveling about the Delta Quadrant in a giant warp-speed cube, assimilating other cultures. According to Guinan, the bartender aboard the *Enterprise* in *The Next Generation*, the Borg almost succeeded in exterminating the El-Aurian race. Several celebrated battles between the Borg and Starfleet have taken place, including, most importantly, the battle for Earth in *Star Trek: First Contact*. The Borg even succeeded in assimilating Captain Picard, who was renamed "Locutus" and helped launch an attack against the *Enterprise* (though, fortunately, he only spent the summer as a Borg; he was assimilated in a season three–ending cliffhanger and rescued and deprogrammed in the season premier for the fourth season).

There have been splinter groups of the Borg, including one that was commanded by Data's evil twin Lore, and another which was discovered by Voyager, made up of former drones who had become separated from the collective and degenerated into internecine cyborg warfare. No matter what their particular circumstances, the Borg were always predatory, ruthless, inhuman villains, ready to drain the life from the nearest warm body. When the Borg succeeded, there was no hope for the victim, just a monstrous future as a life-draining zombie, prowling through cold, dark space, seeking fresh blood.

OF TALES AND FANGS

Stories about vampire-like beings rising from the dead and sucking the very life from their victims were common throughout the Middle Ages and into the period known as the Enlightenment, but it wasn't until a short novel titled *The Vampyre*, by Lord Byron's physician, John Polidori, that the paper trail begins.

As an example of literary greatness, Polidori's tale — spawned during the same stormy retreat that generated Mary Shelley's Romantic-era masterpiece, *Frankenstein* — is rather slight. Yet its mixture of established vampire folk legend (Polidori was a sort of amateur vampirologist) and mesmerizing central character, Lord Ruthven, struck a nerve with some readers. Ruthven — allegedly based on Byron himself — is a moody, charismatic, seductive protagonist with a creepy, supernatural aura of danger and an odd habit of walking in the moonlight and then killing people by sucking their blood:

There was no colour upon her cheek, not even upon her lip; yet there was a stillness about her face that seemed almost as attaching as the life that once dwelt there: upon her neck and breast was blood, and upon her throat the marks of teeth having opened the vein: to this the men pointed, crying, simultaneously struck with horror: "A Vampyre! a Vampyre!"[3]

Polidori's story was taken up by several dramatists in the nineteenth century who recognized a bankable stage persona when they saw one. All the elements were there for a first-rate literary treatment of the subject, which it would receive in the middle of the century at the hands of an Irish horror-story writer named Joseph Sheridan LeFanu, whose novella *Carmilla* advanced the literary myth another notch by including elements of personality transfer and metamorphosis. LeFanu's female vampire, Carmilla, doesn't just suck the blood of her victims, she absorbs their personality as well. And when necessary, Carmilla morphs into a catlike creature — establishing for the first time the link between vampires and their shape shifting forebears from folk-tale tradition. Both of these concepts — personality transference and shape-shifting — became codified in the literature of vampires, largely through the popularity of Bram Stoker's *Dracula*. But *Trek* also made good use of these vampiric traits, as can be seen in *The Next Generation* episode "Sub Rosa," and the *Deep Space Nine* character of Odo, the shape-shifting constable.

Timeless Romance

Part of the vampire's appeal to modern readers has been the element of seductiveness that has increasingly attached itself to the character since Polidori's story. In fact, creators of vampire fiction have often sought to portray vampires as highly attractive beings who exude sexual magnetism. A vampire's mix of power, confidence, exoticism, and often striking good looks makes them truly irresistible.[4]

That's the paradigm behind *The Next Generation* episode "Sub Rosa," a Latin phrase translatable to "Not Out in Light."[5] Indeed, this darkly lit, dark-themed episode hits many of the classic vampire-story benchmarks, beginning with a funeral and including lots of seductions, thunderstorms, candles being blown out by unseen winds, mesmerism, whispered voices and nighttime sexual visitations by ethereal beings.

Dr. Beverly Crusher finds herself to be the victim of visitations from a vampire-like entity named Ronin, who is centuries old and has managed to survive by feeding off the energy of Dr. Crusher's female ancestors — for the past 800 years. Beverly finds herself drawn to this creature, and she resigns her position in Starfleet to be able to continue to live in the village of her female ancestors, communing nightly with the dashing and dangerous Ronin. Only through the intervention of Captain Picard and the *Enterprise*'s plasma detection devices does Beverly discover the truth about Ronin, who admits to being an "anaphasic" being, dependent on the Howard women (Crusher's family name) for survival.

Rationalism triumphs — though just barely. (Given the erotic thrill ride Beverly's nights have become since she started communing with Ronin, one must admire her sense of duty in returning to the cold regions of empty space aboard the *Enterprise*.)

"Sub Rosa" draws deeply from the lore of vampires, appropriating many Gothic-era touches, such as the dilapidated family cottage lit only by candlelight, the disembodied voice which can fill a room, crazy laughter and lightning bolts which shatter stately elms — a sign of the vampire's roots in the tumult of the natural world. "Sub Rosa" has all of that (as well as a musical score which underlies the plight of the heroine with every dissonant chord progression). It's a fun episode, different in style from the usual *Trek* fare, but true to a vampiric tradition that stretches back to the time when flight was possible only if you could change into a bat. And that brings us to another *Trek*-vampire connection: the mysterious character Odo.

SHIFTY CHARACTERS

The idea of shape shifters is as old as literature itself. Homer gave us an early, celebrated example in the perpetually changing Proteus, a truly slippery guy from the *Odyssey*. Throughout Egyptian, Greek and Roman myth we meet other masters of the quick change. Arthurian literature is full of stories about characters who change from old hags to beautiful princesses, or from fierce beasts to genteel woodcutters.

These characters often changed shape to advance a plot point or to teach a lesson, but these were not recurring characters. Story over, character gone. Prior to the vampire, only one other famous shape-shifter recurred in literature with any regularity: the Devil. But he, of course, was found primarily in religious texts. The vampire, though he embodied many devilish traits, was a largely secular character. Most vampires don't represent a religious point of view. These bloodsuckers are generally non-denominational (though they do, of course, recoil from crucifixes — although garlic often works as well).

When a vampire changes shape, it's usually into some sort of animal — most often a bat-like creature, or sometimes a cat. Their shape-shifting ability adds to their mystique, and also aids them in acquiring secret knowledge of their victims. They can, for instance, observe their victims undetected while in their transformed state. It also makes getting away in a pinch easier... the very qualities that one might wish to have if one were, say, a chief of security on a busy space station among a number of suspicious and scheming races. In other words, Odo.

The character Odo is one of the best written and most satisfyingly complex among all of *Trek*'s many major characters. Over the course of the seven year-run of *Deep Space Nine*, little bits of Odo's background leaked out, never betraying the overall mystery surrounding his character but giving us just enough to humanize him — even though he was not, technically, human. As a shape shifter, Odo was able to get into lots of places unobtrusively and observe suspects under his surveillance. Unlike many shape shifters, Odo wasn't limited to animal avatars. He could become anything: a chair, a lamp, a brick wall. And then, magically, he would melt back to his more familiar form (though in actuality, he *had* no form; he slept in a bucket in his natural, liquid state).

Odo's ability to metamorphose at will, to avoid peril or seek advantage, is drawn directly from vampiric tradition. When Dracula needed to scale the heights of a garroted turret, he became a bat. When Carmilla needed to slink into bed with her victims, she became a lithe black panther. When Odo needed to discover who was behind an illegal swap of gold-pressed platinum, or a murder on the space station, he became a door, or a coat rack, or a wall safe. When necessary, he could also become a Cardassian, or Romulan, or a human. It is perhaps in his essential formlessness, in his inability to be completely whole that he most resembles his vampire forebears, who also depended on others to sustain them. Without a fresh "host" they would perish. Interestingly, in the *Deep Space Nine* writers' guidelines, Odo is described in the suitably vampiric phrase, as "an unfinished man."[6]

Shape-shifting plays a key role in the one episode most *Trek* fans think of when they think of vampires, "The Man Trap," an early episode of the original series which features a creature many fans have come to refer to as "the Salt Vampire." Before looking further at this best known *Trek* vampire, a brief look at the best known vampire *ever* created is in order.

Down for the Count

Without doubt, the best known and most widely imitated vampire is Count Dracula, the creation of Bram Stoker, who based his suave and salacious bloodsucker on an amalgam of previous vampire fiction and a bit of gruesome reality. Stoker did a lot of research before penning his classic, reading travelers' accounts of their trips through Transylvania and researching the life of Vlad Tepes, the ruthless Romanian Prince of the Middle Ages who was nicknamed "Vlad the Impaler," a model of sorts for Stoker's Count Dracula. Stoker also researched Slavic legends and folk beliefs and sprinkled lots of long-held superstitions into the mix when he cooked up the Count.

There's also quite a lot of blood, an undeniably grotesque element of the book's enduring appeal. Here's a scene where a visitor to Dracula's castle discovers the Count in his coffin, appearing to be asleep, after a draining round of necking the previous evening:

> I raised the lid and laid it back against the wall; and then I saw something which filled my very soul with horror. There lay the count, but looking as if his youth had been half-renewed, for the white hair and moustache were changed to dark iron-gray; the cheeks were fuller, and the whiter skin seemed ruby underneath; the mouth was redder than ever, for on the lips were gouts of fresh blood, which trickled from the corners of the mouth and ran over the chin and neck. Even the deep, burning eyes seemed set amongst swollen flesh, for the lids and pouches underneath were bloated. It seemed as if the whole awful creature were simply gorged with blood; he lay like a filthy leech, exhausted with his repletion.[7]

Count Dracula's need to gorge himself on fresh blood for sustenance is not very different from the biological imperatives which drive the salt vampire in "The Man Trap"— with the obvious difference being that one requires blood, the other salt (though the difference can be argued to be largely irrelevant; as vampire scholar J. Gordon Melton has noted, "[I]t is not necessarily the blood itself that the vampire seeks, but the psychic energy, or 'life force' believed to be carried by it"[8]).

Like Count Dracula, *Trek*'s "salt vampire" is a shape shifter who can assume a multitude of forms. In fact, it is the creature's ability to represent the dead wife of a lonely scientist that earns it its daily bread— heavily salted, of course. The salt vampire has entered into a symbiotic relationship with the scientist, Professor Robert Crater: life-giving portions of salt for the daily delusion of human companionship (in the form of his dead wife, Nancy, whom the salt vampire killed years earlier). When the crew of the *Enterprise* beams down to Crater's planetary outpost, the relationship is exposed and threatened, causing the salt monster to feast on a couple of Federation security officers. And though monstrous, the salt vampire is also an intelligent and victimized being, one whose need for salt is as pronounced as the human need for air, water and food. Its actions, if viewed sympathetically, cast Dracula's own dietary demands in a more problematic light. Blood sucking is gruesome, yes, but what if that's the only way to sustain life? A more complex view is needed, even in the face of such apparent, cold-blooded villainy.

Thus, *Star Trek* breathes new life into the literary treatment of the undead.

FOURTEEN

Underneath, We're All the Same

Does difference make a difference?

The surface distinctions between people — racial, religious, geographical — have created the requisite conflict to propel many a "classic" work of literature. Most of the works that explore these differences end up endorsing the idea that deep down we're all the same. The idea of equality is a powerful and recurrent theme in literature, perhaps deriving its power from the very reason that drives us to read in the first place: to explore one's connections to his or her fellow human beings, to reaffirm the ties that bind one to society, to assure us we're not alone.

Arguably, there are lots of other reasons writers have addressed the theme of equality, many of them culturally conditioned. Growing up in a country in which notions of equality are inscribed in the civic discourse, one must also grant that equality can be seen as a "national" value (even if the ideal has often been more articulated than achieved). Regardless, the very concept of all people having equality — that is, being worthy of respect, dignity and the full rights of civic enfranchisement — has proved creatively fruitful for novelists, poets, and social theorists who envision a future of nondiscrimination and full equality between men and women, and among all races sharing space on the third planet from the sun.

That brings us to *Trek*.

One of series creator Gene Roddenberry's stated aims in producing *Star Trek* was to provide a blueprint for a world in which the petty squabbling—or even all-out wars—which arose because of often inconsequential differences was replaced with a world of greater acceptance and understanding. He might not have won the Nobel Peace Prize, but in his way, Roddenberry's gestures in favor of greater equality had a real and lasting effect. *Star Trek*, which first aired in 1966, gave viewers a multicultural cast long before such concepts were considered to be politically acceptable or commercially viable. The crew of the Starship *Enterprise* was far more representative of the melting pot ideal which ostensibly undergirds U.S. society than any other mainstream television show ever produced. There have been lots of testimonies from contemporary, high profile entertainers about the positive impact, for example, of seeing a black female (Nichelle Nicols as Lt. Uhura) in a position of authority every week. And though Uhura often had little more to do than simply open a hailing frequency, actors such as LeVar Burton and Whoopie Goldberg both have spoken movingly about what it meant to have African-Americans represented as part of a command structure for a starship of the future.[1]

But *Star Trek* certainly did not originate the idea of equality among all peoples. In fact, the franchise borrowed freely and frequently from the intellectual stream whose source was the movement known as "the Enlightenment." One of the most prominent proponents of equal treatment of all citizens was the seventeenth century British philosopher John Locke, whose work was a major influence on Thomas Jefferson's draft of the Declaration of Independence. The notion that "all men are created equal" resonates throughout the Federation of Planets as well as the nascent American Federation of the eighteenth century. It's worth a closer look.

CIVIC DUTY

As antiquated as it may seem today, one of the concepts that held sway a few hundred years ago among even the highly educated was something termed "the Divine Right of Kings." Most British subjects vowed allegiance to the idea that their sovereigns were designated by the Almighty to rule over them, and that in the exercise of their royal decrees, the Kings were merely carrying out "God's Will." One of the reasons John Locke's name is remembered today is that he was one of the first public intellectuals to oppose that idea, arguing that God endowed all people, not just the king, with a right to decide how best to live. Locke, in a famous essay on the role of government in people's lives, argued that everyone deserved freedom, autonomy and the right to possess property — and that any government that would infringe on those rights was illegitimate:

> To understand political power right, and derive it from its original, we must consider, what state all men are naturally in, and that is, a state of perfect freedom to order their actions, and dispose of their possessions and persons, as they think fit, within the bounds of the law of nature, without asking leave, or depending upon the will of any other man.[2]

Locke made lots of other groundbreaking statements in his famous treatise on government, including urging people to revolt against their governmental leaders if the God-given rights of the citizenry, their "life, liberty, health, limbs or goods," are ever abridged. His notions of equality — "And that all men may be restrained from doing hurt to one another, and the law of nature be observed, which willeth the peace and preservation of all mankind"[3] — were widely adopted by the revolutionaries in eighteenth century Europe and America, and his phrases were closely echoed in the American colonists' Declaration of Independence, which enunciated in Lockean style that "all men are created equal."[4]

Of course, much has been written and said over the years regarding the inherent contradiction between Jefferson's words and the true state of equality in America. It would take another century for the freedom of *all* people to become prescribed in the law — with the Emancipation Proclamation and, closer to our time, various civil rights laws addressing inequities between majority and minority populations. What's important in this discussion is not the extent of the achievement of the ideal, but the ideal itself, and the ways in which *Star Trek* has adopted the stated aim of universal equality. Some of *Trek*'s most compelling hours are built around episodes which reiterate the idea that all people should be free from domination of any sort. One of the best examples of this principle dramatized is the *Deep Space Nine* episode "Captive Pursuit."

Fourteen. Underneath, We're All the Same

GAME FOR THE CHASE

Starfleet officers are taught to follow rules. One of the most important is the fabled "prime directive," a strict policy of non-interference in the affairs of other cultures. Though this dictate has frequently been broken over the course of four decades of storytelling, the rule nonetheless holds: even if alien behavior is repugnant (by human standards), it is not Starfleet's place to impose change on others.

So what happens when this non-interference pact comes into conflict with a severe breach of human rights — or, to be more reflective of *Trek*, the rights of any sentient species? "Captive Pursuit" answers that question.

Here's the situation: an unidentified spaceship from the Gamma Quadrant arrives at Deep Space Nine carrying a mysterious, lizard-like humanoid who calls himself "Tosk"— though it's unclear to Station Chief Miles O'Brien if "Tosk" refers to the creature himself or to his race in general. O'Brien tries to calm the nervous-acting alien, making small talk and sharing some personal information. O'Brien assures him there's nothing to be afraid of, and convinces him to leave his damaged ship and come aboard the station. He explains to Tosk that Starfleet's mission is to "seek out new life forms"— a nice nod to the original series.

Soon, three other visitors arrive at the station from Tosk's planet, looking to capture him and return home. The *Deep Space Nine* crew learns that Tosk is a member of a race of people who are bred only to be hunted by the "superior" inhabitants of his planet. Tosk escaped his captors, but was followed through the wormhole that leads to the space station. DS9's commander, Benjamin Sisko, is disgusted by the concept of such primitive "blood sport," but as a Starfleet officer he is bound by the "Prime Directive" from interfering.

O'Brien's conscience, however, won't allow this "game" to continue, so he changes the rules of the game. Pretending to be acting on orders from Sisko, O'Brien tells Tosk's hunter-escort that the Federation wishes to give them an "official" send-off, and that he, O'Brien, will escort Tosk to the waiting ship. He then tampers with the station's security devices to deliver a debilitating "stun" to the hunter — after which he also administers a punch to the jaw, allowing Tosk to escape, reclaim his vessel in space dock, and get a head start on his pursuers.

Security Chief Odo sets out after O'Brien, but Sisko tells him, pointedly, "There's no hurry."

Clearly disobeying orders, O'Brien receives the requisite dressing down from Commander Sisko, but the way the scene is played makes clear that Sisko (who, as portrayed by African-American actor Avery Brooks, brings a simmering sense of indignation to the idea of one race enslaving another for sport) endorses O'Brien's actions. The tip-off comes when O'Brien mentions to Sisko that he was surprised that neither he, nor Odo, thought of simply employing a forcefield around Tosk's vessel, which would have delayed his escape and allowed him to be returned to his hunters. Sisko's stoic delivery provides an ironic contrast to his answer, as he tells O'Brien, deadpan: "I guess that one got by us."[5] (As most fans of the show know, little ever "gets by" the famously efficient Commander.)

The writers of the episode chose to endorse the idea of freedom over the idea of rigidly adhering to the code of non-interference. This is not unheard of in *Trek*. The breaches of the so-called Prime Directive occur only when all other options have failed, and the disregarding of that order is seldom cavalier. And in this case, the appearance of following orders is partially maintained. Sisko, in his failure to *take* action to prevent the escape, was really acting on behalf of the captive prey, Tosk. Yet he preserves the illusion of strict military protocol, even "formally" reprimanding O'Brien — which also preserves the dramatic integrity of the episodes which question the Prime Directive. If Starfleet officers were free to disregard the directive at will, its restrictive (and well-intentioned) authority would carry little weight. In this particular balancing act, the dictates of conscience prevailed over the dictates of Starfleet headquarters. And a fundamental notion of universal equality was reaffirmed.

Perhaps it can be argued that coming down against slavery and exploitation is not very radical, but *Trek* has also explored some complex issues regarding basic human rights, such as whether non-human beings qualify for full civic enfranchisement. In one of the most important and informed of any *Trek* episodes, the question of whether machine-based life forms are entitled to rights was explored from a variety of perspectives. The episode draws deeply from issues raised in one of the classic pleas for equality in the history of the American nation: Martin Luther King's "I Have a Dream" speech.

Fourteen. Underneath, We're All the Same

Just what does an African-American Baptist preacher's 1960s oration have to do with a *Star Trek* episode about the rights of androids in the twenty-fourth century? Quite a lot, actually.

I, Robot

The best *Trek* episodes combine taut, stand-alone stories with messages of social relevance. That's always been *Star Trek*'s metier, the reason the whole franchise remains much greater than the sum of its episodic parts. In its appropriation of a courtroom drama–style story, *The Next Generation* episode "The Measure of a Man" offers a compelling narrative with a high-stakes legal face-off. Yet the whole episode hinges on Captain Jean Luc Picard's indignation at the concept of slavery and the idea that, even in the twenty-fourth century, some beings are considered superior to others.

In his famous clarion call for universal rights and a society which judges people "not on the color of their skin but on the content of their character,"[6] Martin Luther King rallied a nation — and put in place the rhetorical benchmarks against which a society's progress could be measured. Jean Luc Picard takes King's message of equality and uses its rationale to fight for the android Data's rights against exploitation, against being treated like a piece of property in the hands of a dominant majority culture. In language that could have been ripped from the pages of King's famous 1963 address, Picard seeks to convince a special court that Data is entitled to the full rights of person hood, rather than being treated like a species apart. What King said about the state of the African-American in the 1960s, who has "languished in the corners of American society and finds himself in exile in his own land... a shameful condition,"[7] is true of Data's uncertain status as a member of the Federation. He is part of Starfleet but not respected as an autonomous being, capable of directing his own affairs.

Here's the premise of the episode: a noted Starfleet research scientist in cybernetics has requested that Data be transferred to his command for the purpose of dissembling the android and learning precisely how he works. When presented with these orders, Data's commanding officer, Captain Picard, objects, protesting that "Commander Data is a valued member of my bridge crew."[8] However, the Starfleet JAG officer agrees with the scientist that Data is Starfleet property, and that he must be given over for study. Picard formally objects and demands a hearing on the matter. Picard will represent Data, and, under Starfleet regulations, the prosecutor must be the second in command — Will Riker. (Though Riker tries to avoid this distasteful assignment, he is by regulation forced to do it or the case will not be tried and Data will lose out on his only chance — an implicit commentary on how certain repressive systems can sometimes compel people of good conscience to act contrary to their will.)

The arguments at the hearing focus on whether Data, as a machine, has any more rights than a toaster or a computer. With the case going badly, Picard seeks solace in the *Enterprise*'s lounge. He vents his frustrations to the bartender Guinan (played by Whoopie Goldberg) that the case is probably lost, and that soon the researcher will get his wish, dissembling Data, whom Picard knows and admires, and making hundreds, or thousands, of copies of this super-computing android. Guinan listens, and then adds the following comment: "In the history of many worlds there have always been disposable people. They do the dirty work ... you don't have to think about their welfare."[9]

Picard has an epiphany: "You're talking about slavery. *That*'s the uncomfortable truth behind the euphemism 'property'!"[10]

Seeing Data's quest for autonomy now as part of a long line of historically wronged racial oppressions, Picard marches back into the hearing, stating: "A single Data is a curiosity. A thousand Datas? Wouldn't that be a race? And won't we be judged by how we treat that race? ... Are you prepared to condemn him, and all who are like him, to servitude and slavery?"[11]

Not too surprisingly, the answer is no. The JAG officer agrees, claiming she can't say for certain that Data has no soul, and therefore she can't rule that he be treated like a soulless mechanism. Martin Luther King's call for equality was built on the same foundation, the recognition among all people of those qualities that connect us beyond mere physical attributes. (In Data's case, Picard is able to demonstrate that the android possesses the qualities of "sentience" — intelligence and self-awareness.)

Just as there were people — emboldened by laws — who once proclaimed that Negroes were less than full persons, so too this Starfleet cybernetic researcher, who sees in Data's yellow-hued skin and mechanistic agility a creature undeserving of full rights and legal protection. But Data is *different*, not lesser — a distinction which *Star Trek* has always presented as Exhibit A in its courtroom of the future.

"The Measure of a Man" took seriously the issues at stake: whether Data deserved rights. The arguments made on either side were intellectually defensible. But one of the first *Star Trek* episodes to deal with the issue of equality wasn't quite so deep, aiming only to show how pointless, destructive and downright kooky the divisions of "race" really are. In an entertaining but none-too-subtle stripping away of the veneer of racism, the original series episode "Let That Be Your Last Battlefield" put all of its egalitarian cards on the table.

Lefts and Rights

Diehard *Trek* fans will admit that, while they were delighted the original series was saved from cancellation after the second season, many of the episodes produced for the third season lacked the nuance and thoughtfulness of the previous two seasons. Roddenberry had left the show as executive producer, and the show simply failed to maintain the exceedingly high standards of writing and producing which had made *Trek* so popular in the first place. Still, the series provided a steady stream of entertaining and usually socially conscious episodes. "Let That Be Your Last Battlefield" is an example of what happens when the commitment to social activism trumps dramatic subtlety.

The plot is this: the *Enterprise* comes across a stolen Federation shuttlecraft carrying a humanoid named Lokai, from the planet Cheron. Lokai is half-black, half-white, as if painted right down the middle. Shortly after the *Enterprise* rescues him, another inhabitant of Cheron, also exactly half-black and half-white, is found racing through space in pursuit of Lokai. The *Enterprise* transports him on board just before his vessel explodes. Though the new arrival, named Bele, tells Kirk that he's there to arrest Lokai for being a political traitor and murderer on Cheron, Kirk refuses to relinquish Lokai.

When Kirk and Bele visit Lokai in sickbay, Kirk hears two sides of the same story. Bele accuses Lokai of being an ungrateful, scheming, low-class murderer who betrayed those who accepted and educated him, while Lokai says Bele and his people have educated Lokai and others like him "just enough to be of service,"[12] claiming that he lives as a slave back on Cheron.

As Kirk ponders their stories, he is told the ship has inexplicably changed directions and is now headed to Cheron. When he investigates the reason for this unexplained change of direction, Bele tells him he has taken control of the ship. Phasers are useless against the two Cheron inhabitants. In a desperate move to regain control of the ship, Kirk threatens to initiate the *Enterprise*'s auto-destruct sequence. After the mandatory, white-knuckle, "who-will-be-the-first-to-blink?" 30-second countdown to destruction, Bele relents, and Kirk aborts the destruction order.

With control regained, the ship resumes its former course. Kirk lectures both Bele and Lokai that he could put them in the brig but he won't because they are new to this part of the galaxy. He tells them the *Enterprise* and its crew are governed by the United Federation of Planets, which respects the rights of all beings. He invites them to wander about the ship and observe his crew, so that they might see firsthand how tolerance and cooperation are manifested in this quadrant of the galaxy.

Both Lokai and Bele try to win converts to their points of view, expressing to whomever will listen the defects and deceit of the "other" race. Just why do Lokai and Bele hate each other so? Because they can't abide the differences in their appearance: half the race is black on the left, white on the right. The other half is black on the right, white on the left.

For anyone who might have missed the message regarding the stupidity of skin-color prejudice, Lokai and Bele grip each other in a stranglehold while derisively hurling the epithets "half-white" and "half-black" at each other. And just so viewers are made aware of how deadly such racial differences can be, the *Enterprise* arrives at Cheron at the end of the episode, where it is revealed that all the inhabitants have killed each other in a civil war. Not a single inhabitant of Cheron remains alive—except for Bele and Loaki, who beam down to their home planet, where they continue their hate-fueled chase.

In the twenty-third century, will humans have risen above such pettiness? *Trek*'s answer is always optimistic, if sometimes overly obvious.

FIFTEEN

The Wonders (and Dangers) of Technology

Star Trek has embraced so many themes and ideas that any talk of the franchise's "main theme" or "moral" ought to be received with skepticism. Five series, ten movies, and hundreds of plots have given the show's creators countless opportunities to offer social commentary on contemporary culture. And yet....

If one was pressed to choose a theme which seems to have engaged the show at the deepest and most passionate levels across its multiple incarnations, that overriding theme might be the double-edged sword of technological progress. *Trek* has illustrated, time and again, that humanity stands to benefit greatly from continued scientific advances, but the potential cost of such development does not go unremarked. In the wrong hands — or even the right hands, sometimes — technological "progress" becomes highly ironic, with threats of universal consequence sometimes resulting from new technologies. Though *Star Trek* has occasionally provided viewers with a Dr. Strangelove–type villain who is threatening to deploy some super-weapon, the most interesting variations on the technology theme tend to involve the Federation itself. Watching the various *Enterprise* crews wrestle with the consequences of their own technological capabilities has provided some splendid and insightful *Trek* moments.

This theme is a natural for *Star Trek*, practically the show's raison d'être. Only through technological advancement — principally, the development of faster-than-light warp speed flight — is humanity able to explore the stars. So the *Enterprise* is dependent on technology. But as every fan knows, the deeper into space the ship ventures, the more the crew's "human" qualities are needed. In fact, the ship and its crew have often been spared by alien entities not because of the *Enterprise*'s technological capabilities, but by their demonstration of human value (which strikes some advanced species as "quaint").

The questions raised by such encounters have been addressed in some classic works of literature, primarily in the genre of science fiction. Questions such as "How does one reconcile the desire to go beyond what is known with the danger of unleashing something which can't be controlled?" or "Do humans have the right to 'play God' merely because they can?" have infused many sci-fi narratives. These questions apply in our own time to issues from nuclear development to cloning, and in *Trek*'s time, from cybernetic mutations to terraforming dead planets. As forward thinking as *Trek* has been, the template for navigating this delicate balance between the wonders and the dangers of technology was established in a literary classic written by an eighteen-year-old girl after a night of ghost stories, Mary Shelley's *Frankenstein*. Closer to contemporary times, Shelley's themes were adapted into one of the best-known works of science fiction in the past few decades, Michael Crichton's *Jurassic Park*. Both works have a lot to say about the use of technology and the dangers of unchecked creation — themes that *Star Trek* has debated thoughtfully for almost 40 years.

A MONSTROUS DECISION

Among the great writers whose artistic visions have been drastically changed by Hollywood adapters, Mary Shelley is practically in a league by herself. Say the name "Frankenstein" to anyone who's ever been to the movies, and what comes to mind is a big, hulking, bolt-necked creature who swings his gangly arms and glares dumbly at the screen. The popular conception of Frankenstein could not be more different from what Shelley wrought — starting with the basic misconception that the monster himself is named Frankenstein. Shelley's masterpiece never names the creature, only his creator, Dr. Victor Frankenstein. In typical filmic shorthand, Frankenstein's monster became "Frankenstein." It would further shock many movie buffs who've never read the novel *Frankenstein* to learn that the monster as originally written is a thoughtful and highly intelligent being who educated himself about humanity by reading Milton's *Paradise Lost*, among other works. And when he speaks, he sounds more like creator than creation:

> Oh what a strange nature is knowledge! It clings to the mind when it has once seized on it like a lichen on the rock. I wished sometimes to shake off all thought and feeling, but I learned that there was but one means to overcome the sensation of pain, and that was death.[1]

Frankenstein is often considered the first science-fiction novel. Its youthful author — wife of Romantic poet Percy Bysshe Shelley — successfully wed the scientific concerns of her day to the rising interest in stories of the supernatural. *Frankenstein*'s many "what ifs?" are still being debated today. Shelley's Doctor doesn't just sustain life, he creates it — a decision he comes to regret, extremely. Cautioning a fellow scientist on a polar expedition who claims he's willing to sacrifice human lives to conquer "the elemental foes of our race," Victor Frankenstein pleads for restraint: "Unhappy man! Do you share my madness? Have you drunk also of the intoxicating drought? Hear me; let me reveal my tale, and you will dash the cup from your lips."[2]

That's a keynote theme in *Frankenstein*, and in much science fiction: the idea of having over-reached, of having tinkered with something taboo. The (sometimes) good intentions of science can result in a catastrophe. In Shelley's novel, the tragedy involves both creator and creation. In the process, the very idea of who is "creator" and who is the creature is interrogated, with the scientist eventually being dominated by his own beast: "You are my creator, but I am your master," Victor is told by the monster. "Obey!"[3] That idea too is at the heart of much modern sci-fi, a tables-turning reordering of the creator-creation paradigm. What we make can unmake us if we're not careful (philosophers call this the "law of unintended consequences").

The story ends, like all tragedies, with the deaths of the principal figures. Shelley's fable of the consequences of playing with fire (the subtitle of the novel is "The Modern Prometheus," a reference to the

Greek hero-rebel who disobeyed Zeus and stole fire from the heavens) is not ambiguous. Victor Frankenstein's Faustian bargain wrought only hellish results. Critics have found lots of things in *Frankenstein* worth commenting on. Some see it as a treatise on the Romantic era's embrace of rebellion, others as a cautionary tale about scientific advances and the nineteenth century's crisis of faith. Fans of *Star Trek* will also find an early formulation of some of Gene Roddenberry's questions about the responsible development of science and technology. And, as we'll explore shortly, the important debate about the "Genesis Project" in *Star Trek II* and *Star Trek III* had its genesis in *Frankenstein*.

PAW PRINCE

Though the questions which often arise about the use of technology are subtle and nuanced, many of the narratives that offer answers are not. Best-selling author and Harvard educated physician Michael Crichton has frequently addressed the delicate balance between technological development and self-imposed restraint in his novels. In perhaps his best-known work, *Jurrasic Park*, Crichton weighs in with his opinion — with several thousand pounds of it, in fact — tearing into the notion of unchecked progress with the ferocity of a velociraptor devouring a meaty mortal snack. After watching his reconstructed inhabitants of Dinotopia stomp through almost 400 pages of his book, living testaments to man's desire to out-create the creator, it's difficult to miss his point.

Crichton, however, is no chicken-little alarmist, poised to see threat under every new advancement of science. As a man of science himself, he seems keenly aware of just how *human* most technology blunders are:

> Scientists are actually preoccupied with accomplishment. So they are focused on whether they can do something, They never stop to ask if they *should* do something. They conveniently define such considerations as pointless. If they don't do it, someone else will. Discovery, they believe, is inevitable. So they just try to do it first. That's the game in science.[4]

Jurrasic Park's notions about the perils of ill-considered technological "advancements" gained wide currency through the movie ver-

Fifteen. The Wonders (and Dangers) of Technology   131

sion of the book. The film became one of the most successful "blockbusters" in the history of cinema; and though the movie's subtext sounds a cautionary note, it was the action, adventure, and chomping that engaged moviegoers more than the message. But in the book, that message is broadcast from the very first paragraph. *Jurassic Park* is not a book about dinosaurs so much as it's an extinction parable for our times:

> The late twentieth century has witnessed a scientific gold rush of astonishing proportions: the headlong and furious haste to commercialize genetic engineering. This *Enterprise* has proceeded so rapidly — with so little outside commentary — that its dimensions and implications are hardly understood.[5]

Again, that theme of not looking before one leaps, of pushing the envelope without knowing where it will lead, is what connects *Frankenstein* to *Jurassic Park*, and both of them to *Star Trek*. In both novels, a nascent scientific marvel ends up running amok, threatening not only its creator but also the world at large. Though neither *Frankenstein*'s monster nor *Jurassic Park*'s dinos were created with the best of intentions (ego, curiosity, and greed), neither was created by a villainous character trying to rule the world. That's the seed that takes root in the great *Trek* explorations of the proper use of technology. It's generally not "what will happen if Evil Dr. X gets ahold of this thing?" as much as it's "What happens if *we* deploy this?" The place to look for the answers, if any are to be found, is the Genesis planet.

BACK TO THE GARDEN

Life from lifelessness. That's how the "Genesis Project" is tersely defined in *Star Trek II*, the movie which first introduced us to this scientific marvel which had been developed and nearly perfected by Dr. Carol Marcus, a molecular biologist who is also the mother of James T. Kirk's son, David. The project is shrouded in secrecy until Khan, Kirk's nemesis, learns of it and tries to acquire it. Acting to prevent that, Kirk undertakes the mission that forms the heart of the movie, the battle against Khan. But before we get the rousing, climactic space battle, we get an intellectual battle over whether the very idea of a "Genesis Device" is defensible.

The debate ensues after Kirk shows Spock and McCoy a classified video file about the project. As we watch Dr. Marcus' presentation along with Kirk, Spock and McCoy, we discover that the Genesis device — a kind of life-bringing torpedo — must first annihilate a "dead" planet and then re-assemble the atoms according to a matrix which puts the pieces back together in a way which engenders new life. Literally, life from death.

Spock finds the idea intriguing, while McCoy finds it repugnant. The good doctor's objections are based on several factors, including the likelihood that if the device were used where life currently thrives, the opposite effect might occur: everything would be wiped out. Further, McCoy expresses his discomfort with humans "playing God," giving tacit acknowledgement to the existence of the law of unintended consequences — we simply don't know what will happen once this chain of events begins. Spock the logician refuses to moralize, merely observing that such a device could have great benefits. Though he concedes there is a danger if it falls "into the wrong hands" (to which McCoy famously responds, "Do you mind telling me whose hands are the *right* hands?").[6]

What is the viewer to think? Typical for *Trek*, this complex issue gets complex treatment. Khan launches the Genesis Device — the torpedo itself — as a final act of vengeance as he seeks to destroy the *Enterprise* itself. So there would seem to be support for the argument that such technologies will inevitably doom their creators because they could fall into the wrong hands. But as a result of Khan's actions, the device is launched and a new, habitable planet is formed from the remains of a dead one. And it is that planet which receives Spock's body after it is launched through space to conclude his funeral on the *Enterprise*— and makes possible his "resurrection" in *Star Trek III*. So that is clearly a positive. Yet, later in that same movie, we discover that the unstable nature of "proto-matter" used in the matrix of the device leads to natural disasters and, eventually, the destruction of the newly-born world. So, it's back to where we started.

But not exactly, because now we have something more than theorizing. After having watched Khan acquire the weapon, and the Genesis planet's ultimate cataclysmic collapse, who can argue that Genesis is a good thing? Yet, after having watched Spock's body be "re-born" and after seeing the natural beauty and remarkable species diversity in the new Eden of the Genesis planet, who would say such developments ought not be pursued? And that's *Star Trek*'s point. While acknowledging the horrific potential of new technologies, *Trek* yet manages to celebrate the impulse leading to their creation, reinforcing the need to look, and also, occasionally, to leap.

THE GOOD OLD DAYS

In the movie *Star Trek: Insurrection*, the ante is upped. The debate between the advancement of technology and the perils of such development gets a very interesting twist, and requires a bit of watching-between-the-lines.

The movie tells the story of a race of humanoids called the Bak'u. These people live simply, in an agrarian lifestyle, which suggests an almost Amish-like disdain for the modern world. When Captain Picard and his crew encounter them (on a mission to retrieve a malfunctioning Data, the film's first symbol of both what's right and what's wrong with technology), the space explorers are stunned to discover that the Bak'u live this way despite their advanced knowledge. They know about things like positronic neural nets (data's "brain") and warp drive, but they have chosen to turn their backs on such twenty-fourth century commonplaces and live a slower, more land-connected existence.

The movie seems to be setting us up for a message about how to live simply, what the "essence" of pleasure really is, how to turn our explorer instincts inward to discover our true selves. These themes are further reinforced by the menace posed by a much more technologically literate race called the Son'a, who want to drive the Bak'u from their planet and exploit their resource-rich world.

So, all the signals have been sent to the viewer that the Bak'u have it right — a life of simple joys, a tightly knit community living in harmony with the land. This, surely, is the way to be. And though the movie never suggests that *isn't* the way to live, the issue is problematized by one simple fact: without the intervention of Picard and his crew, the Bak'u would be easy prey for the Son'a. If we are to empathize with the Bak'u — including their pacifist ideology — we are faced with quite a dilemma. Like it or not, in the twenty-fourth century, other cultures will have technology, and they might not subscribe to the same moral code as peace-loving cultures.

Star Trek: Insurrection never gives you a scene or even a snippet of dialogue to help sort out this dilemma. If Picard had ended up giving a speech about how these people should better arm themselves, of if the Bak'u had lectured the *Enterprise* crew on their militaristic and spiritually-empty way of life, the film's power would have evaporated. There are no eleventh-hour foxhole perorations about "better to die with principles than to raise a hand against my enemy" sort of thing. The Bak'u want to live, and they cooperate with Picard and Company as they fight off the Son'a.

In the end, of course, the Son'a are beaten back, but the film's central tension is unresolved: a peace-loving rural society needed twenty-fourth-century space warriors to save their bacon.

TECHNOLOGY, (IN)HUMANITY

That unwillingness to endorse one particular approach as *the* way is wrought from a variety of factors, many discussed previously. It is also rooted, like so many other themes that penetrate the *Star Trek* corpus, in the wide embrace of Gene Roddenberry's humanism. *Trek* has always eschewed easy answers for any social problem. Seeking simple answers in *Star Trek* is as dangerous as many of the missions undertaken by the Starship *Enterprise*. But it is fair, and accurate, to say that *Trek* has always recognized the value — the necessity, even — of exploring the unknown, of reaching beyond one's grasp. But *Trek* also acknowledges that humanity is a necessary ingredient in every technological concoction. Victor Frankenstein wrought destruction not because he tried to create a human being, but because he put too little of his own humanity into the equation for life. The for-profit scientists at Jurassic Park created theme park attractions, not creatures whose needs and habits were understood or respected. So if *Star Trek* has anything to add to the rich, centuries-long legacy of debate over technology, it would be that no technological development stands apart from the people who will deploy it. Innovations aren't "good" or "bad," they are the products of human ingenuity and culture, a marriage of necessity of opportunity, as humane or inhumane as their creators.

SIXTEEN

Fantasy vs. Reality

There are things that are "real" and things that are "made up." Fiction, which exploits readers' notions of what is "real," is made up, invented, a fantasy. But sometimes, fiction makes real people cry real tears, or laugh out loud. In many stories, the fictional characters themselves are trying to determine what's real or what's fake. And though these characters have no "real" existence outside of the book, TV show, or movie screen, when the story ends we sometimes feel a real sense of loss. Literature is sometimes credited with being a form of "escapism," but some readers feel more connected to Ishmael, Hester Prynne or Holden Caulfield than to the "real" people in their own lives.

Trying to untangle the knot of what's real and what's not can be a difficult enterprise indeed. Perhaps for that very reason, writers have been drawn to create situations that challenge and expand our current notions of reality. The universe of *Star Trek* is, technically speaking, not real. It exists in the literal future, and in the figurative imaginations of its fans. And yet those fans — breathing, flesh and blood humanoids — attend *Star Trek* conventions, write fan letters, publish magazines and evidence a very "real" attachment to *Trek*. If not impossible, let us at least grant that it is daunting to sort out where fantasy ends and reality begins. And maybe such a compromise could serve as a springboard to a discussion about how *Trek* has portrayed this battle between fantasy and reality, and how literature, stretching back to the beginnings of storytelling, has also addressed this dichotomy.

When fantasy and reality collide, a couple of different things can happen. You might get disoriented. Or you might get some really great literature. One of the most significant and greatest of fantasy-reality melds comes from the oldest poem in Western Civilization. It was Homer who gave us the first look at how dangerous and alluring "fantasy" can be — a motif which *Star Trek* adopted in its conception of the "Nexus." Following in his footsteps — almost three millennia later — was James Thurber, who, in his classic story "The Secret Life of Walter Mitty," provided the idea of fantasy as necessary release, a motif adopted by *Star Trek* in its conception of the holodeck and the holosuite. And, in one of the most brilliant and perplexing works of imaginative literature in any (or every) language, James Joyce's *Finnegans Wake* offers the blueprint for the impact on the psyche of rapid changes between planes of reality, the interpenetration of fantasy and reality, a motif adopted by *Trek* in its use of the reality-challenged character known as "the Q."

FLOWER POWER

In *The Odyssey*, we get the prototypical reasonable man, Odysseus, whose keen intellect and resourcefulness help him survive the perils of a monstrous world. Homer seems to have understood, long before the invention of depth psychology, that people (to paraphrase Oscar Wilde) can resist all perils except temptation. After surviving the carnage of the Trojan War and the wrath of some highly placed Greek gods, it is the human predilection toward pleasure which poses Homer and his men one of their most serious threats. Homer's allusion to the mesmerizing influence of the Lotus petal is replicated in *Trek*'s concept of the "Nexus." Here's the original reference in the text of the *Odyssey*:

> They started out at once, and went about among the Lotus-eaters, who did them no hurt, but gave them to eat of the Lotus, which was so delicious that those who ate of it left off caring about home, and did not even want to go back and say what had happened to them, but were for staying and munching lotus with the Lotus-eaters without thinking

further of their return; nevertheless, though they wept bitterly, I forced them back to the ships and made them fast under the benches.¹

Like most of the *Odyssey*, this passage is remarkably compact, but it does contain several discreet concepts that bear pointing out — especially as they bear directly on *Star Trek*. The Lotus represents, first, freedom from pain. Homer feels compelled to note that the Lotus-eaters "did them no hurt but gave them to eat of the lotus." Once secure from threat, Homer's men (and by extension, humanity) are free to indulge their innate hedonism, for Homer tells us the lotus "was so delicious." This gluttonous feast of the senses overpowers Homer's men, clouding their minds and making them forget their responsibility, for "they left off caring about home and did not even want to go back." Finally Homer, indulging his appetite for understatement, conveys the reluctance of giving up this physical sensation by informing the reader matter-of-factly that his fierce, battle-tested warriors "wept bitterly" when they had to give up the lotus.

Each of these ideas finds its corollary in *Star Trek VII: Generations*, a film whose villain isn't so much a person but a concept, a kind of a space age Lotus blossom called "the Nexus." This "energy ribbon" flies through the universe, absorbing life forms into its electrical emanations of pleasure, an experience described for Jean Luc Picard by the character Guinan , who spent some time in the Nexus, this way: "It was like being inside joy — as if joy were something tangible and you could wrap yourself up in it like a blanket. And never, in my entire life, have I been so content."² She goes on to say that she didn't leave the Nexus, she was "pulled away, ripped... none of us wanted to go" (recalling Homer's admonition that "though they wept bitterly, I forced them back to the ships"). She warns Picard: "If you go, you're not going to care about anything. All you'll want is to stay in the Nexus. You're not going to want to come back."

Picard does go into the Nexus, where he also discovers Captain James T. Kirk, who was thought to have been killed seventy-five years earlier in a space catastrophe (but was really just gobbled up by the Nexus). Interestingly, the Nexus for him (a farm in Iowa) is different than the Nexus for Picard (a Victorian-era hearth and family in England). The Nexus is different for everyone — perhaps an acknowledgment that the Lotus which figures so prominently in Homer's narrative also means different things to different cultures.³

The common denominator in both stories is really the blissful forgetfulness imparted by a mind-altering sensation. In both Homer's *Odyssey* and *Star Trek: Generations*, there seems to be an equating of a worry-free Paradise (Lotus/Nexus) with the ability to wipe clean the life one has led and to start anew — as if the "burden" of choices we've been forced to make as human beings is what creates our reality — and our need for relief. Yet, in both Homer and *Trek*, true heroes accept that burden and turn away from the fantasy.

Of course, everyone can use a break now and again. And when primitive desire for release meets twenty-fourth-century technology, the result is suitably impressive. It's time to enter the Holodeck.

SEEMING IS BELIEVING

The original voyage of the *Enterprise* was supposed to last five years — a long time, even by the standards of twenty-third century intergalactic travel. Although the original series was canceled after only three-fifths of its voyage was completed, subsequent spin-offs provided a way for weary space travelers to unwind during their extended journeys: the holodeck. (Holodeck technology wasn't available to Kirk and his crew; the first glimpse viewers got of the holodeck was the pilot episode for *Star Trek: The Next Generation*, "Encounter at Farpoint." Apparently, all "galaxy class" starships come with holodecks as standard equipment.)

The holodeck is a virtual reality suite which allows the user to program any scene which he or she can conjure up, from pastoral valleys or languid beaches to swinging jazz clubs or swashbuckling adventures. *Star Trek* has gotten lots of dramatic — and comic — mileage from the use of the holodeck, but the idea of a quick escape from the rigors of modern life didn't originate with *Trek*'s technicians. It found its first and greatest expression in the brief comic masterpiece "The Secret Life of Walter Mitty," by the twentieth-century writer/humorist James Thurber. "Walter Mitty" bequeathed to modern fiction the notion of fantasy as a means of escape from the mundane world, and a quick reconsideration of his plight — or, more accurately, his triumph over his plight — should help illuminate the corridors of *Trek*'s holosuites.

Thurber's Walter Mitty is an endearingly henpecked husband who spends most of the story imagining himself to be enmeshed in heroic, life-or-death circumstances. With no commentary, Thurber simply presents Mitty's alternating "realities": a middle-aged man who must buy dog biscuits and, galoshes, and then meet his wife in the lobby of a hotel ("She didn't like to get to the hotel first; she would want him to be there waiting for him as usual"[4]). In Mitty's life in the real world he is a practical nonentity, mumbling to himself and trying to drive his car without clogging city traffic or getting into an accident. But the real action takes place in Mitty's other reality, where in his mind he's a fighter pilot engaged in a dogfight, a world-famous surgeon, even a condemned man defiantly eyeing the firing squad. Mitty, in his fantasies, is the polar opposite of Mitty in his meek married existence.

Thurber's deft touch as a writer keeps Mitty from degenerating into a total milksop or delusional neurotic. Rather, he's simply an average guy, feeling unappreciated, battling the indignities of the modern world and finding greatness and acclaim in the only place he can: his own mind. Implicit in the story is the *necessity* of Mitty's fantasies. One suspects it's what keeps him humming along in his marriage as well. If he didn't have these delusions of grandeur, there's no telling what kind of psychopath he might otherwise become. If he's going to be a murderer, better to restrict it to the confines of his imagination, as in this fantasy, after a newsboy runs by, shouting some breaking news about a trial:

> "Perhaps this will refresh your memory." The District Attorney suddenly thrust a heavy automatic at the quiet figure on the witness stand. "Have you ever seen this before?"
> Walter Mitty took the gun and examined it expertly. "This is my Webley-Vickers 50.80," he said calmly. An excited buzz ran around the courtroom. The judge rapped for order. "You are a crack shot with any sort of firearms, I believe?" said the District Attorney, insinuatingly. "Objection!" shouted Mitty's attorney.
> "We have shown the defendant could not have fired the shot. We have shown that he wore his right arm in a sling on the night of the fourteenth of July."
> Walter Mitty raised his hand briefly and the bickering attorneys were stilled. "With any known make of gun," he said evenly, "I could have killed Gregory Fitzhurst at three hundred feet with my left hand." Pandemonium broke loose in the courtroom....[5]

Thurber would no doubt enjoy the many *Star Trek* episodes where the holodeck was used to construct many Mitty-like fantasies. In one such episode in the Mitty mold, a meek engineer finds himself transformed into a swashbuckling swordsman. In another, a highly competent doctor becomes a highly competent secret agent, a la James Bond. Here's a peek at their fantasies.

THE MEEK SHALL INHABIT THE HOLODECK

What's the most outrageous fantasy that you can imagine? How about Jean Luc Picard in a Louis XIV wig, brandishing a sword as one of the Three Musketeers? Or Deanna Troi as a Greek goddess, seductively smoothing her toga? How about earnest Dr. Julian Bashir, cautious man of science, as a James Bond–style secret agent?

Star Trek holodecks have seen it all.

In one of the most entertaining and memorable episodes (*The Next Generation*'s "Hollow Pursuits"), the nervous and maladjusted engineer Reg Barclay regularly seeks escape into the holodeck to do battle with the Three Musketeers: Captain Picard, First Officer Riker and Chief Engineer LaForge, in full musketeer plumage. His reward for his inevitable and impressive victories? The affections of goddess Deanna Troi, temptress of the master swordsman Barclay.

Tearing a page right out of Thurber, the episode focuses on a crew member who is suspect in his fitness for duty and capacity for responsible behavior. Reg Barclay is a modestly capable engineer but a bumbling human being. Geordi Laforge, his supervisor, scolds him, Riker lectures him and Picard doubts him. But in the holodeck, they fall before him, humbled by the finesse of his foil. Like Walter Mitty, Barclay bounces back and forth between the "real world" of the *Enterprise* and the world of his own making. His use of the holodeck's fantasy is borne of more than a desire to pass a few fanciful hours. He uses fantasy to cope with reality. Reg Barclay, human being, might fully disappear if he weren't occasionally bolstered by the better Barclay inside him, the one who dispatches enemies with the élan of a master dueler.

Of course, the holodeck also hosts master spies as well. In the fun and provocative *Deep Space Nine* episode "Our Man Bashir," the station's committed and competent physician, Dr. Julian Bashir, indulges his fantasy as a 1960s-era British Secret Service spy. In an episode filled with intrigue, danger, surprises and dashing, last-minute escapes, Bashir gets to experience life as a secret agent and still return to his rather mundane job as space station physician in the same day.

Unlike Barclay, Bashir is a character who would seem to be reasonably fulfilled in his life. And, in fact, that is the case. But Bashir's holodeck adventure provides a nice bookend to Barclay's swashbuckling. In the *Trek* universe, fantasies aren't just for the incompetent or the insecure. *Everyone* is entitled to unwind after a hard day at work. The need for release through fantasy is not only hard-wired into holosuites but also into human psychology. People need to get away from their day-to-day lives, and in space that means the holodeck. *Trek*'s acknowledgment of humanity's need for escape is only one side of the story, however. With opportunity comes risk. And if it's fantasy we need, then there are certainly those who would play on that need, manipulating people through fantasy.

Playing with people's fantasies? Casting them about randomly in space and time? Putting them in thrilling situations that force them to survive in unfamiliar, challenging environments? In *Star Trek*, that can only mean "the Q." That impish cosmic deity has troubled the sleep of many Starfleet officers. But the ability to inhabit multiple times and multiple identities doesn't originate with *Star Trek*, but rather with a work of literature penned by a writer who also created many strange new worlds: James Joyce.

Waking Up in a Whole New Place

Although *Star Trek* has always traded on the latest intellectual currents, it owes a portion of its appeal to an early twentieth-century movement called "modernism." Embracing a wide range of thinkers and artists, "modernism" was distinguished by its conscious obliteration of accepted norms in the arts and sciences. Modernists drew on ideas put forward by Freud (especially his advancement of an interior consciousness separate from one's "public" self), Einstein (who showed that one's perception of an object is conditioned by space and time) and Picasso (whose cubist approach to painting represented the modernist idea of a "fragmented" reality). In literature, the high priest of modernism was James Joyce. In his masterpiece *Finnegans Wake*, Joyce provided the template for a recurring figure of importance in the *Trek* universe, "the Q."

Finnegans Wake is among the most complex, bizarre and controversial books ever published, yet it's founded on a fairly simple (but troubling) idea: identities are unstable, and our "reality" is constantly in flux, shifting among various historical periods, geographical locales, even physical incarnations. For example, a man can experience in one afternoon what it is to be Julius Caesar, a caveman, a bartender, Jack the Ripper, and an object like a dung heap or a tree. In fact, we all move among these various temporal realities, gathering our atoms together at one place and then rearranging them later in different configurations.

In Joyce's world, the snap of a finger, the snippet of a song or a stubbed toe can be the catalyst for a leap into another dimension. Without warning, one can be ripped from one millennium and transported to the next, an instantaneous, unpredictable dislocation. It is impossible to represent by excerpt Joyce's magnum opus. No single passage or page makes much sense when removed from the entire work (and not even then, Joyce's detractors would argue). But the book, which borrows phrases from dozens of languages and figures from hundreds of myths, novels, legends, court trials, patriotic poems, saloon songs, Shakespeare plays, and sacred books like the *Tibetan Book of the Dead*, the *39 Thesis* of Martin Luther, the *Bhagivad Gita* and the *Rites of Osiris and Isis*, makes its point. The here and now only *seems* stable. We are in a state of perpetual flux.

"The Q" might never have read *Finnegans Wake*,[6] but he dramatically embodies the idea of perpetual flux. He embodies lots of other ideas as well.

CUE THE ANTAGONIST

The entity known as "the Q" first revealed himself during the pilot episode for *The Next Generation* series, "Encounter at Farpoint." Throughout the next seven years, and even in the sister series *Deep*

Space Nine and *Voyager*, "Q" (the definite article was generally omitted in subsequent episodes) created extreme havoc for the Federation. His playful and irreverent personality, combined with his omnipotence and time-bending abilities, made for some turbulent times in space. In the "Farpoint" episode, he transports the crew from the bridge of their ship to a kangaroo court trial, populated by dwarves, samurai warriors and medieval peasants, and puts them on trial for crimes of humanity — in general. Over the course of the episode, he stops time, erects a barrier in space to prevent the *Enterprise* from going anywhere, snaps his fingers and changes into the clothes of King Henry VIII or a World War II infantry soldier, or simply freezes a member of the bridge crew by pointing his finger at her. With a wave of his hand he rearranges scenes and resets time.

In later episodes he does much the same, sometimes showing up out of thin air to startle Captain Janeway in her bed, or Picard in his ready room. He once tempted Commander Will Riker with a taste of godlike omnipotence, and in the series finale of *The Next Generation* he threw Picard back and forth through a variety of time frames, ending up ultimately at the point in geologic history when the first microbes in the primordial ooze were about to merge to create life.

In Joyce's *Finnegans Wake*, we get similar rapid and disorienting dislocations. The principal agent of these movements through time is Humphrey Chimpden Earwicker, a pub keeper whose drunken dream provides the impetus for the peripatetic narrative. Earwicker's sleep is troubled by the shame of having committed some unspecified lewd act, which plagues his conscience. The Q takes a page from Earwicker's plight, for he too once committed an unacceptable act: spreading chaos through the universe. For this, his omnipotent powers were suspended by the "Q continuum," a sort of committee of ruling cosmic supergods. Until Q showed himself capable of true selflessness, he had to live as a mere human among the Starfleet crew he had so enjoyed tormenting for so many years (in *The Next Generation* episode "Deja Q").

Joyce's point — well, one of many points made by Joyce — is that the modern world, with its discoveries of psychology, physics, and communications technology, is a very difficult place in which to feel "grounded." Telegraphy, radio waves, telephones and air travel destroy distance. Hypnosis, psychotherapy, even dreams destroy linear time.

Mass media and mass migration destroy identity. All of these "advancements" help to obliterate the formerly reliable sense of who we are. "Q" is an advanced being, too, and he frequently chides the mere humans of Starfleet for their hubris in thinking they understand the universe because they fly around in their man-made starships. The world is not what you think it is, Q often warns. Time, space, the mind... there's more to these things than you can possibly conceive of.

It's a sentiment that Joyce — and *Trek*'s creator Gene Roddenberry — spent the better part of a career promoting.

SEVENTEEN

Gods, True and False

An encounter with some sort of deity — either by accident or by design — has formed the basis for many of the *Enterprise*'s most memorable *Trek*s. On the one hand, that seems rather unsurprising. Since mankind first sought shelter in the cave to hide from the thunderous voice of God, the quest for spiritual knowledge has been a driving force for individuals and societies. In a show about the various journeys taken by intrepid explorers of the future, it would seem odd indeed if their travels never raised some fairly common questions about the almighty: Does God exist? What happens when we die? Do other races/species share human belief systems? Do moral absolutes exist in the universe?

And on and on. Yet, as many fans know, the series' creator, Gene Roddenberry, was an avowed secular humanist who had great disdain for organized religion.[1]

In the original series there is not a lot of talk of God, Heaven, prayer, or even the performance of routine religious rituals.[2] Though exceptions occur (including Captain Kirk's brazen rebuff of pantheism in the episode "Who Mourns for Adonais" that "one god is enough" for humans of the twenty-third century), the post–original series spinoffs deal much more frequently and directly with the nature of spiritual experience than the original series episodes.

The instructive and complex overlap between *Trek* and religion can perhaps be analyzed best in those movies and episodes in which a "god" is reportedly discovered. This has been a fairly common recurring motif, especially in the post–Roddenberry years (he died during the fifth year of production of *The Next Generation* in 1991), though there were many episodes and movies which dealt with this theme while Roddenberry was firmly in control of the franchise.

Trek's notion of God is built largely upon the image bestowed to Western Civilization by literary tradition. Therefore, it's worth examining those texts that have established in the mind of many viewers the image that informs our collective conception of God. The list of works which have helped etch an image of God in the modern psyche would itself take up a whole book, but there are some which are clearly more important than others. The Alpha and Omega of religious texts in Western Civilization is the Hebrew Bible, or Old Testament. First, then, we'll look at some of those lasting images which can be traced back to the Old Testament, and then at how those images gained currency and were reflected back in one of the greatest and most influential works of imaginative literature even written, John Milton's late Renaissance epic, *Paradise Lost*.

HE'S GOT THE WHOLE WORLD IN HIS HANDS

"In the beginning, God created the heaven and the earth." So we are told in chapter 1, verse 1 of "Genesis," the first of the Old Testament books and the one which purports to chronicle — literally or metaphorically, depending on one's school of religious thought — the creation of human life upon the former void now called earth. The entire Old Testament, which was written in Hebrew, recounts not only the creation of the earth, but also provides a history of Israel, the formation of its laws as given by God, and an overview of God's covenant with the people of Israel, often referred to as "the chosen people." One can, if one wishes, read a lot into a line of any text — especially the Old Testament. Religious and literary scholars have argued for two millennia about the meaning of certain Bible passages, but from just that first line of Genesis, we can glean a great deal about the God of Biblical tradition. He is, first and foremost, all-powerful.[3] Nothing exists that was not created by Him. Yet, he existed before all that we now call creation, before Heaven, before everything—except he has no definable origin. He is and has always *been*. That leads to the second most important quality of God: he is mysterious. An enigma. God and his ways cannot be discussed rationally, leading to a related, critical aspect of his being: he requires that his worshippers have *faith*.

Star Trek, as we shall see, has played off those qualities when it's presented a deity to viewers: God's power, his mysteriousness, and the implicit requirement that people accept him on faith.

From this lone, introductory verse (and, of course, a wealth of supporting material), a sort of profile of God—both psychological and physical—has taken root and become engraved in our culture. God is often portrayed in art as an old man, bearded, sitting on a throne or surrounded by naked angel babies, engaged in some act of creation or vengeance. From Michelangelo to Albert Brooks, this image has been widely promulgated—a physical manifestation of those qualities enumerated in Genesis: power (seated on a throne), timelessness (surveying the void, reaching out to Adam, judging the dead of every generation), and demanding the suspension of reason (speaking through a burning bush, turning people into human salt licks). Our notion of who God is owes much to artistic representation derived from the Old Testament.

An awareness of how firmly these attributes are engraved in so many peoples' minds helps illuminate many of *Trek*'s Godlike encounters. On the one hand, when a Federation crew comes across a being purporting to be the Almighty, he/she/it will generally demonstrate some or all of the qualities discussed above. This kind of beatific shorthand helps establish in the minds of the viewers that the entity in question could reasonably be mistaken for God. Hence, we share the crew's fear and awe at whatever being is claiming to be God because, to be somewhat flip, we recognize the type. On the other hand, some episodes offer us a look at super-powerful entities who are clearly *not intended* to be seen as a Judeo-Christian God, and it's interesting to see how different these "gods" act. They may manifest a sense of humor, for instance (as is the case with that meddlesome, sarcastic deity "Q"), or they may reveal ignorance about some aspect of humanity, or about the universe (the God of the Old Testament knows everything about everything because he created everything; to question himself, or others, is not in his nature).

The God of the Old Testament is always right, then, but not always easily understood. The questions that have been raised since the beginning of recorded time by rational human beings expressing skepticism have not gone away, but some writers have been so bold as to speak on behalf of the almighty in answer to those questions. The most famous articulation of God's side — and an epic attempt to "justify the ways of God to man" — is John Milton's *Paradise Lost*, a lengthy and meticulously crafted poetic retelling of God's battle with Satan for the souls of Adam and Eve.

LOOKING FOR PARADISE

Milton's *Paradise Lost,* published in 1667, may not be every undergraduate English major's favorite work, but it's generally found at or near the top of lists with titles like "the Greatest Works in English" or "Top Ten Epics." Its form (written in twelve "books") and its subject matter (Adam and Eve's expulsion from the Garden of Eden) qualify it for the status of "epic," which generally denotes a very long poem retelling the tale of some heroic struggle (other well-known epics include Homer's *Iliad* and *Odyssey*, Virgil's *Aeneid* and Dante's *Divine Comedy*). The opening lines give away, more or less, what the next several thousand will be about:

> Of Man's first disobedience and the fruit
> Of that forbidden tree, whose mortal taste
> Brought death into the World, and all our woe,
> With loss of Eden.[4]

Milton — who was blind and therefore had to dictate the poem to his daughters — gives us all our favorites from the Old Testament: God, Satan, Adam and Eve. And, savvy author that he was, Milton mentions Jesus Christ at the very end in teasing anticipation of a sequel, which he published five years later as *Paradise Regained*.

In *Paradise Lost*, Milton tows the party line. He saw his job as helping to cement the establishment belief that God is who the Old Testament says he is: mighty, just, omnipotent. Milton' achievement was poetic, not prophetic. He challenged readers' attention spans, not their theological presumptions. His epic underlines how important it is for mankind to follow God's dictates, to have faith that His governance is just and to avoid at all costs running afoul of Him by disobeying or questioning his intentions.

In both scriptural text and sculptured poesy, then, the message has come down pretty much the same: God exists, unchallenged in his power, worthy of praise and tolerant of no dissent from his ways. The price of non-belief is the loss of paradise. Because God tolerates no dissent, some people who extol a belief in Him often exhibit a similar intolerance of dissent. *Star Trek* has given us many worshippers who are unshakable, even zealous, in their faith. But in the world of *Star Trek*, zealotry is often the source of ignorance, error, violence and even death. Let's take a look at what happens when a person claims to know the mind of God and manages to get control of the *Enterprise*—with the hope of using the ship to get closer to Heaven.

LOOKING BEFORE YOU LEAP

In *Star Trek V: The Final Frontier*, we are introduced to a charismatic character named Sybok, a highly intelligent Vulcan rebel who, we discover, turns out to be Spock's half-brother. Sybok is something of a mentalist in that he seems to be able to sense people's pain, and then help them release it. This therapeutic power helps him establish a close bond with those he meets. In addition to his powers of empathy, Sybok is in possession of the belief that God is speaking to him, and that the Almighty is waiting for him at a place called Sha-Ka-Ree — the Vulcan equivalent of heaven.

Sybok persuades his followers to assist him in a plan to hijack the *Enterprise* and fly off to find Sha-Ka-Ree. He succeeds, even persuading many of the crew of the *Enterprise* that he's truly on a religious mission sanctioned by God (though significantly, Kirk never buys into it; he remains a skeptic to the end, articulating what some might call irreverence toward the apparent God at Sha-Ka-Ree but what Gene Roddenberry surely would have seen as rational resistance to some high-tech hocus-pocus).

When Sybok and the hijacked crew encounter the "God" at Sha-Ka-Ree — a previously undiscovered planet just beyond a forbidding part of space called the "Great Barrier" — they are presented with a variety of images which could have been culled from the pages of the Old Testament. Bearded, longhaired, powerfully etched features of an elder male figure, wrathful in countenance, appear magically before the dazed crew. A voice purporting to be the Almighty addresses the assembled onlookers and demands that the *Enterprise* be turned over to it so that His message can be spread throughout the galaxy. The scene succeeds because the viewer sees exactly what one might expect to see when encountering God. The visage, the voice, the awe-inducing power of the God of Genesis is manifesting before our eyes. But amid the wind, thunder and blinding light of this apparition, Kirk remains unconvinced, asking for further proof that this phenomenon is really "God." McCoy — a convert to Sybok's spiritual pain-release program — chastises Kirk: "You don't ask the almighty for his ID,"[5] McCoy scolds.

Yet, this movie and many of the episodes of each of the series endorse precisely that kind of pragmatism, that unbending application of logic even when a leap of faith is being called for. Kirk — and fellow captains Picard, Janeway, Sisko and Archer — always demands proof before making a leap. This is not to say that each of the respective *Star Trek* captains lacks human passion or emotion. But in matters of faith — traditional religious faith, anyway — *Star Trek* places a premium on proof. Kirk, at the foot of Heaven, remains a doubting Thomas. His skepticism is well founded, by the way, as the God of Sha-Ka-Ree turns out to be merely a powerful, and bitter, entity who has remained "trapped" in this planet and is seeking escape. His wrath is Godlike, but his essence is decidedly secular. Sybok was deluded, and but for the implacable skepticism of Kirk, his crew would have been annihilated (as Sybok is, fittingly, at the end of the movie when he tries to heal the entity's pain).

Sha-Ka-ree, which is also called Paradise by Sybok, is not lost because of a lack of faith, but rather because of misplaced faith. Milton's convictions in *Paradise Lost* were the same as Sybok's, with Kirk functioning as a hybrid of questioning Adam and disobedient Satan. In the literary epic, that mix results in the expulsion from Eden, but in the cinematic epic, modern skepticism triumphs over religious myth.

MANY ARE CALLED BUT ONLY I'VE BEEN CHOSEN

It would be wrong to characterize *Star Trek* as anti-spiritual, or even anti-religion. From Vulcan meditation ceremonies to Klingon vision quests, the franchise has illustrated many paths towards spiritual truth. It is not religion, per se, that engenders conflict, confusion or despair, but rather a perversion of the religious ideal. There is a sort of loosely observed equation regarding spirituality in *Star Trek*. The more public the religious impulse, the less pure and more suspect. Characters who exhibit private religious impulse — or even overt superstition — are generally regarded positively. No one thinks ill of Worf because he believes Kahless the Klingon Savior has returned. He's not determined to make *everyone else* believe. In the true spirit of the Prime Directive — the policy of noninterference in the natural development of another culture — inhabitants of the *Star Trek* world usually live and let live. However, when a private religious impulse turns into a public mandate, problems arise. Sybok provided an example of how far astray one man's private delusions can lead him, but notwithstanding the potential destruction of the *Enterprise*, Sybok truly meant no harm to anyone around him. (He is genuinely disturbed when the entity he was seeking engages in hostile behavior toward the *Enterprise* crew.) Such was not the case with D'Jamat, the creepily compelling character in the *Enterprise* episode "Chosen Realm."

What "Chosen Realm" lacks in nuance it makes up for in menace. The episode is a showcase example of how one man, who deems himself anointed by the Almighty, becomes a living example of bigotry, hatred, intolerance and violence — all in the name of God. After being rescued by Captain Archer and his crew, D'Jamat and his fellow crew members — identified as "Triannons" — expose themselves as combatants in a holy war on their home planet. From sabotage to suicide bombings, all in the name of following God's mandate, they wreak havoc on the *Enterprise*, very nearly killing Archer and the crew in the process.

And in the clearest indictment of petty and irrelevant religious bickering perhaps ever displayed in the franchise, it turns out that the Triannons' holy war — a war, which we discover at the end of the episode, has destroyed their home planet and millions of its inhabitants — is based solely on whether "creation" took place in seven days or eight days. That such an insignificant difference could lead to a wholesale holocaust would seem preposterous if modern religious schisms over interpretations of sacred text weren't so common, and frequently violent, in our own time. That implicit message is made explicit in the final shot of a smoking planet reduced to rubble, with even the morally pugnacious D'Jamat exhibiting inexpressible shock and sorrow over what his holy war has wrought.

Although "Chosen Realm" aired more than a decade after Gene Roddenberry's passing, its basic premise, and the premise of *Trek* from its inception, remains true to the vision Roddenberry outlined from the start of the series. As he explained in 1968's *The Making of Star Trek*, Roddenberry felt that human beings — and any species we might encounter beyond the boundaries of our world — would have to move beyond the petty bickerings over religious minutia and embrace those commonalties which really bind us. He saw *Trek* as a way to accelerate that movement: "This approach expresses the 'message' basic to the series: we must learn to live together or most certainly we will soon all die together."[6] That sobering prospect has under-girded many of the best hours of *Trek*, a show whose many differing journeys towards universal enlightenment end not in a church, synagogue or mosque, but in the temple of the human heart.

EIGHTEEN

The Rise of the Machine

Say the words "science fiction" to some people and what pops into their minds is an image of a robot with lights blinking, mechanical limbs awkwardly flailing and a telephone-answering-machine voice muttering some generic phrase of distress like "Danger!" or "That does not compute." Or perhaps, for those weaned on more modern sci-fi, the image might be of a cyborg-type humanoid, with latex flesh and superhero strength, armed with an automatic weapon and fighting terrorist hit squads from the future. The images differ in degree but not in kind: electronic circuits giving "life" to a mechanical man.

But can robots — or their inevitably more advanced progeny — ever lay claim to being more than mimics of their creators? Can laughter, tears, love — or genuine "consciousness" of their own existence — be bred in a machine? And if so, is that a good thing? What are the limits of artificial intelligence? Are humans ultimately irreplaceable, or will they one day be replicated on a futuristic assembly line? And would they differ in personality? And who would decide how these beings act, think, or even look?

Sci-fi writers sure have had a lot of fun trying to figure out the answers to those questions. The uncertain evolution of machine-based life forms — living computers, robots, cyborgs, androids — has attracted writers, musicians, and filmmakers like a magnet. *Trek*, too, owes some of its most memorable hours to the exploration of the limits of artificial intelligence. Each of the various series has featured plots and characters built squarely upon the questions raised by "thinking machines." *Trek*'s appropriation of this time-honored theme pays tribute not only to the genre of classic "science fiction," but also reflects an advancement of the arguments put forward by the forebears of robotic fiction. *Star Trek* is at its smartest when it's dissecting the intersection of humanity and machinery.

All the "giants" of the sci-fi genre seem to have tackled the subject. And what they had to say was not lost on *Trek*'s writers — or generations of sci-fi devotees. Nobody had more to say about the subject than Isaac Asimov, the avuncular guru of the "golden age" of sci-fi. His classic work *I, Robot* is the most famous fictional rendering of a world seeking the balance between the eclectic and the electric.

Rules of the Game

Once in a rare while, an idea is put forth with seeming casualness that, by accident or design, becomes *the* idea which must be deferred to, acknowledged, argued against or grudgingly accepted. Such was the case with Asimov's *I, Robot,* a collection of previously published robot stories which gave book-length gravitas to the now-famous "three rules of robotics" (which Asimov employed but did not completely originate; that distinction belongs in part to pioneering sci-fi publisher John Campbell, a fact Asimov happily acknowledged whenever he was asked about the origin of the rules[1]). The rules soon came to be sort of a sci-fi lingua franca among people writing (and reading) robot-themed science fiction. One could no sooner ignore them than someone writing a story about whaling could afford to ignore the influence of *Moby Dick*.

Here they are, still intriguing writers and readers more than half a century later:

> Rule One: A robot may not injure a human being, or through inaction, allow a human being to come to harm.
> Rule Two: A robot must obey the orders given it by human beings except where such orders would conflict with the First Rule.
> Rule Three: A robot must protect its own existence as long as such protection does not conflict with the First or Second Rules.[2]

Eighteen. The Rise of the Machine

Asimov uses these rules for all they're worth, designing plots which place various robots in situations where the rules would seem to be in conflict, or at least create a dilemma for a purely preprogrammed mind. While all of the stories in 1950's *I, Robot* revolve around the "rules," Asimov also frequently promotes his personal belief that robots not only pose no threat to humanity, but also that they'll render a great boon to mankind. In fact, the book suggests robots are, in many ways, "superior beings." At the very least, our tin-plated brethren deserve more respect and affection than Asimov's peers were wont to give them, he implies. Here's an excerpt from the first story in *I, Robot*, called "Robbie," about a young girl's robot companion/plaything. Though the girl's mother finds the whole idea of a robot companion unnatural and not a little threatening (plus the neighbors are beginning to talk), the father sees it as an asset:

> Well, what have the neighbors to do with it? Now look. A robot is infinitely more to be trusted than a human nursemaid. Robbie was constructed for only one purpose really — to be the companion of a little child. His entire "mentality" has been created for the purpose. He just can't help being faithful and loving and kind. He's a machine — *made so.* That's more than you can say for humans.[3]

The girl herself is even more direct. When the mother, who engineered Robbie's "disappearance" and replaced him with a dog, tries to console her daughter by pointing out that "Robbie was only a machine, just a nasty old machine. He wasn't alive at all," Gloria, the little girl, screams, "He was a *person* just like you and me and he was my *friend*."[4]

While *I, Robot* is legendary for its iteration of the "Three Rules," it's this sub-theme of a machine's "humanity" and the repulsion some people feel for robots that has provided the most dramatic mileage for *Star Trek*'s writers. (Though Asimov's "rules" are not alluded to specifically in *Star Trek*— presumably because any "robot" in service aboard a starship would be beholden to Starfleet's code of conduct rather than to the rather simplistic, twentieth century "rules"— Asimov himself *is* credited, in *The Next Generation* episode "Datalore," as the conceiver of Data's "positronic"-type brain.) The question of whether an artificial life form can ever seamlessly take its place in human society hangs over the heads of two of *Star Trek*'s most popular regular characters: Data the android, from *The Next Generation*, and the Doctor, the computer-program-come-to-virtual-life on *Voyager*. Both characters have typically unnerved many of their Starfleet peers — though no history of violence or erratic behavior had been associated with them.[5] Machines that replicate human behavior simply seem to make some people uneasy — as Data discovered when he received his first command.

GET WITH THE PROGRAM

In the two-part *The Next Generation* episode "Redemption," Captain Picard is ordered to assemble a fleet of Federation starships to form a blockade to keep the villainous Romulans from trying to clandestinely cross the "neutral zone." He summons his senior officers to his ready room and announces who will take control of each of the ships in the blockade. But he neglects to give Data a starship to command, and the android — exhibiting the rather human quality of resentment at being overlooked — asks the captain why he wasn't chosen. Picard awkwardly fumbles for an answer, suggesting that Data is too valuable to the *Enterprise* to assign him elsewhere. But as Data presses his case Picard relents and gives him a ship of his own to command. Picard's failure even to consider Data for a captain's assignment might have been unintentional, but it represents the fundamental "different-ness" Data himself (itself?) represents. The outward resentment of the Starfleet crew Data is assigned to lead leaves no doubt that there is some latent fear and hostility toward artificial life forms — even in the twenty-fourth century.

"Excuse me sir, I'd like to request a transfer," says Data's new first officer when Data walks onto the bridge of the U.S.S. *Sutherland*. "I don't think I'd be a good first officer for you."[6] When Data points out that the officer's record suggests otherwise, the officer repeats, with special emphasis, "I don't think I'd be a good first officer — *for you.*" He tells Data he doesn't trust his judgment and that he believes an android is unfit as a captain.

Of course, Data is an exemplary captain, and his cleverness and experience help save the day for the *Sutherland*. At the end, his detractors among his crew have become his fans, recognizing his unique computer-generated "gifts" as assets, not liabilities.

Eighteen. The Rise of the Machine

This was Asimov's optimistic message: Give them *a chance*, and you'll find robots to be rather useful, if not outright necessary, to the human race.

Who's more useful to us humans than a doctor? Well, don't ask Beverly Crusher — herself a doctor — about non-human medical practitioners, such as the holographic physician from *Voyager* known as the EMH ("Emergency Medical Hologram"). In *Star Trek: First Contact*, Crusher says, "I swore I'd never use one of these," before grudgingly activating the on-line program which will bring forth the doctor (who was a regular on *Voyager*, but technically resides in the computer program in the Starfleet databanks, not on board a particular ship). Her distaste for the idea of virtual health care providers is temporarily outweighed by the needs of the moment: a bunch of Borg (a ruthless army of drones) are trying to bust down the door of the sickbay and turn Crusher et al. into one of the cybernetic undead. Aside from being exciting, the scene provides a commentary on the pros and cons of artificial life forms. Here are the borg — cyborgs, after all — threatening humanity, and here is the EMH — a hologram, after all — coming to the rescue. A little something for both the technophobes and the computerphiles in the audience. (And in a winning nod to the original series doctor, Leonard "Bones" McCoy, the EMH tells Crusher he's not programmed to hold off the Borg by reminding her that "I'm a doctor, not a doorstop!" — an echo of one of McCoy's famous rejoinders.) He does, however, manage to divert the Borg long enough for Crusher and her medical staff to escape, thus successfully saving a few lives (and perhaps changing Beverly's mind about EMHs).

One of the recurring themes in many of the episodes which feature Data or the Doctor is the quest by both artificial life forms to become more "human." The *Trek* writers have ground away at the idea that, though the machines have superior capabilities, they still imagine themselves incomplete. That's a notion that can be played for laughs — and a little bit of genuine pathos. But what if these "thinking machines" really *did* acquire humanity? What if machines and mankind merged? What would the result be? Would such a coupling represent an advancement in human intelligence — or a step *away from* what makes one human in the first place? And would the hybrid of human/machine be bothered by the same things that have always plagued humanity, such as the need to be loved, or the desire to connect with a "higher power"?

Man and machine do in fact merge, in the climactic scene of the first — and most controversial — of all the *Star Trek* films, a cinematic journey inspired by a classic piece of robotic fiction.

Now, Voyager

Ask any two *Star Trek* fans what they think of the first big-screen adventure of the *Enterprise*, and you're likely to get what seem like critiques of two completely different movies. The film remains a lightning rod for the *Trek* community, which has debated ad nauseum whether the film is a brilliant and visionary cinematic version of Roddenberry's original vision or a disappointing and dull rehash of some warmed over original series ideas, presented with beauty but little dramatic sizzle.

Of course, those who have seen the movie and read the voluminous criticism are forced to conclude *both* views are defensible. But the film becomes much less schizophrenic when it's viewed, primarily, as a movie about the limits of artificial intelligence. That's the real thrust of the film, which seeks to explore the future of the man-machine relationship. Despite what its harshest critics say, *Star Trek: The Motion Picture* does indeed plumb the depths of this central question — but at the cost of the character-based humor and sentimentality associated with the franchise (and particularly the Kirk-Spock-McCoy triumvirate). In an irony that almost undid the franchise, the first and most-eagerly awaited film in the *Star Trek* franchise was arguably the most "sci-fi" and the least "*Star Trek*" of any of the 10 *Star Trek* films. Perhaps those first audiences for the movie should have been handed a copy of the short story "Robot's Return" along with their ticket stubs, for that pioneering 1939 story by Robert Moore Williams provided the blueprint for the *Enterprise*'s big-budget blastoff.

The behind-the-scenes battle to bring *Star Trek* to the big screen was circuitous, delayed, complex and artistically grueling — all of which has been documented in some previous studies.[7] The voyage of the script itself was worthy of a film about an epic journey: from a story treatment written by Roddenberry for a series tentatively titled "Genesis II," to a story treatment of the same material by another writer, then a new version of the story as a script for the never-produced "*Star Trek Phase II*" series, which was then ultimately reworked as the script for the movie.[8] Roddenberry's original treatment, written in 1973, was called "Robot's Return," drawing upon themes suggested by the short story of the same name, written 35 years earlier by Robert Moore Williams.

Williams' "Robot's Return" is set eight thousand years in the future and involves a group of robots in a far-off planetary system who set off on a quest to find their ancestral homeland, which they believe might hold for them the key to some enduring puzzles of their existence, such as why they sometimes revert to spoken language (as opposed to communication by radio waves, which is how they usually do it). They are seeking the land of their creator in search of fuller knowledge of who they are and how they evolved. Their high-tech search — aided by oral legend and some ancient maps — leads them to Earth, now decimated and lying in ruins. They wander among those ruins and find some old structures intact, stumbling across buildings with elevators, furnaces, and various other machines. But they are puzzled, because if their origins really are of this place, "how could lifeless, dead metal build itself" into the thinking and feeling creatures these robots represent, leaving them to wonder, "Where had robots acquired their ability to dream?"[9]

They come across a plaque which reveals the bitter truth, forcing them to accept that something called "Man" had once designed robots for his use, and it is from this advanced technology which was wrought by man that a planet-full of thinking machines apparently evolved. The plaque, "a tough metal, almost completely rust-resistant," tells the story:

> Now Man dies. A mutant bacteriophage, vicious beyond imagination, is attacking, eating, destroying all living cells, even to dead animal matter. There is no hope of escape on Earth. The only hope is to flee from Earth.
>
> Tomorrow we blast our first rocket ship off for Mars, ourselves in suspended animation to withstand the acceleration, the ship manned by Thoradson's robots.
>
> It may be we shall live again. It may be we shall die.
> We go, and may God go with us.[10]

After the shock of the discovery, they try to connect the missing pieces of their ancestry, with one robot concluding, "An organism —

an animal — Yet obviously they must have created us, used us as slaves. They manned their ship with robots."

The robots return to their ship while they continue to speculate, bitter that their origin appears to have begun in servitude to man. Yet they have solved the mystery, and they feel the awe and pride of ownership of their origin: "They may have eaten the flesh of other animals; they may have been weaklings; they may have arisen out of slime, but somehow I think there was something fine about them. For they dreamed...."[11]

It's a short leap across the fictional cosmos from "Robot's Return," with machine-based life forms seeking out their creators, to *Star Trek: The Motion Picture*, with a machine-based life form (here called "V'ger") seeking out its creator. In the *Star Trek* version, the visitor seeking to "return" to Earth is really a late twentieth-century NASA space probe, "Voyager VI," which ultimately was discovered by a planet of "living machines," who grafted their technology onto the probe to enable it to fulfill its mission: investigate the universe and report its findings to its "creator." Now enhanced — and ravaging everything in its wake that is *not* its creator — V'ger (as the probe calls itself) seeks its origins.

There's a significant subplot in the movie which involves Spock's interest in, and communication with, V'ger that really drives home the theme of both the movie and Moore's short story. Namely, pure brilliance, perfect emotionless-logic is not enough, even for an advanced race of superior beings. Existence derives its meaning from "human" qualities: friendship, love, joy, even pain. Supercomputers have no soul, and soul is precisely what's needed to make life worth living. Spock, who spends most of the movie disavowing such "human sentimentality," comes to this conclusion after he has a space-walk "mind-meld" with this massive technological orphan and discovers that for all its bulk, it is spiritually "empty."

Eventually, V'ger gets what it came after: knowledge of its origins — and more. A member of the *Enterprise* crew, Commander Will Decker, willingly "sacrifices" himself to V'ger in a sort-of high-tech cosmic consummation. V'ger has already "absorbed" Decker's former lover, Ilya, during an earlier abduction from the *Enterprise*, so Decker's sacrifice is not completely selfless — though it does lead to one of the strangest love triangles in movie history. The film suggests that this joining of mankind and machine could lead to the creation of a more advanced — and humane — species.

So the mission is complete. The thinking machine that generated so much fear and misunderstanding was really just looking for love. Spock finds it too. Kirk is back in the arms of the machine he loves: the *Enterprise*. Man and Machine in harmony. A robot story with a happy ending. Somewhere in the cosmos, Isaac Asimov must be smiling.

NINETEEN

That Old Gang of Mine

Barrel-chested, gun-toting criminals dressed to the nines in double-breasted pinstripe suits. Fedora-bedecked cigar chompers riding shotgun on the sideboards of vintage automobiles. Slash-tongued dialect, peppered with subtle warnings like "Don't be a wise guy" and "Shut up, if you know what's good for ya." Hoods. Molls. Scarred faces and baby faces. Bank jobs, G-men, lookouts, payoffs. Speakeasies and gin joints, passwords and Fifth Amendment rights.

Capone's Chicago. Dutch Schultz's Newark. Nicky Scarfo's Philly. Lucky Luciano's waterfront.

Murder Inc., and made men. FBI and Teamsters. Overcoats and turncoats, cement shoes and pinky rings.

The Starship *Enterprise*.

Something wrong with that list? You gotta problem with that list? You think that last item don't go with the others? Fugghetaboudit. It fits like a listening device in a Mafioso's buttonhole.

Book 'Em (And Film 'Em, Too)

As visionary and futuristic as *Star Trek* has always been, it has never shied away from wrestling with real-life history. Many of *Trek*'s best and most moving hours have come as a result of its archeology of the past, sending its characters back to mingle with their brethren from an earlier — and usually less enlightened — time and place. And though *Trek*'s excursions into the mobster-run eras of America's golden gangland age might be less weighty than its trips to Nazi Germany or ancient Rome, *Trek*'s writers have faithfully — even minutely — captured the sights, sounds and shots (gun, gin) of the era of organized crime syndicates. And those times when Kirk or his cronies had to strap on a snub-nosed revolver reveal a surprising depth of knowledge about the intricate workings of the underworld as it's been detailed in books and film.

Though there have been countless narratives about life in the Mafia, and hundreds of cheaply made, by-the-numbers movies, a couple of benchmark works stand out for the impact they've made, and the image they've created in the public mind.[1] Many of the mobster images *Trek* has traded on find their best expression in two works: *The Untouchables*, a non-fiction account by famed crimefighter Eliot Ness, and the screenplay for the 1932 movie *Scarface*, written by legendary Chicago newspaperman-turned-screenwriter Ben Hecht.

The Untouchables is the inside story of the famed group of G-men who waged war against Al Capone on his home turf. The book's author, Eliot Ness, was the leader of the so-called crew of "untouchables" — a nickname that derived from their inability to be bribed (unlike many of their less scrupulous counterparts in the office of prohibition enforcement). The book recounts the story of how a young Eliot Ness and a dozen cohorts found themselves trying to do what hundreds of local and federal law enforcement agents had failed to do: namely, put Capone's bootlegging operations on ice.

Told in the self-serving, somewhat melodramatic style that probably typifies the kind of personality who would take on Al "Scarface" Capone, the narrative captures the thrill and danger of life in the roaring 20's, Chicago style. Some readers and critics have found the book to be a somewhat overblown account of the actual work of the "untouchables" — who, it should be noted, didn't really have a hand in bringing Capone to justice; he was ultimately brought down by tax evasion, not bootlegging — but in terms of the picture it paints of gangland Chicago, the book is irreplaceable. If Ness was exaggerating his own role in the war against organized crime, his portrait of a city run amok with gangsters does retain an aura of authentic menace:

Possibly time has dulled the satanic memory of the ruthless gangster known as "Scarface Al." But in that year of 1929 he was at the height of his career — that of the most powerful criminal of all time.

On the day when we gathered for the organizational meeting in my office in the Transportation Building, he already had killed — or ordered killed — an estimated three hundred men. Wholesale murder was his favorite method of eradicating both competition and opposition. It was an alternative of almost positive certainty on occasions when his attempts at bribery failed.

In this year alone, I thought as I sat there drumming my desk with nervous fingers, he had already cost the lives of ten men in three well-publicized blood lettings. These were only the sensational slayings, because gang killings of minor figures in the underworld were so commonplace that the ordinary "bumping off" drew little attention. But the Capone mob had been butchering with a callous flourish in 1929, defiantly heedless of whether the victim was a person of consequence or an ordinary "hood." Nobody was too big or too little to feel the Capone wrath, usually for the last time.[2]

The Untouchables, which inspired a long-running television series in the 1950s (starring Robert Stack in the lead, as Eliot Ness) and a film of the same name in 1987 (starring Kevin Costner as Ness, and Robert DeNiro as Al Capone), rivets the reader's attention, with its no-holds-barred prose celebration of the good-guys-vs.-bad-guys struggle for survival. Ness reveals a world where criminal bosses are utterly impervious to threats or sanction — though they could use a little more schooling, he notes, pointing out, "[m]ost criminals are very limited in intelligence or they wouldn't be outside the law." Those twin attributes — ruthlessness and gullibility — are important as gangland character traits in the original *Star Trek* series' treatment of the underworld theme in the episode "A Piece of the Action," and in *Deep Space Nine*'s over-the-top mob episode "Badda-Bing, Badda-Bang." And although both episodes are played largely for laughs, the tyrannical character of the episodes' crime bosses, their desire for any advantage over an opponent, and their shiftless and shabby moral code is evident on almost every page of Ness's narrative.

Of course, *Star Trek* was not the first entertainment vehicle to make dramatic use of mobsters. As noted above, an entire series was based on the exploits of Ness & Co., and to this day Hollywood producers continue to mine gangster life for its undeniably compelling view of killers, payoffs, speakeasies and double-crosses. Like Ness's *Untouchables*, the best entertainments have often been those which hew closest to the historical record. Although Ness's book reads like a novel, a good deal of its page-turning quality derives from the truth of its content. The same can be said about one of the first — and still best — films about Capone and his grip on Chicago, the 1932 movie *Scarface: Shame of a Nation*, a thinly veiled story about Capone (here called Tony Camonte) and his ruthless rise to power. The movie was ostensibly based on a novel about Capone's exploits, but it is the screenplay of Chicago newspaperman Ben Hecht — who was witness to so much of the 1920's Windy City mayhem — that gives the movie its dramatic heft. Only someone who had a front seat during Capone's reign of terror could have captured the frenzy and the fear of life in the underworld as fully as Hecht, who earned his journalistic chops covering Chicago in the Capone era. Though the film has been eclipsed in the public mind by director Brian De Palma's bloody retelling of a mobster's rise to power in the 1983 film *Scarface* (the remake is dedicated to Ben Hecht), the original remains, well, completely original.

In the first few minutes of the 1932 film (which was actually shot by director Howard Hawks in 1930, but couldn't be released until concerns by censors about the film's glorification of violence could be resolved),[3] most of the major leitmotifs of the gangster-on-film were established: sharp-dressed cigar-chomping mobsters, a "boss" giving orders to his henchmen in heavily accented Italian-English, a shadowy hit man in a fedora, phrases like "Here come the coppers!" shouted in advance of police raids, Tommy guns brandished by drive-by shooters squatting on running boards, and newsboys blaring about the latest "hits" on local gangsters. This is Chicago in the grip of underworld thugs. (In the original series episode "A Piece of the Action," an entire society is modeled on the book "Chicago Mobs of the Twenties"— a book which serves as a sort of guide to life for this particular society.) Early in the film, a newspaper editor spells it out for the viewer as he dictates the next day's headline after the shooting of mob boss "Big Louis" Costillo:

> Do you know what's happening? This town is up for grabs. Get me? You know, Costillo was the last of the old-fashioned gang leaders. There's a new crew coming out. And every guy that's got money enough to buy a gun is gonna try to step into his place. You see? They'll be

shooting each other like rabbits for control of the booze business. Do you get it? It will be just like war. That's it! WAR! You put that in the lead! WAR — GANG WAR!"[4]

Hecht's screenplay crams all the chaos of mob rule into a story with clearly defined characters battling the authorities (nominal) and each other (considerable) for control of the bootleg bonanza that was Chicago under Prohibition. Long before Mario Puzo's *Godfather*, Hecht's screenplay laid out in chilling detail how dangerous it was to cross the reigning local crime boss — yet how quickly gang members were to switch allegiances when it suited their economic interests. As Tony "Scarface" Camonte explains to a fellow member of the Johnny Lovo gang:

> TONY: There's business just waiting for some guy to come and run it right. And I got ideas.
> GUINO: We're workin' for Lovo, ain't we?
> TONY: Lovo? Who's Lovo? Just some guy who was a little bit more smart than Big Louie, that's all. Hey, that guy is soft. I could just see it in his face. He's got a set-up, that's all, and we're gonna wait. Someday, I'm gonna run the whole works.[5]

"Scarface" Tony Camonte, of course, gets his wish. He becomes leader of the crime syndicate that controls Chicago — much to the displeasure of rival gang leaders and law enforcement officials. This idea of jockeying for control of a "territory" has provided the dramatic tension for many mob-related stories, and it is the basis for the story in the original series episode "A Piece of the Action."

CAPTAIN KIRK GETS MOBBED

One of the great strengths of *Star Trek* is its consistency of theme. No matter where the *Enterprise* might find itself, there are certain keynote ideas upon which the plot will generally turn. One of the most prevalent of these themes is the double-edged value of advanced technology. In "A Piece of the Action," *Trek* is able to pay homage both to this crucial theme in *Scarface* and its own ideological bearings. In the 1932 movie, gangster Tony Camonte's rise to power is married to his discovery of new technology: the "Tommy gun," a machine gun fondly referred to by mobsters in the film as a "typewriter." The use of such an efficient killing devices alters the landscape in favor of the lawless hoods who would slaughter with indiscretion. In the first look at the society of gangsters which populates the planet Kirk and crew visit in "A Piece of the Action," everyone is brazenly brandishing a "Tommy gun." As the viewer soon discovers, this is merely a variation on a common theme in *Trek* wherein rival factions seek to gain the advantage over their opponent by gaining possession of more potent, more lethal, technology.

The first look at the society on the mafia-flavored planet Iota confirms a close familiarity with gangland zeitgeist. One sees flappers, vintage 1920's automobiles, and shadowy men wearing Zoot suits and fedoras. This is Hecht's Chicago, for sure. There is even the requisite colorful dialect of the gangster, as in this request by an Iotian mobster to Mr. Spock: "I wanna see ya put your hands over your head, or you ain't gonna have a head" (Spock, logically, complies). In the first 10 minutes of "A Piece of the Action," there is a remarkably comprehensive assemblage of gangland motifs.

That's fitting, as we'll discover, because the entire Iotian society has been built around a book, reportedly published in 1994, titled *Chicago Mobs of the Twenties*. The book was left behind on the planet by a Federation starship, the U.S.S. Horizon, a hundred years before the *Enterprise* came along. A century later, the habits, lifestyle and philosophy of the Iotians reflects a complete immersion into the seedy underworld of racketeering—complete with rival crime bosses "Bela Oxmyx" and "Jojo Krako." Each leader tries to persuade Kirk to instruct him in the use of the Federation's weaponry—phasers and communicators—so that an advantage in the gang wars might be gained (just as those gangs which first possessed machine guns were able to gain the advantage in Chicago's gang wars). The rivalry between Oxmyx and Krako mirrors the split in Chicago between the factional bosses—who often had colorful names as well. As Ness explains:

> In those days, Chicago was cut up into various "territories" by sectional mobs which worked without liaison. One of the strongest gang leaders was "Diamond Jim" Colosimo, who specialized in gambling, white slavery and crooked labor unions.[6]

Oxmyx and Krako each use persuasion, blackmail, kidnapping and other means of coercion to get Kirk to reveal the secret of the newfangled weapons (which the mobsters call "heaters"—more slang for "guns"). But Kirk quickly deduces the rules of this society, and in a classic power play (using the only language the Iotians really speak), turns the tables on the gang leaders with threats of his own: "We're takin' over the whole ball of wax. You cooperate with us and maybe we'll cut you in for a piece of the action," Kirk informs the mob bosses. "The Planet is bein' taken over by the Federation... we need one guy who pulls the strings, then we pull his, ya see?"[7] He convinces the rival factions to unite as one all-powerful planet-controlling criminal cabal.

The *Enterprise* escapes intact—almost. Dr. McCoy forgets his communicator on Iota, leaving Kirk to worry about what might happen when this society of mobsters finally figures out how to use twenty-third century technology.

The episode's recipe of suspense, alleviated by large doses of humor—(a favorite moment: Scotty the engineer threatens Krako to mind his manners or he'll be wearing "concrete galoshes." The puzzled gangster asks, "You mean 'cement overshoes'?" Scotty pauses, mindful of his mistake, and sheepishly intones, "Aye"[8])—and with a touch of philosophy thrown in along the way, also helped flavor one of the most enjoyable hours of the *Star Trek* spin-off series, *Deep Space Nine*, as it paid tribute to the world of the mobster in the delightfully menacing season seven episode "Badda -Bing, Badda-Bang."

Lounge Lizards and Rat Finks

By the time *Deep Space Nine* came along as a series, the holodeck concept had become a reliable storytelling tool, evolving from mere novelty during *The Next Generation* series to a truly integral part of a space ship (*Voyager*) or space station (*Deep Space Nine*). As such, the stories and characters associated with the holodeck became increasingly sophisticated and dramatically useful. The most well-developed recurrent holodeck character in any of the series was Vic Fontaine (played by singer James Darin), a lounge singer and raconteur whose "connections" to the underworld provide the humor and tension of the *Deep Space Nine* episode "Badda-Bing, Badda-Bang."

As with many holodeck-based episodes, this one follows the fairly standard blueprint of "something's-gone-wrong-and-now-what-do-we do-'cause-we-can't-end-the-program-and-we're-all-trapped-in-here" motif. What elevates this episode above the usual fare is the fact that the only character in jeopardy is Vic — who is not real, after all, but whom the crew of *Deep Space Nine* nonetheless rallies to help out. The plot of the episode can be stated simply: A new crime family is moving into Las Vegas and is determined to get Vic out of the way, one way or another, so they can take over all the action. The mere fact that Vic is a holographic projection, and that his entire Vegas showroom setting is the result of computer programming, doesn't offset the crew's genuine affection, and concern, for this character's well being. It's an implicit and powerful commentary on the nature of "reality" in the future, when cybernetic beings and holographic projections can seem as real as the "real" beings aboard ship or space station.

Like "A Piece of the Action," the episode is more fun than fearful, with fans getting the chance to see the *Deep Space Nine* crew pull a classic "caper" in the B-movie style of countless "Wiseguy" films. The plot is a collection of contrivances to bring everyone — including a reluctant Jake Sisko — into the action, focusing on a "heist" to steal some of a crime boss's loot from a safe (with the Ferengi character Nog, of all people, as our heroic safecracker).

The writing of the episode honors the genre, with lots of dutiful nods in its Ben Hecht–inspired gangland-speak (as in this first scene, a confrontation in a nightclub after hours, which is how "Scarface" begins):

> FRANKIE: Well, look who's here — the pretty boy singer himself.
> VIC: Frankie Eyes. What are you doin' in Vegas?
> FRANKIE: Whatever happened to "Hello. Frankie, long time, no see. Can I getcha anything?" (Turning to his bodyguard) How d'ya like this guy?
> BODYGUARD: No manners.
> FRANKIE: We're a long way from South Philly, ain't we Vic?
> VIC: You here on business or pleasure?
> FRANKIE: Let's just say that I'm here to stay, while you, pretty boy, are about to take a powder.[9]

That kind of classic confrontation, right at the beginning, sets up the inevitable power struggle which usually leads to a protracted gang war and leaves only one "boss" standing. That's essentially the plot of "Badda-Bing, Badda-Bang," a fun, taut episode peppered with classic mob taunts, fedoras, not-so-innocent cigarette girls, payoffs, rubouts, crooked casinos and small-time hoods looking to move up in the "family." There is, however, a brief, important sub-plot involving Sisko's refusal to, at first, "play along" and join the others in their effort to help Vic, based on his awareness that Vegas clubs such as Vic Fontaine's used to exclude blacks and other minorities. He's not sure he wants to revisit that time and place, still seething over what it once represented.

Generally, though, the episode is pitched pretty lightly and is played mostly for laughs. It's an entertaining descent into the grime and frivolity of organized crime, with shapeshifting "untouchables" and space age scarfaces.

To ignore the delights of *Trek*'s mob-inspired episodes because they lack the weight of more substantive, more philosophical outings would be a crime. Taking their inspiration from some seminal works in the history of gangland criminality, these episodes provide a universal translation for anyone seeking to know the risks, and thrills, of living in dangerous times.

TWENTY

The Quest for Perfection

The ancient Greeks imagined it. Renaissance artists painted and sculpted it. Modern writers have given it voice and explored its complexities. Still, many people question whether it truly exists.

The idea of "perfection" has drawn the interest of humanity's greatest creative minds. From antiquity, the quest for perfection has intrigued the literary minds of each generation. What constitutes the "perfect?" Is perfection attainable? Do our imperfections keep us from greatness — or are they what makes us great? If a "perfect" world existed, would everyone want to live there? Would anyone?

The notion of the "perfect place," free from the problems which have always plagued humanity, has been addressed by writers and thinkers such as Plato (in his famous prescription for a perfect society, *The Republic*), Plutarch, Sir Thomas Aquinas, and Francis Bacon, up to such modern-day writers as H.G. Wells, George Orwell, and Aldous Huxley. Such "perfect places" have come to be called "utopias," and it is from the work that gave utopias their name that our most complete and compelling look at a perfect world originates.

Sir Thomas More's *Utopia*, written in 1516, remains the benchmark for all serious discussions about creating the "perfect world." His mix of social satire, reformer zealotry and humane interest in the improvement of the life of his fellow man — along with a natural gift for storytelling — combined to create one of the more provocative and enduring works in the history of literature. So omnipresent has More's work become in the discussion of the "perfectibility of mankind" that works on similar themes that predate his by thousands of years (such as *The Republic*) are also called "utopias," even though More is the one who coined the phrase.[1]

There would seem to be a natural parallel between More's seminal work and Gene Roddenberry's creation. Like *Utopia, Star Trek* often seeks to provide a blueprint for a better way of living. More wasn't shy about putting forward ideas that he knew would rub the aristocracy the wrong way. Much of his work can be read as an attack on the pomposity of Renaissance rule and the folly of politicians and theologians who think they have all the answers. Roddenberry was not so very different, using the mainstream vehicle of television to critique mainstream public vices like war, racism and sexism. Both *Utopia* and *Star Trek* provide a level of entertainment that subtly masks their reformer intentions. Both use stories of distant worlds as a prompt to re-imagine our own world. And both point to the perils of excess that can lead one from the path of genuine improvement to the path of extremism.

More's work is rich in its philosophical complexity and naturalistic detail. Many books have been written about just what More was up to, and whether he wholeheartedly endorsed the ideas he put forth. Some see More as a greater satirist than social engineer, suggesting the very name of the work, *Utopia*, reveals Moor's tongue-in-cheek approach to the reforms he suggests (utopia comes from the Greek words for "not," *ou,* and "place," *topos*; hence, utopia is, literally, "no place"). But if that's so, then More's nuanced look at the perfectibility of the world only draws him closer to *Trek*, which eschewed easy answers and often suggested its own wry take on improving the world.

Despite its importance in the development of the utopia subgenre, More's work, it must be admitted, is not exactly beach reading. Few modern readers have felt the need to pick up the volume for consolation or diversion, and it has become increasingly the province of graduate students in English and political philosophy. A brief brush-up with More's main lines of thought, then, is probably in order before looking more deeply at *Trek*'s own utopian impulse.

MORE OR LESS

Utopia is divided into two main sections, with the first serving as a sort of justification for the second. More spends the first part of his narrative offering a critique of the Christianized Europe of the sixteenth century, attacking the greed and vice of its ruling classes. Couched as a tale being related by a traveler named Raphael Hytholoday, Book I of the *Utopia* savagely skewers the laws and lawgivers of More's time, showing how widespread vice has poisoned the body politic:

> Moreover, there is no chance for you to do any good because you are brought among colleagues who would easily corrupt even the best of men before being reformed themselves. By their evil companionship, either you will be seduced yourself, or keeping your own integrity and innocence, you will be made a screen for the wickedness and folly of others. Thus you are far from being able to make anything better...."[2]

It's in Book II, however, that things really get going. Narrated by the traveler Hytholoday, the book turns into a travelogue for the eponymous land of the title. There are a number of features which stand out immediately as central to More's idea of a perfect place, and many of them have been appropriated by later writers in the construction of their own perfect worlds (or turned on their heads by writers of what have become known as "dystopias"—works which paint a picture of the worst possible civilizations). The now-standard list of utopia features derived from More's work include:

- A lush landscape, filled with gardens of Eden-like beauty, though usually these landscapes have been engineered by the Utopists themselves. (This calls to mind the whole idea, incidentally, of the Genesis Project, and *its* aim to create natural paradises where once was nothing but barrenness.)[3]
- A communal society in which everyone contributes something and everyone receives something. Or, as More puts it, "In Utopia, everything belongs to everybody... the individual will lack nothing for his private use. In Utopia, there is no poor man and no beggar. Though no man has anything, yet all are rich."[4]
- A system of hierarchical government, led by an individual deemed most worthy to govern, "a man whom they judge most useful."[5]

- A philosophy which inclines them toward the pursuit of pleasure as the highest human goal. As the book states, "They lean more than they should to the school that espouses pleasure as the object by which to define either the whole or the chief part of human happiness."[6]
- The pleasure the Utopians seek can only be found by living in harmony with nature, and if there is an inviolable utopic commandment, it's this: "The Utopians define virtue as living according to nature since to this end we were created by God."[7]

Star Trek has borrowed liberally from that recipe to explore the idea of utopia, poking a few holes in the conception as articulated in More's book. However, it didn't take Gene Roddenberry to point out that More's prescription is somewhat flawed, if not outright hypocritical. For one thing, in the Utopia More describes, much of the grunt work is performed by slaves. As More explains it, "All menial offices which to some degree include heavy labor or soil the hands are performed by slaves."[8]

In addition, *Utopia* is not a pacifist society, choosing war as one of the means to deal with their growing population and their ever-expanding need for more space. When they encounter a different culture residing on abutting lands, the Utopians encourage them to join in the community of Utopia. Somewhat shockingly to those who have always believed that utopic societies were less martial in character, More tells us that "the inhabitants who refuse to live according to their [Utopian] laws, they drive from the territory which they carve out for themselves."[9]

Most readers and critics generally remark upon the "ideal" qualities of literary Utopias, often downplaying the more egregious lapses in these perfected societies, such as the aforementioned aspect of unequal treatment. Still, More's book is weighted heavily in favor of those qualities which would appeal to most modern readers: a world of natural beauty, serenity, contemplation, hedonistic pleasures, freedom from economic worry, the support of a vast community, and on and on.

Perhaps it is the all-too-easy embrace of the utopia ideal which made Gene Roddenberry want to establish, and then skewer, the notion of a "perfect world." That's exactly what he did in *The Next Generation* episode "The Masterpiece Society."

Twenty. The Quest for Perfection

NOTHING BUT THE BEST

In More's *Utopia*, Nature is almost a "god." To live as one with nature ensures that you are following God's will (who, after all, created all that nature), and that you are moving towards experiencing transcendent bliss that comes from being one with your natural surroundings:

> We have achieved a fully integrated existence. Not just among ourselves, but with our environment. We don't just live here, we are part of our environment. It's a part of us. Every plant life, every microscopic life form is part of the master design. We cannot separate ourselves from it.[10]

That excerpt, however, is from *Star Trek*, not More's *Utopia*, and it sets up the conflict in an episode that at first seems to support the idea of a perfect society but ultimately reveals its flaws and its futility. Yet, as can be seen from that opening speech from the governor of a Utopia-like colony inside a biosphere to an *Enterprise* crew that has just beamed down, this episode is as rooted in More's sixteenth century as it is in the twenty-fourth.

Briefly, the plot of "The Masterpiece Society" has the *Enterprise* discovering a colony in space comprised of descendants (eight generations' worth) of Earth residents who fled their home planet 200 years ago, seeking to establish a "perfect world" through "controlled procreation"— or genetic engineering. Through selective breeding, the very best qualities (leadership, say, or physical strength, or even musical ability) were enhanced in certain bloodlines, while traditional human "weaknesses" were minimized or eliminated. This perfect world — with all of More's A-list qualities, like lush vegetation, communal living, well bred governors, etc. — is threatened by a giant asteroid hurtling through space, headed right for their biosphere. At first, the colony's leader is reluctant to allow the Federation's engineers to assist in preparations to try to avert the disaster — the colonists have had no outside contact to "corrupt" them, you see. But reason wins out, and the governor allows them to work with the biosphere's scientists.

As ship's counselor Deanna Troi gets chummy with the colony's governor, she discovers what a placid, artistic, worry-free idyllic paradise this biosphere really is. And she's impressed. But Captain Picard is not, and he delivers a stinging rebuke to the colonists' way of life — which marks the temperamental shift in the episode. Speaking about selective breeding, Picard tells Troi that "It's a bad idea whose time has long passed. They've given away their humanity with this genetic manipulation. Many of the qualities they've bred out — the uncertainty, self-discovery, the unknown — these are many of the qualities which make life worth living."[11]

The writers of the episode drive the point home when they allow the biosphere's scientists to avert the disaster by adapting on a large-scale technology from Geordi LaForge's visor (which allows him to see). Further reinforcing the episode's point about our imperfections making us what we are — and should be — Geordi points out the irony that "the answer to all of this comes from a visor for a blind man who never would have existed in your society."[12]

Beyond a simple critique of this one utopic colony, "The Masterpiece Society" implicitly assails the notion of the "perfectibility" of any human enterprise — or of humanity itself. The vanity and shortsightedness of any such effort to create a race of "supermen" can only breed problems. When fans of *Star Trek* consider the ethics of genetic manipulation, they need only think of one character, and the dangers of such schemes come stirringly into focus.

He's such a magnetic and disturbing character that it's easy to forget that Khan Noonien Singh — the villain in the big-screen blowout *Star Trek II: The Wrath of Khan*— has a long history. Fans of the series probably know that he made his first appearance in the original series episode "Space Seed." However, Khan's real roots can be traced to a literary tradition in which humans have been the subject of many types of efforts to create "the perfect person." From Mary Shelley's *Frankenstein* to modern day accounts of sports heroes transforming their bodies through steroid use, the quest for human perfection has engaged many writers. One of the prototypes of this genre came from the pen of one of the greatest American writers ever, and though his words are more than 200 years old, his story's moral remains relevant for understanding Khan, and ourselves.

THE MARK OF EXCELLENCE

Nathaniel Hawthorne helped create a literature that was truly American. Grafting European "sophistication" and tradition onto

American expansionism and the journey into the unknown, Hawthorne created a rich literature that is haunted by many intellectual spectres. His short stories reflect a mind trying to resolve the tensions of the new republic: Puritanism vs. freedom of conscience, revolution vs. the need for stability, the city vs. the frontier. And as the new country aimed for some measure of perfection, Hawthorne perched at his writing desk and spun stories about characters wrestling with their inherent imperfections. One of his greatest statements about man's inability to fully accept his imperfections is "The Birthmark." The story also communicates a moral lesson that is relevant to understanding Khan's wrath.

"The Birthmark" is, like most of Hawthorne, deceptively simple-seeming. It's the story of a man named Aylmer who is married to a beautiful woman named Georgiana. She is smart, sensitive, loving, and gorgeous. In short, the perfect mate. Well, *almost* perfect. She has a small birthmark on her cheek, a "crimson stain upon the snow" that was shaped like "a human hand, though of the smallest pigmy size."[13] Aylmer is unable to accept his wife's tiny imperfection, sharing what he believes to be all men's wish that "the world might possess one living specimen of ideal loveliness, without the semblance of a flaw."[14]

Alas, Aylmer — who is a scientist — concocts a potion that he tells her will remove the blight, assuring her that "its virtuous potency is yet greater than its harmful one."[15] She accedes to his wishes, drinks the potion — and dies. Aylmer sinks into despair, berating himself for failing to appreciate just how "perfect" his wife was. "He failed to look beyond the shadowy scope of Time, and living once for all in Eternity, to find the perfect Future in the present."[16]

Hawthorne's story contains lots of allegories about the dangers of overreaching, of trying to play God. His story drives home the idea that such genetic tinkering can lead to no good. It's a tribute to Hawthorne's genius that the reader is made to realize long before Aylmer that the relationship will be destroyed no matter what the outcome of the operation. Even if Georgiana were to survive, she'd be welcomed back into a marriage with a man who has been shown to be superficial and vain. (Perhaps that's why she consents so readily to risk her life to remove her small blotch.) In shooting for perfection, both the target and the archer are destroyed.

That brings us round to Khan — without doubt, the franchise's most renowned villain. In the original series episode "Space Seed," we learn that he is a genetically-altered "superhuman" who tried to take control of earth in the 1990s during a conflict termed the "Eugenics Wars," in which a group of scientists helped create a select group of superior beings. Khan was one of them, and his larger-than-life abilities allowed him to rule a large swath of the globe, from Asia to the Middle East, though his proportionately-sized ego led him to rule as a tyrant. He was eventually deposed, and he chose to escape ignominy by fleeing earth in a "sleeper ship," in which his body, along with a group of fellow genetically engineered humans, was preserved in a state of suspended animation. His ship, the Botany Bay, was discovered by the *Enterprise* more than 200 years later. He is awakened, but again, over the course of the episode, his arrogance and his ambition offset his superior physical and intellectual mien. After spending most of the episode insulting the inferior humans who make up the crew (he tells Kirk, "I'm surprised how little advancement there has been in human evolution"[17]), Khan seizes control of the *Enterprise*. However, he is eventually defeated by Kirk's resourcefulness. The captain releases a knockout gas that neutralizes Khan's fellow superhuman mutineers. He and Khan then have an old-fashioned fistfight, with Khan reminding him, "I have five times your strength — you are no match for me!"[18] But as Kirk is getting knocked around, he pulls a pipe-like lever out of the console he's just been slammed into, and uses it to whack Khan. (It's a bit of a cliché, harkening back to the dirty tricks practiced in many B-movie barroom brawls and prison yard fights, but it is effective and it *does* demonstrate resourcefulness.) The episode ends with Khan and his small band of followers being exiled to a distant planet — a thread that is picked up in *Star Trek II: The Wrath of Khan*.

Khan's plight — his deposal, exile in space during the late twentieth century, subsequent rescue and exile again — are due to the hubris in believing himself to be a sort of god, just as Aylmer thought he could do the work God left undone in creating Georgiana. Khan's quest for perfection blinded him to the fact that enhanced physical strength and mental agility do not alone constitute superiority. Khan was as morally bankrupt as he was physiologically enhanced. His *idea* of perfection was, itself, an imperfect one. Just as Aylmer mistakenly presumed that a blemish-free wife would provide a blemish-free life, Khan has staked his whole being on the notion that genetic alterations can create a *better* man. Kahn may be lots of things, but this popular villain is certainly not a "better" man than Kirk or any of his crew.

And therein lies a big part of *Star Trek*'s appeal. The crew, its vessel, and its chances for success were always far from perfect. Mission after mission found the *Enterprise* supremely disadvantaged — against more "advanced" civilizations, more militaristic foes, more ruthless opponents. Yet this all-too-human crew made up of imperfect people (or half-imperfect, in the case of the half-human Mr. Spock) often triumphed over their "superior" combatants. *Trek*'s imperfections, reflected both within the action of the series and outside of it (poor time slots, lack of network support, early cancellation) helped to make it, for many fans, the perfect entertainment experience.

TWENTY-ONE

Growing Old

The idea of aging — with all of its related psychological baggage — has not only been explored in dozens of *Star Trek* episodes and movies, but it also hovers over the franchise itself. *Star Trek*, its spin-offs and decathlon of movies, has aged in a way that raises the same questions and issues individuals face as they age.

Longtime fans of *Trek* have watched characters age in many 50-minute episodes through the use of makeup and prosthetics, but we've also seen the actors grow old in real life. There's a complex byplay among the episodes (which never age, but remain frozen in time), the characters (who age, but within the safety of subsequent films and series), the actors (who, of course, age in real life and have become, in some cases, infirmed or deceased) and the fans, some of whom have used *Star Trek* as signal buoys in their sail through life. And, to make matters even more complex, the series has had a lot to say about aging which is drawn from some ageless sources of literature, such as Shakespeare. But rather than be overwhelmed by this inchoate stew of ideas about aging, the franchise has often entwined with clarity these disparate strands of philosophy about growing old. At the end of the day, there are some *Trek*-sanctioned truths to cling to which might help one understand and cope with the aging process.

As a theme, "growing old" could be represented by dozens of episodes from each of the series. The *Enterprise*'s voyage through the cosmos can easily be made to stand for humanity's voyage through our own realm of consciousness — from Earth to the stars, from birth to death. Pick any of the series and you could find a well-developed story arc about how "Character X" deals with growing old, beginning with callow Chekov in the original series, and including Sarek, Wesley Crusher, Kes, Jake Sisko, and just about every other major or minor character. The clock ticks for everybody.

Yet the character who seems to serve for most *Trek* fans as the franchise's chief timekeeper is Captain James T. Kirk. It is Kirk who we see really wrestling with the issues of growing old, and it is Kirk whose ultimate acceptance of time's unstoppable handiwork has given the franchise's forays into aging such heft and poignancy. Kirk's various reactions to the aging process have served as a psychological Greenwich mean time to the *Star Trek* faithful, as they wrestle with issues of aging, loss and journeying into the unknown.

But before there was Jim Kirk — before even Gene Roddenberry — there stretched back to the roots of literature a string of works which dealt with the difficulties of growing old. I will deal with only two such works, but for sheer power of expression or insight, these two are unbeatable. The first is Shakespeare's *King Lear*, the granddaddy of cautionary tales and a still-unexhausted vault of the wisdom of the aged. The second, though a relatively short poem, harkens back to Homer and picks up the story after his hero has entered the twilight of his life: Tennyson's "Ulysses." Kirk's chronological travails are really no different than Lear's or Ulysses' ("Odysseus" in the Greek): concern about loss of bodily strength, failed relationships, preoccupation with mistakes made and a growing concern for how one might be remembered.

KING ME

A Shakespearean critic writing about *King Lear* once noted the following: "There is a very real sense in which the whole action of the tragedy might be described as a projection of the conflicting issues supremely present in the mind of the central protagonist."[1] Couldn't the same be said, in part at least, about Kirk in the *Trek* canon's best known exploration of aging, *Star Trek II: The Wrath of Khan*? Beyond some neat coincidences which connect these two decidedly different works of art (*King Lear*, by the way, is considered Shakespeare's greatest achievement, while many fans revere *Star Trek II: The Wrath of Khan* as the best of the [so far] ten films), there is a more profound connection. Those who know Shakespeare's opus will recognize a measure of Lear's agony in Kirk, and at the end of each drama the viewer will have relearned some hard truths about what it means to grow old.

Thematically, as I have suggested, the two works share much of the same genetic material: the encroachment of age and the subsequent loss of one's power; the need to feel useful; the compulsion to learn what is real and true; the savoring of those loves which are most faithful and abiding. In *Lear*, the king cedes his power by stepping down from his throne. Kirk, ironically, gives up his real power when he acquires the admiralty of Starfleet. Both men made tragic mistakes about which direction to go when faced with "retirement," and both pay for those mistakes with a sense of regret and mourning (Bones McCoy even likens Kirk's funk over growing old to seeming "like a funeral"[2]). Both productions follow different story arcs, of course. *King Lear*, being in the genre of tragedy, marches somberly towards its required unhappy ending. *Star Trek II: The Wrath of Khan*, being in the genre of the action-adventure popcorn chomper, detours from tragedy to triumph. Nonetheless, these respective meditations on aging illuminate and inform each other in ways helpful to the student of either.

A bit more background on *King Lear* might be useful here. The play opens with the aged monarch having decided to retire, as it were, from active kingship, and divide up his land among his three daughters. Each of the three — Goneril, Regan and Cordelia — is asked to profess her affection for her father; tell me how much you love me and I'll tell you how much land you get. The first two daughters, who turn out to be scheming, insincere opportunists, really lay it on dear old dad. He, being a vain and foolish old man, is subject to the vicissitudes of flattery and so he carves out for each of them a healthy swath of his kingdom. But the third daughter, Cordelia, is not interested in fleecing her father. A dutiful daughter, respectful and proper, she tells her father that she loves him according to her bounds to him, "no more, no less." This displeases the aged patriarch. Say more, he implores her. Tell me what a great guy I am. She says again that she loves him as any daughter should love a father, but she also adds that she can't lie and say he's the greatest love of her life because, as a single woman on the market, she knows that she will love some other man more. She chastises her sisters for their embellishments. How could they be in love with their husbands if they only have eyes for you, dad, she questions. She does love and honor her father — more obvious upon every rereading — but won't sink to platitudinous pronouncements just to get his wealth. Cordelia, a principled woman of conscience, finds herself in one of literature's stickiest "no-win" situations. (Interestingly, *Star Trek II: The Wrath of Khan* also begins with a reenactment of a "no-win" situation, the officer-testing scenario called "Kobayashi Maru."[3]) Lear rebukes Cordelia and then petulantly announces she's out of his will.

Lear will live to regret his forsaking of Cordelia, and his rewarding of the mendacious Goneril and Regan. By the end of the play, when he has been kicked off his own land and forced to wander the heath, attended only by fools and beggars, he will have learned a hard lesson about himself, about how vain and deluded he was, and he will even regain something of a youthful defiance in his nascent wisdom.[4]

Throughout the long business of the play, the king discovers the vanity of human desires and the unreliability of the human vessel. The play is filled with wonderfully bleak observations about the difficulty of maintaining one's dignity in a world so inhospitable for our weak, unsteady frames: "What is man," the dispossessed King asks famously in Act III, "but a poor, bare, forked animal?"[5] Images of the loss of potency attend every one of the King's scenes. Shakespeare makes sure we get it: growing old ain't easy. We cheer for Lear's fortunes to change, though they don't. Yet, by the end of this unrelenting and sometimes-gory tragedy, Lear possesses a wisdom which — should he survive (he doesn't) — would serve him well.

Captain Courageous

When fans think of *Star Trek II: The Wrath of Khan*, most of them probably recall the scenery chewing of Ricardo Montalban's Khan Noonien Sing, or the seat-of-your-pants space battle at the climax, or perhaps the cringe-inducing earwig scene (analogous, one could argue, to the similarly hard to take "blinding" scene of Gloucester in *King Lear*). But this film's principal concern isn't dispatching with the bad guy — though he is dispatched, with great, teeth-gritting glee. The second *Star Trek* film is about Kirk's journey through time, not through space.

As the movie begins, this is hardly the Kirk we've come to know. He's somber, a bit withdrawn, almost tentative (which for Kirk is a fate worse than death). His mood is explained by the circumstances: it's his birthday, though as alluded to above, McCoy notes that it seems more like a funeral. Kirk is sullen, reflective, and in need of glasses to read Spock's gift, Charles Dickens' *A Tale of Two Cities* (the glasses are one of the few outward signs of Kirk's loss of potency). And he is no longer in the business of racing star ships around the galaxy — the *Enterprise* is now in the hands of Captain Spock. Kirk is a desk jockey, marking time, feeling useless. He is evincing the philosophy of those great sages, the Rolling Stones: it *is* a drag getting old.

The movie explores this theme in the depth it deserves without lots of somber digressions or overt signs of the aging process. What we really watch for the next two hours is a test of just how aged Kirk has become — mentally, and physically. His battle against Khan is like Lear's battle against his rebellious daughters. It's aimed at showing what our protagonist is made of, and whether the mistakes of his past will overwhelm his ability to act in the future. Kirk is older, to be sure, but also wiser, and in this battle with Khan, the Captain relies as much upon his accumulated wisdom as his vigor. The film asks the implicit question: what is it to live? Kirk, after a period of avoidance and despair, faces the question squarely, and in dealing with it, dispenses with it. He says "yes" to life, to action, to accepting his fate, to aging — even if it means, ultimately, that he will lose his friend Spock. Kirk, unlike Lear, lives to fight another day. And in the willingness to fight, in the desire to engage the world, he rediscovers his lost self. For all that has happened to him during the movie, he expresses a remarkable epiphany at the very end of the movie, and expresses it in one of the most famous lines the good captain has ever spoken: "I feel young."[6]

There are other connections between *King Lear* and *Star Trek II: The Wrath of Khan*, but the most significant are those which deal with the preoccupations of aging, such as family, friendship, legacy and self-knowledge. Both of these works deal with men in positions of authority who walk away from being "in charge," though they come to regret their decision; both find themselves aware, for the first time, of the limitations of their bodily strength; both discover something about their children they never knew (or, to be more accurate in Kirk's case, a child he had never met); both learn the true meaning of friendship, with Gloucester willing to sacrifice himself for Lear, as Spock sacrifices himself for Kirk and the *Enterprise*; and both experience a psychological transformation that helps them see the vanity and foolishness of their positions (with Lear realizing what a sham royal authority really is, as Kirk concludes, similarly, the pointlessness of marking time as a bureaucratic desk jockey with an important sounding title).

If Kirk comes to conclude that growing old doesn't have to mean growing irrelevant, it's a lesson that's been hard earned, for as fans of the original series remember, Kirk's first brush with old age left him far less reason for optimism.

KILLING TIME

Fans of the original series were able to peer into the future and view a very old Captain Kirk way back in 1968, in the episode "The Deadly Years." The view of old age was not complimentary, as even the title of the episode communicates a grim truth: time is killing us. The story is this: the crew beams down to a scientific outpost to check up on the inhabitants and administer a routine physical exam. They discover the 20-something science crew has morphed into elderly men and women, aged shells of their former selves. As Kirk and his cohorts try to puzzle out what's happened, they find that they have also become "infected" with rapidly encroaching old age.

The dramatic tension of the episode revolves around Kirk's refusal to step down as Captain, even as his dementia and his physical weakness manifest themselves in his dealings with an increasingly alarmed crew. Kirk is put on "trial" by one of his science officers who has not been affected by the mysterious aging anomaly to determine his fitness to continue captaining the *Enterprise*.

Just as Lear's travails can be seen in some ways as inevitable — we all grow old, we must all bequeath some part of our worldly lot to those left behind — Kirk's "trial" can be seen as emblematic of the trial we must all endure. The prosecution amasses a litany of complaints against Kirk that reads like a bill of particulars in the inescapable course of living: Kirk is forgetful, weakened, his reflexes dimmed, his focus distracted, more weary than wary, increasingly stubborn and more than a little resentful that people are questioning his fitness for command. Even though the episode ends with McCoy devising an antidote and Kirk returning to "normal," the future has been glimpsed, and it's pretty grim.

The Kirk we get in most of the *Star Trek* movies may be nearly as old as the one in "The Deadly Years," but he's nowhere near as fragile or useless. He's different in his outlook and his ability, largely because he's drawn from another literary strain. Instead of the age-brings-decline motif of *King Lear* et al., the "mature" Kirk is derived from the "old soldiers never die" theme in literature. This school of thinking finds its most eloquent articulation in a poem which harkens back to Homer's hero, Odysseus, after he's entered the twilight of his life, and it feeds directly into both *Star Trek VI*, which is the last movie the original cast made, and *Star Trek VII*, in which Kirk fights his last battle.

"To Strive, to Seek, to Find..."

Victorian-era poet Alfred Lord Tennyson may have lived a hundred years before *Star Trek* came into existence, but his poem "Ulysses" (Latin for "Odysseus") so captures the spirit of the "second phase" of the original *Star Trek* gang that he could be given story credit for some of the *Star Trek* films. The 70-line "Ulysses" is one of the most rousing defenses ever offered for the impulse to stay in the game, to forge ahead even though tide — and time — is against you. The sentiment, and even the phrasing (archaic diction aside), of many passages of the poem sound remarkably like the things Kirk might say to his crew: "Come, my friends, 'tis not too late to seek a newer world"; "Some work of noble note, may yet be done/Not unbecoming men that strove with Gods"; "My purpose holds/To sail beyond the sunset, and the baths/of all the western stars, until I die...."[7] The poem is a recreation of how Tennyson imagined the great hero of the Trojan War, Odysseus, at the end of his life, forswearing the leisure of living on one's laurels and asking his former shipmates to join him as he seeks new adventure. The ending of the poem is one of the most Trekkish passages of poetry ever written:

> That which we are, we are;
> One equal temper of heroic hearts,
> Made weak by time and fate, but strong in will
> To strive, to seek, to find, and not to yield.[8]

Those words haunt a scene in *Star Trek VI*, in which Kirk confides to Spock that just maybe they have outlived their usefulness. For a moment, Kirk seems to be seriously considering whether he still belongs out there, cruising through the hinterlands of space as he once did in his youth. Fortunately, he concludes otherwise — in time, as it happens, to foil a universal conspiracy and ensure galactic peace.

OK, so the movie had to have a happy ending. But beyond that scene, Tennyson's words seem to hover over many of the latter-day incarnations of the original series, with an aged crew choosing to look forward rather than behind. The change in thinking that announces this philosophical shift — from fear of old age to an embrace of time's gifts — takes shape in *Star Trek II* when Spock dies, and the crew is forced to confront, for the first time, their own mortality. It's a shock that could have unmade them, but they soldier on, keeping his memory alive in their renewed determination to continue exploring. In doing so, they resurrect themselves from their existential funk about aging (and, as fans know, they also resurrect Spock). Kirk and his crew continue to deal with issues of aging in a "Ulysses"-like manner right through *Star Trek VII*, when Kirk accepts Captain Picard's plea that he leave the nexus of perpetual pleasure to fight the evil Dr. Soran. Kirk, emulating "Ulysses," turns his back on a life of leisure and plunges into the future, phaser in hand.

Trek's multifaceted exploration of the perils of growing old exposes the viewer to many possible approaches to the final act in the human comedy. At the end, however, *Star Trek* offers an optimistic view of human life, even in its twilight. Existence is meaningful, right up to the end — if we have the courage to continue to strive, to seek, to find, and not to yield.

TWENTY-TWO

The Final Journey

Star Trek is a great TV show, but can it save your soul?

All right, that question is a bit grandiose. As a piece of popular entertainment, its primary aim is not to achieve metaphysical significance. Sure, many of the episodes and films deal with the world of metaphysics: religious experience, heightened consciousness, the afterlife. But does merely mentioning those things, incorporating them as parts of a 50-minute teleplay, really count as a metaphysical exercise? Can *any* soul be saved by just watching TV?

One doesn't have to be a theologian to realize the answer is no. People turn to lots of institutions for spiritual guidance, but few seek genuine transcendence through the medium of television. But while many television shows have mirrored spiritual exercises in the secular world — they might feature a priest as a main character in a drama, for example, or show some soldier praying in a foxhole — in the world of *Star Trek* there really is an attempt to translate some metaphysical ideas which have been bequeathed to the modern mind from antiquity and portray them in a way which preserves their integrity and allows for genuine reflection.

A question that has likely occupied human thought more than any other is "What happens after death?" The classic works that have sought to address this question tend to be in the "heavyweight" category — a not-unexpected result given the weightiness of their subject. But to *Star Trek*'s credit, the show has not flinched from appropriating the complex ideas which animate these works, and in doing so, the show offers its own amalgam of answers about the afterlife — answers which usually mirror the insights of the deepest and most daunting works in Western Civilization. The two most important of those works — the New Testament, and Dante's *The Divine Comedy* — provide answers about what happens to the human soul on the final leg of one's journey through time. Much of what these works have to say might be surprisingly familiar to fans *of Star Trek*'s continuing journey.

Although *Star Trek* creator Gene Roddenberry was a secular humanist who eschewed traditional religious dogma, he wasn't afraid to embrace the idea of an afterlife. In the *Trek* universe, the metaphysical longings of many races of creatures is respected and explored. And frequently their visions of an afterlife seem to draw from the same source that has fed Western Civilization's notions.[1] The prospect of a state of existence, modeled something on the Christianized conception of "heaven," is common in *Trek*, so it's worth taking a look at how that conception has developed over the last two millennia.

KINGDOMS IN THE SKY

The idea of "heaven" in the human imagination is not limited to Western Civilization or the modern mind. From the Native American's idea of a "happy hunting ground in the sky"[2] to the Buddhist notion of nirvana,[3] a state of blissful existence for the human soul after death seems almost hardwired into human DNA. Countless cultures across the globe have partaken of this ideal, so it's something everyone, everywhere, seems able to understand, if not necessarily believe.

So pervasive is this assumption of an afterlife that it's easy to forget just how wild, surreal and bizarre-sounding is the typical description of heaven (and its necessary opposite, hell). The picture of a light-filled, placid and perpetually joyous "heaven" is axiomatic in Western Civilization, and it owes its popularity to the best-selling and perhaps most widely read book since the advent of the printing press, the Bible. The second half of the Bible, the New Testament, deals with the life, death, and resurrection of Jesus Christ. It is from these pages that the "modern" idea of heaven has been delivered, and though many of the various "books" of the New Testament speak in some way (often abstract) of the afterlife, I'll look at three parts of the New Testament which paint a pretty vivid picture of heaven. Together, they provide a comprehensive overview of what awaits mankind for all eternity.

The first is a letter that St. Paul wrote to a small but devout group of recent converts called the Thessalonians. (It's considered the first of the Bible's many "epistles"— letters written in an effort to expand Jesus' fan base.) He was trying to give them some direction regarding how to live as Christians. Paul went right for the good stuff: eternal life in the warm glow of heaven, if y'all can just hang in there. The wording of the King James Version is a touch more impressive:

> For the Lord himself shall descend from heaven with a shout, with the voice of the archangel, and with the trump of god: and the dead in Christ shall rise first; Then we which are alive and remain shall be caught up together with them in the clouds, to meet the lord in the air: and so shall we ever be with the Lord.[4]

In that very short paragraph to a newly formed Christian sect, Paul hit most of those heavenly notes which have continued to reverberate through the ages: true believers shall rise from the dead, head to the clouds, and live blissfully in a kingdom in the sky. Notwithstanding the mountainous biblical commentary that has allegorically interpreted such descriptive phrases, the idea is simple and, perhaps for that reason, has remained prevalent: a heaven in the clouds, a life with God "up there."

The Thessalonians had to take Paul's word for it, but readers of the New Testament get to hear it from a source closer to home, as it were. In the gospel according to Matthew (one of the four big guns of the New Testament, whose work purportedly captures the words of Jesus himself), the Messiah paints a similar picture of life in the kingdom of heaven — or hell, for those who don't rate a ticket for the trip north:

> The Son of man shall send forth his angels, and they shall gather out of his kingdom all things that offend, and them which do iniquity; And shall cast them into a furnace of fire: there shall be wailing and gnashing of teeth. Then shall the righteous shine forth as the sun in the kingdom of their Father.[5]

For readers who respond to that sort of imagery, the last book of the New Testament offers a dazzling payoff: a vivid, graphic, surreal portrait of the final furious days of humanity. Known both as the book of "Revelation" and the "Apocalypse," this richly wrought book is high on symbolism and low on clarity. No two biblical scholars agree on what it all means, but for two thousand years people have been mesmerized by the wildness of the narrative. Amid all the noise, smoke, swirls and separation of the children of light from the children of darkness (you know what a commotion *that* can create), a picture of heaven emerges that is consistent with the more sedate passages of the New Testament:

> After this I looked, and, behold, a door was opened in heaven: and the first voice which I heard was as it were of a trumpet talking with me; which said, Come up hither, and I will shew thee things which must be hereafter. And immediately I was in the spirit; and, behold, a throne was set in heaven, and one sat on the throne. And he that sat was to look upon like a jasper and a sardine stone: and there was a rainbow round about the throne, in sight like unto an emerald. And round about the throne were four and twenty seats: and upon the seats I saw four and twenty elders sitting, clothed in white raiment; and they had on their heads crowns of gold. And out of the throne proceeded lightnings and thunderings and voices.[6]

Again, heaven is portrayed as a place of light which rewards the righteous, though here it is further associated with a courtly setting, with a sort of royal cabal ruling the celestial kingdom. It's perhaps pointless to note that many people, believers and nonbelievers, see such New Testament descriptions of heaven as merely metaphorical, and that they believe no such physical place actually exists. The picture has been etched, the image enshrined. And it has been adapted in works of secular literature by countless writers, including one of the most important creative and forceful minds in the annals of Western Civilization: Dante Alighieri, who in addition to demonstrating the unsuspected linguistic richness of the Italian tongue, gave the world the first guided tour of hell, purgatory and the promised land.

TO FORGIVE, DIVINE

Dante's massive epic, the 100-canto *Divine Comedy*, is broken into three parts, each offering a medieval Baedeker of some aspect of humanity's potential end: hell, purgatory or heaven. Like the book of *Revelation*, Dante's masterpiece is a rather chewy affair, filled with complex allegories and a theology drawn from Thomas Aquinas — himself no simpleton. In addition, Dante worked in lots of allusions to contemporary political figures, choosing to even some political scores throughout his work (he spent the last two decades of his life as a political exile in his own country). The entire poem is pretty tough going — though even first-time readers are likely to respond to the sheer beauty of Dante's elegant phrasing and visual imagination (which comes across in even the most workman-like translation).[7]

The poem consists of a walkthrough of hell, then advances upward toward the celestial kingdom of God by way of purgatory. Far and away the most popular of the three sections has always been the "Inferno," filled with clever tortures and uncomfortable resting places in perpetuity for swindlers, liars and heretics. But for the purposes of *Star Trek*, it is Dante's development of the idea of purgatory that is the most useful.

Souls stuck in Dante's purgatory — a kind of free-floating mountain in the air — experience both the torment of their human sins and the delight at the prospect of entering God's sanctum. His purgatory is a strange amalgam of painful and pleasant, a holding pattern for souls in transition. As one critic has put it: "[T]he predominant image is one of homesickness... a yearning to return to man's real home...."[8] Many critics have likened Dante's purgatory to a way station for the soul (and *only* the soul; drawing on Aquinas, Dante accepted the idea that souls in purgatory have no corporeal aspect).

This idea of "not-quite-in-heaven-but-not-back-on-earth" has found its way into works from Shakespeare's *Hamlet* (remember Hamlet Sr., the murdered king who is "forced to walk the earth" as a ghost?) to Charles Dickens' *A Christmas Carol*. And of course, into *Star Trek*. *The Next Generation* episode "The Next Phase" demonstrates nicely how *Trek* translated the notion of Dante's purgatory and created its own model for a "holding pattern" after death that is both painful and pleasurable.

JUST A PHASE

At one point in Dante's purgatory, the narrator's friend and guide, the spirit of the poet Virgil, states: "If now I cast no shadow on the ground you should not be surprised. Think of the spheres: not one of them obstructs the others' light."[9] That idea seems to have been much in the mind of the writers of the episode "The Next Phase."[10]

"It's like I'm here, but I'm not here." So says Geordi LaForge, the chief engineer on board the *Enterprise*, who after a transporter malfunction finds himself, along with his crewmate Ensign Ro Laren, seemingly alive but invisible to everyone around him. Geordi and Ro discover, much to their horror, that they are "dead." While still able to see each other, and everyone around them, they move about without any physical substance, passing through doors, or other people, trying to make contact but unable to arrest any attention whatsoever. The episode plays on both the fear and the sublimity of such an experience, watching as their former colleagues conduct a memorial service for them, feeling loved yet feeling completely lost, metaphysically detached.

"What are you saying? We're some sort of spirits?" Geordi asks.

"Spirits, souls... My people used to call them borhyas," Ro says.[11]

Ensign Ro is a Bajoran, a race of people who have a rich and deeply mystical faith-based society. Fortunately for Geordi and Ro, it turns out they aren't technically dead — just "cloaked" so no one can see them. They discover a way to concentrate the small amount of radiation their cloaking emits to get Commander Data's attention — just in time to rematerialize at their own memorial service. Yet the episode doesn't hinge on the mystery of their death or the technology behind their disappearance so much as the poignancy of their suspended status as souls without a place to go. Wandering about in the purgatory of space, Geordi and Ro ache to either go back, or to pass on to the next phase. In this desire, they are like Dante's purgatory dweller who is told, "You are like a woman very sick, who finds no rest on her soft, sumptuous bed, but turns and tosses to escape her pain."[12]

"The Next Phase" captures some of the Dante-esque feel for the state of purgatory, but for the full-blown heaven and hell experience, complete with gods, devils, swirling lights and celestial tumult, one needs to consult the series *Deep Space Nine*, which over the course of seven seasons approximated the afterlife experience with all of the New Testament trimmings — and a few extras thrown in just for kicks.

NETWORK PROPHETS

Some television pilot episodes do little more than set the stage for future development, but the two-hour *Deep Space Nine* pilot, "The

Emissary," covered an immense amount of ground, creating back story for its characters, establishing multiple plot threads that would take years to unwind, and adding a heavy dose of spirituality to the generally secular *Trek* franchise. The creators of *Deep Space Nine* lay it all out in "The Emissary": religious prophecy, angel-like creatures who watch over humanity, a high priestess with immense political and spiritual power, holy books, sacred artifacts, miracles, visitations, time travel, alternate states of existence, skeptics and true believers who are willing to die — or go to war — for their religious ideals.

The New Testament spoke of a kingdom in the sky, and that's exactly what *Deep Space Nine* offered viewers in the form of a "stable wormhole." While scientists have theorized that actual wormholes — cosmic tunnels which serve as a sort of shortcut between vast distances — might actually exist, the wormhole from *Deep Space Nine* is an artificially generated space tunnel which has acquired great religious significance. Bajorans call the wormhole the "celestial temple," and believe it to be home to the Prophets, the god-like overseers of the Bajoran people who anoint the "Emissary" (a kind of Bajoran pope) and who have gifted their people with the mystical Orbs, which generate religious visions and help keep the population on the right spiritual track.

Where the New Testament warns of torments for those who do evil (in the eternal lake of fire in hell), and the temptations of Satan himself, *Deep Space Nine* answers with the Pah-Wraiths, evil energy-based life forms who are forced to live in the fire caves because they were banished by the Prophets from the celestial temple for their malevolent ways. Like their biblical demonic counterparts, the Pah-Wraiths can occasionally "possess" a soul in an attempt to do evil. (For instance, in the episode "The Assignment," the Pah-Wraiths took over Keiko O'Brien, the wife of Station Chief Miles O'Brien, but they were successfully exorcised.)

Perhaps the most interesting connection between the New Testament and *Deep Space Nine* can be found in the central figures of each story. In certain retellings of the gospels, Jesus expresses a sense of reluctance, of "cold-feet" if you will, about his coming crucifixion. So too *Deep Space Nine* commander Benjamin Sisko, who is told in the pilot episode that he is the "Emissary" of the Bajoran people. Sisko, a career Starfleet officer, is naturally skeptical — and he holds on to that skepticism for the seven-year run of the series (though the fact of his divine anointment as "Emissary" turns out to be true, we learn at the end of the series).

BIBLICAL MANDATES

It's just a coincidence that the writers' guides for each of the *Star Trek* series were referred to by the production staff as "the Bible." But like that "good book," the *Trek* writers' bibles offered a set of generally inviolable guidelines that sought to maintain the integrity of a particular worldview. It's simplistic to say merely that "good triumphs" in the world of *Star Trek* and that evil gets punished. Yet it's equally disingenuous to suggest that *Trek* doesn't adhere to a strong moral code and a belief that people, from all races and planetary systems, ultimately get what they deserve.

Though suspicious of organized religions and their claims of exclusivity, *Star Trek* draws on conceptions of life and death that are, perhaps, archetypal in the human imagination. It's a broad-based theology that's rooted perhaps as much in a pre–Christian past as it is in the inventions of theologians. It is perhaps best exemplified by something that a leader of a Native American–like tribe of settlers once explained to Wesley Crusher after learning that Starfleet was going to relocate his entire race:

> Everything is sacred to us. The buildings, the food, the sky, the dirt beneath your feet. And you. Whether you believe in your spirit or not, we believe in it. You are a sacred person here, Wesley.[13]

Gene Roddenberry didn't set out to create a heaven on earth — just an entertaining, thoughtful show. Along the way, however, his creation became the vehicle for the discussion of some important and enlightening points of theology. But to return to the original question posed at the beginning of this chapter, has *Star Trek* ever saved anyone's soul?

Heaven only knows.

TWENTY-THREE

Seize the Day

When a literary theme becomes a bumper sticker, whatever powers it once had to entice or charm would seem to be long gone. Yet *Carpe Diem*—"Seize the Day"—remains both a shamefully overused cliché and a potent philosophical statement which continues to inspire great art. Perhaps it's because the simple-seeming entreaty to live each day fully is more than a literary theme; it's a *human* theme, connected in some way to our survival instinct, or our innate awareness of the shortness of our mortal journey. For whatever reason, the concept of "carpe diem" roils the imagination, and its echoes sound in the farthest reaches of Federation space.

Both Western and Eastern philosophers have preached the value of living in the moment, urging one to find hints of the eternal in the ephemeral. Some of the best—and a good deal of the worst—of literary culture revolve around variations on that theme. Poets especially seem drawn to the idea of seizing the day, perhaps because the form of a poem requires the kind of compression of thought that mirrors the "carpe diem" philosophy: discard the extraneous, focus on the immediate. A well-wrought single line (consider, as just one example, William Blake's abruptly instructive line, "Hold Infinity in the palm of your hand/And Eternity in an hour")[1] can drive home the point better than a full-blown novel. The poetic idiom, then, is where one should look to find this theme most memorably crystallized. Not surprisingly, the greatest poets in English have found this theme worthy of their grandest and most moving poetic statements. *Star Trek*'s creators seem to have been similarly inspired, with a handful of examples representing the theme, and two—*The Next Generation*'s "The Inner Light" and the original series two-parter, "The Menagerie"—offering powerful, even sublime uses of the "carpe diem" theme. To fully appreciate the ways in which *Trek* has traversed this theme, it's necessary to revisit some early poetic masterworks which urge readers to live fully, *now* (even if the poets often equate "living fully in the moment" with sexual gratification, the principle remains the same, more or less). Robert Herrick's "To the Virgins, to Make Much of Time" is as fine an example of "carpe diem" thinking in print as can be found in the annals of imaginative literature—though his contemporary, Andrew Marvell, has achieved the greater measure of fame for his carpe diem–esque "To His Coy Mistress." Both poets deserve a wider contemporary readership, as does the master who first coined the phrase *carpe diem*.

Roman Through the Canon

Though his full name, Quintus Horatius Flaccus, might be known to Latin scholars only, many readers have some familiarity with the life or work of the Roman writer generally called "Horace." His works, dating from about 45 BCE, comprise the usual Roman retinue of literary genres: orations, satires, lyric poetry, epistles and hundreds of "maxims" (short, witty sayings, usually drawn from longer works). In a series of books of poems he called "Odes"—a form borrowed from the Greeks, and hence worthy of imitating—Horace dispenses life wisdom, touching on everything from wine to Roman rulers. The Odes represent a kind of "to-do" list for the well-placed Roman of his time. It would be impossible to establish which of Horace's hundreds of maxims have achieved the greatest currency in contemporary thought, but the idea of "seizing the day" would certainly have to make the cut for any short list of Horace's greatest hits. The actual phrase, "carpe diem, quam minimum credula postero," appears in Book 1 of the *Odes*, Number 11, and is generally translated this way: "Seize the day, and put as little trust as you can in the morrow."[2] From there, it tumbled through the centuries of recycled Western thought, finding new expression in the works of the late Renaissance poets—who were, of course, in love with all things antique, Roman and Greek.

One of those poets, Robert Herrick, rephrased Horace's exhortation so memorably that one would be hard pressed to find a greeting card store which didn't feature dozens of examples of the following on wall plaques and wedding announcements:

> Gather ye Rose-buds while ye may,
> Old Time is still a flying:
> And this same flower that smiles to day,
> To morrow will be dying.
>
> The glorious Lamp of Heaven, the Sun,
> The higher he's a getting;
> The sooner will his Race be run,
> And neerer he's to Setting.
>
> That age is best, which is the first,
> When Youth and Blood are warmer;
> But being spent, the worse, and worst
> Times, still succeed the former.
>
> Then be not coy, but use your time;
> And while ye may, goe marry:
> For having lost but once your prime,
> You may for ever tarry.[3]

The first line of that poem has come to the rescue of many a nuptial toastmaster. And why not? It translates Horace's hard-edged axiom into a more soft-hued suggestion for how to get the most out of life: live... live *now*. Herrick, a late Renaissance poet writing at a time when English scribes were busy cannibalizing Greek and Roman sages, is not widely read today, except by scholars. His "Gather ye Rosebuds" contribution to poetry makes him kind of a one-hit wonder with contemporary readers. Notably, his advice in the poem is in the service of love. To live fully means, apparently, to live lovingly. That idea was taken even further by Herrick's near-contemporary, Andrew Marvell, who argued in his famous poem "To His Coy Mistress" that to live fully means to live lustily.

Driving Home the Point

Marvell's "Coy Mistress" is widely anthologized in literature textbooks, coming as close to sexual frankness as most textbook editors are comfortable with. Once his lofty-sounding metaphors are decoded, the poem becomes literature's slyest come-on. It's nothing more than a forceful argument for immediate sexual gratification, nothing less than a lyrically-arresting reminder of humanity's ephemeral nature. It's perhaps the most eloquent extended pickup line in literary history. The speaker in the poem is trying to persuade his love that she should put aside her modesty and join him in sexual congress. Yes, your beauty is worthy of extended praise, he assures her, but the clock is ticking. Let's strike while the iron is hot, so to speak. That's Marvell's game. But he dresses up his come-on in such mellifluous and decorous language that one can mistake the libidinous energy that drives the poem for mere linguistic virtuosity. The whole thing is marvelous. Here's a taste:

> Had we but world enough, and time,
> This coyness, Lady were no crime.
> We would sit down, and think which way
> To walk, and pass our long love's day....
>
> My vegetable love should grow
> Vaster than empires and more slow;
> An hundred years should go to praise
> Thine eyes, and on thy forehead gaze;
> Two hundred to adore each breast,
> But thirty thousand to the rest;
> An age at least to every part,
> And the last age should show your heart.
> For, Lady, you deserve this state,
> Nor would I love at lower rate.
> But at my back I always hear
> Time's winged chariot hurrying near;
> And yonder all before us lie
> Deserts of vast eternity....
>
> Now therefore, while the youthful hue
> Sits on thy skin like morning dew,
> And while thy willing soul transpires
> At every pore with instant fires,
> Now let us sport us while we may....

> Let us roll all our strength and all
> Our sweetness up into one ball,
> And tear our pleasures with rough strife
> Through the iron gates of life;[4]

Well, there you have your basic, highly literate Renaissance-era objection-deflecting sentimental lyric. But for all its carnal heat, it hews closely to the more general "carpe diem" theme. When one defers life's pleasures, one defers life. And life — Horace, Herrick and Marvell remind us — must not be deferred.

SEEING THE LIGHT

If one were clever enough, he or she could find the "carpe diem" message inherent in the very medium of television itself — and in the one-hour drama specifically. After all, to fully enjoy the experience of watching a satisfying weekly television series, one must commit the time to focus on the show in question, putting all other distractions aside (though whether or not television *itself* is a distraction is another matter altogether). One must invest some emotion in the characters and plot, and become involved enough in the drama to hang around through several commercial breaks each episode to see the action through to the end. To "seize the day" means to live fully in the moment, and good drama — whether in the theater or on television — can often engage one's emotions fully.

Without doubt, *Star Trek* has done that, countless scores of times. Yet it's also a show that has vigorously endorsed the message about the need to live in the moment. The most powerful example of *Trek*'s use of the "carpe diem" philosophy can be found in *The Next Generation* episode "The Inner Light" — arguably the best single hour of *Trek* ever produced. For an episode that tries to promote the idea of living fully in the moment, it practices what it preaches, offering a riveting hour of compelling drama and a bold restatement of Horace's call to live.

The episode begins with the *Enterprise* out trolling the hinterlands of space, when it comes across an innocuous-looking probe. As the ship approaches to get a closer look, the probe emits some kind of radiation stream which appears to lock onto Captain Jean Luc Picard, knocking him into an almost catatonic neurological state. While the crew struggles to revive him — and to analyze the probe's emission — Picard finds himself awakening on an alien world, where he seems to have a wife, friends and a whole life waiting for him. At first reluctant to believe what he deduces is some sort of hallucination, he eventually comes to accept that this place — the planet Kataan — and these people (his wife, Eline, and his friend, Batai) are real, and that his memory of his time on the *Enterprise* is an illusory dream.

The episode gives us the unfolding stages of Picard's life, as he has children, ages, becomes involved in his community's problems and watches his grandchildren be born and grow. Against the backdrop of this other existence is the growing threat of drought and widespread devastation for the planet Kataan, whose sun is preparing to "go supernova," thus dooming the residents of the planet. Picard — an ironworker called "Kaamin" in this other reality — is one of the first on his planet to understand what's happening, and the knowledge of the inevitable demise of his world devastates him. The pathos is wrenching in those scenes where Picard speaks to his daughter about her future, or counsels his son about career choices. He knows their world will not exist much longer. This is not the Picard that viewers had watched for five years, ready to make the kind of sacrifices expected of a military officer. This is a father who can see the end for his children but can't stop it from coming.

What can he do? What can the residents of this doomed world do?

They must seize their day.

In one of the most moving exchanges ever in *Star Trek*, Picard speaks to his daughter, invoking the carpe diem principle in language so simple and wise as to improve upon Horace, Herrick and Marvell in one fell linguistic swoop. His daughter has come to him, unsure of whether or not she's ready to get married (a plot device ripped right from the poetry of Herrick and Marvell). So Kaamin/Picard, the loving father, offers this brief entreaty:

Live now. Make *now* the most important moment of your life, *always*.[5]

But we're not done yet, for the carpe diem idea gets another mind-bending twist in this episode. Years pass on the planet Kataan, and one day, an elderly Kaamin is invited to join his family members and the rest of the community to watch the launch of a rocket carrying a space probe. When Kaamin questions the usefulness of such a mission, wondering who might ever see this probe, he is told by his daughter that he already *has* seen it — that this is the probe that will find the *Enterprise*. The probe contains information about the society which is now several thousands years extinct — information which was sent into space so that one day a future explorer might find it and know of a world which once was and now is no more. The Kataanians seized *their day*, choosing to preserve the record of their civilization and thus attain some measure of timelessness, of immortality in the face of certain alienation.

Once this scene is played out, and the elderly Kaamin realizes he's the one who has received the signal, the probe's beam ends, and Jean Luc Picard reawakes on the bridge of the *Enterprise*— unable to believe that he'd only been unconscious for 20 minutes while he'd experienced a whole lifetime while in the probe's control.

Perchance to Dream

Star Trek has always had an interest in exploring reality, examining how we experience different states of consciousness. Picard's life, it is presumed, will now be enriched by having had a chance to do all those things he would otherwise never have done, such as getting married and having children. "The Inner Light" seems to suggest that fully experiencing a particular *moment* in time — holding your new baby, exchanging marriage vows, watching your children achieve success — is more important than merely accumulating a string of moments which merely fill time. It's about *seizing* the day, not just killing time, *Trek* often reminds us. One of the earliest reminders — and one of the cagiest — comes from the original series episode "The Menagerie."

Upon first consideration, this episode might not seem to be a candidate for a "Carpe Diem" chapter, but that's exactly what the episode is about. Mr. Spock has arranged to transport his former — and now critically injured — captain, Christopher Pike, to a planet whose inhabitants can induce states of virtual happiness (even though contact with the planet is forbidden by Starfleet). Spock is trying to get Pike to a place where he will have the illusion of living a full and happy life, even though, in reality, he will remain a helpless invalid, bound to a wheelchair and imprisoned by a badly damaged body.

Twenty-Three. Seize the Day

The tension in this episode — which was put together with footage from the original, unused pilot episode called "The Cage" — derives from Spock risking a court-martial for his actions, which involve taking control of the *Enterprise* and refusing to explain his actions. Spock's unshakeable commitment here is to the "carpe diem" ideal — to return his beloved former captain to a day when all *was* right with his world, to replay an idyllic moment over and over, thwarting the ravages of time and disease. It's like turning the clock back to return to a day you wish you *had* seized. And in this inversion of Horace, *Star Trek* intriguingly suggests that it may, indeed, not be too late to gather those rosebuds that would have otherwise withered long ago.

For a franchise whose very existence was marked by a series of near-death experiences (the original pilot refused, cancellation threatened, spin-off series and movies shelved indefinitely), one can understand how the concept of seizing the day became such a defining theme. "Carpe diem," said Horace, two thousand years before space travel became possible; *Star Trek*'s best journeys have been marked by that ancient ideal ever since.

TWENTY-FOUR

Socrates Goes to a *Star Trek* Convention

At first glance — or even after several sustained glances — the phenomenon known as the *Star Trek* convention can seem like a rather silly affair. A brief inventory of only the most obvious elements should make the case: mature adults dressed as Klingon warriors; college students who've died their skin gold, or blue, or green, wearing antennas or dressed as alien dancing girls; whole families attired in matching "Beam Me Up Scotty" T-shirts; middle-aged businessmen wearing phaser holsters and com badges; hordes of fans swarming around tables in a raucous "Dealer's Room" set up to sell replicas of Klingon weaponry, or poorly mimeographed scripts of the unproduced pilot for the legendary, ill-fated TV series *Star Trek: Phase II*, or Starship *Enterprise* tie-clips.

Silly, yes?

There is, however, a way to see all of this which adds an almost noble element, an intellectual underpinning — even a link to Hellenic antiquity. *Star Trek* conventions, it can be argued, are the modern equivalent of the kinds of forums for truth-seeking famously established by the Greek philosopher Socrates. The typical *Star Trek* fan gathering is modeled quite closely on the type of encounter first illustrated in the dialogues of Plato.[1] Sound farfetched? Maybe. But the premise deserves to be examined, explored, argued. In other words, let's look at the question of Socrates' impact on *Star Trek* conventions as Socrates himself would.

QUESTIONS, QUESTIONS

What little we know of the philosopher called "Socrates" (469–399 BCE) comes largely from the records of his best known and most influential student, Plato. In his famous "Dialogues," Plato relates many of Socrates' conversation-interrogations — a politely confrontational style of "Q&A" which aims to uncover flaws in logic and to get at the real heart of an issue. The *Dialogues* of Plato have been enormously influential in the development of Western philosophy. They are more than works of literature; they've become modes of assessing reality. Socrates' oft-quoted dictum "An unexamined life is not worth living" is the driving force behind all of Plato's *Dialogues*, with their incessant questing after precision and clarification. Socrates was one of those people who never took "no" for an answer. Or "yes." Or any other succinctly stated assertion. Keep digging away — that's the "Socratic Method."

The literary scholar Clifton Fadiman, in his highly informed and accessible "Lifetime Reading Plan," sized up the situation this way:

> Socrates questioned all things, and particularly the meanings men attached to abstract and important words, such as justice, love and courage. The questioning was real; the truth was finally approached only through the play of minds, that give-and-take we call "dialectic." This mode of thought is exemplified and perfected in the Dialogues. They are not mere exercises in mental agility (except occasionally) but works of art in which the resources of a poetic and dramatic imagination are called into play.[2]

As eclectic in his tastes as Fadiman was, it's a safe guess that he never attended a *Star Trek* convention. Yet his description of the *Dialogues*—what they do, what they are — is a pretty darned good description of a typical *Star Trek* convention. There's the "questioning" he mentions: This process of questioning is at the heart of every *Star Trek* convention, usually taking the form of informal question-and-answer (Q&A) sessions between a *Trek* "star" and the assembled crowd. There are also lots of questions asked during panel discussions about various aspects of sci-fi, or the history of *Star Trek*, or some larger theme which the show addressed.³ There are even trivia contests which features questions from fans to an "expert" panel drawn from convention attendees. And, of course, lots of questions get asked during the informal gatherings of fans in hotel lobbies, nearby cafes, and in convention-hosted "happy hours." This questioning is no different than the kind of questioning Socrates made famous. After all, most everyone attending a convention "knows" the material: the shows, the movies, the history, the behind-the-scenes anecdotes. So they gather to consider the "meaning" of all those shows and movies, to inquire more deeply about (to borrow Fadiman's phrase) "abstract and important words" like friendship (Kirk and Spock), valor (the many episodes and movies which featured personal sacrifice) and even mortality (too many relevant examples to mention, though *Star Trek III: The Search for Spock* is probably the best example). And the conventions themselves are, like Plato's *Dialogues*, "works of art in which the resources of a poetic and dramatic imagination" are called into play. Just think of all those specially produced "video tributes," dramatically hyped stage entrances for speakers like William Shatner and Leonard Nimoy, and even dramatic readings and impromptu singing performances by various cast members. Truly, the conventions are comprised of lots of "poetic and dramatic" moments.

To understand Socrates' style — and how, more than two millennia later, it continues to inform the behavior of *Trek* conventions' standing-room-only crowds (many outfitted with pointed ears or Borg eyepieces) — it's helpful to review the *Dialogues* themselves for their mix of pit-bull inquisition and graceful, extemporaneous philosophizing.

Perhaps the most famous of all of Plato's *Dialogues* is "The Apology," in which Socrates defends himself against charges of corrupting the youth of Athens with his freethinking ways. Here's a snippet, with Socrates slyly mocking his accusers' argument that he, himself, is the only "corrupting" influence in the entire world:

> SOCRATES: Come hither, Meletus, and let me ask a question of you. You think a great deal about the improvement of youth?
> MELETUS: Yes, I do.
> SOCRATES: Tell the judges, then, who is their improver; for you must know, as you have taken pains to discover their corrupter, and are citing and accusing me before them.... Speak up, friend, and tell us who their improver is.

MELETUS: The laws.
SOCRATES: But that, my good sir, is not my meaning. I want to know who the person is, who, in the first place, knows the laws.
MELETUS: The judges, Socrates, who are present in court.
SOCRATES: What, do you mean to say, Meletus, that they are able to instruct and improve youth?
MELETUS: Certainly they are.
SOCRATES: What, all of them, or some only and not others?
MELETUS: All of them.
SOCRATES: By the goddess Hera, that is good news! There are plenty of improvers, then. And what do you say of the audience — do they improve them?
MELETUS: Yes, they do.
SOCRATES: And the senators?
MELETUS: Yes, the senators improve them.
SOCRATES: But perhaps the members of the assembly corrupt them? Or do they too improve them.
MELETUS: They improve them.
SOCRATES: Then every Athenian improves and elevates them; all with the exception of myself; and I alone am their corrupter? Is that what you affirm?
MELETUS: That is what I stoutly affirm.
SOCRATES: I am very unfortunate if you are right.[4]

Socrates goes on to decimate, with several examples, the folly of Meletus' position, concluding: "Happy indeed would be the condition of youth if they had one corrupter only, and all the rest of the world were their improvers."[5]

The "Socratic method" in action results in a scouring of the subject down to the bone, the hard truth underneath the preconceptions. The *Dialogues* generally take place in a public forum so that all might discover the truth. Other interrogators take turns questioning the subject, and at the end of these sessions, everyone has learned something. Add a dealer's room filled with key rings and 8x10 glossies and you've got a *Star Trek* convention.

PRESENT AT THE CREATION

Though Plato's *Dialogues* purport to record what happened during these Socratic forums, no one really knows for sure. There are no official transcripts of these conversations — just Plato's spinning of events (not completely reliable, scholars say). Fortunately for scholars of *Star Trek*, there is an abundance of available documentation to trace the growth and development of the convention phenomenon. The story of *Trek*'s burgeoning fandom is every bit as fascinating as many of the episodes of the original series, and though it's been told many times, the best accounts remain those of the insiders. Readers interested in a single source of information about *Trek* conventions could find no better mix of history, anecdote and insight than William Shatner's own book-length explanation of the craziness that is the *Trek* convention, the wryly-hubristic *Get a Life!*

Significantly, Shatner's book arose from its author's extended use of the Socratic method to understand a phenomenon he had been a part of — yet had been apart from. As he explains in an introductory chapter, Shatner had been appearing at conventions for years but he never really thought about what it all meant. Then, when his character, Captain Kirk, was killed off in the film *Star Trek VII: Generations*, Shatner experienced an unexpected bout of depression. For the first time in his career, he says he began to really need the applause, affection and support from the audiences at *Star Trek* conventions, so he began appearing at every convention he could. His subsequent epiphanies owe their existence to his Socratic interrogations:

> Throughout this extended "Kirkapalooza" tour, I also began consciously squeezing the most out of my convention time, chatting one-on-one with dealers, organizers, and fans whenever I could, while simultaneously arm-twisting my embarrassed co-author [Chris Kreski] into wandering convention floors in search of hard-core fans who'd sit for an interview. At that point tucked away from the crowds in green rooms, kitchens, even glorified storage closets, I'd ask fans why *they* attended conventions, and for their take on why *Star Trek*'s fans feel the urge to occasionally gather and commune with one another. What was it about *Star Trek* that inspires such devotion?[6]

Shatner's book provides lots of answers to that question. He and co-author Kreski trace the history of conventions from the first, hastily organized convention in the mid–1970s, when a trio of women who had become fans of the show produced amateur-tinged events for what they expected might be a hundred fans (thousands came), to the slick and professionally-produced conventions which have become the norm.

Shatner's book is a delight for fans, filled with equal measures of the good captain's self-deprecation and self-aggrandizement. Yet even the book's structure is a monument to the Socratic method, organized around a series of interrelated chapters which explore, respectively, the five questions most frequently asked by fans. Shatner explores the questions in some depth, reflecting on what these questions signify and how his response to them has changed and deepened over the years as he has a chance to reflect on them. It's Shatner's version of a final exam on Socrates, take-home style.

THE FIRST QUESTION

For many long-time fans of *Star Trek*, the most important question they ever demanded an answer to was the one which was likely to determine the future of their existence, *as fans*: would the show be canceled? If fans had let the network simply decide the future of the franchise, there might not have been a second season of the original series, and most certainly would never have been a third season. From the very beginnings of *Star Trek*, long before the fan-based congealed into hordes of convention-attending devotees, the show's most committed viewers were going the Socratic route: questioning the supposed "wisdom" of authority figures — in this case, the network NBC. Endowed with a firm belief in the real "truth" about *Star Trek* — its committed fan base, its seriousness of purpose, its impact on society — individual viewers took a page from Plato's *Dialogues* and opened a dialogue of their own with the network. The results of this grass roots campaign to keep the show on the air have become legendary in the annals of television production.

Several books have retold the story of how *Star Trek* was brought back from the brink of perennial cancellation by the loyal (and vocal) opposition to cancellation. Probably the most reliable information about the famous second season original series eleventh-hour reprieve (1967–68) comes from the book *Inside Star Trek: The Real Story*, by Herbert Solow and Robert Justman, two television veterans who were closely involved in the making of the original show. They explain how Gene Rodenberry's idealism, mixed with the devotion of a growing, and vocal, fan base, convinced the network suits to spare the ax. "The ratings hadn't improved at all.... Prospects for another season looked bleak. But a new force had arrived. Trekkies! (At least, that's what they were called then. Today, they're 'Trekkers.')"⁷

David Gerrold, the writer of one of the original series most popular episodes, "The Trouble with Tribbles," takes a wider view of the "Save *Trek*" campaign in his book *The World of Star Trek*:

> *Star Trek* was renewed for at least the first half of its third season, but not without a fight. As the rumor of impending cancellation spread among the fans of the show, a groundswell of protest began to rise. During the months of January and February that ground swell assumed the proportions of a tidal wave. A highly articulate and passionately loyal fan base participated in what is probably the most massive anti-network programming campaign in television history
>
> NBC-TV (both New York and Burbank offices) were deluged with letters of protest. The furor increased with each passing day. *Star Trek*'s chances for renewal became a topic of discussion in newspaper columns across the country. Student protest movements were organized. Cal Tech students marched, along with other *Star Trek* supporters, against NBC's Burbank office, carrying a petition urging renewal of the series....
>
> On the East Coast, meanwhile, reaction was equally vocal. For the first time in network history, pickets were marching up and down Rockefeller Plaza, carrying placards, handing out leaflets and bumper stickers, publicly protesting the rumored cancellation.⁸

This kind of activism represents a sort of Socratic refusal to accept the "programmed" thinking which often follows a different agenda (money, power, status quo). The kind of questioning which led *Star Trek* fans to mobilize continued to energize the fan base after the show's premature demise. The fan conventions represent the logical outgrowth of that spirit of defiant inquiry. No show in the history of television had ever come close to generating the self-sustaining current of excitement that *Star Trek* generated. As Shatner explains it in *Get a Life!*:

> In 1972, this planet played host to a grand total of one *Star Trek* convention. In '73, there were three. However, even by 1974, conventions were popping up in Los Angeles, Houston, Atlanta, Kalamazoo, even Leicester, England. By 1975, twenty-three conventions dotted the map, including one massive Chicago affair attended by thirty thousand fans. Then in 1976, independent producers and moneymaking corporations were churning out conventions on an average of one a week.⁹

And the lingua franca of each of those conventions was, and continues to be, the "Q and A," the endless back and forth between starstruck audience members and the "talent" from the various *Star Trek* spinoff series and movies. The stakes might not be as high as those in Socrates' time (his failure to persuade his jailers did, after all, lead to his death-by-hemlock), but the underlying notion of the *value* of rigorous questioning remains the same. Though Shatner, Nimoy, et al., admit to being asked many of the same questions hundreds of times, each convention offers an opportunity to discover some new piece of the *Star Trek* puzzle. Convention "reports" are posted on internet-based fan sites and widely circulated among the fans, who then proceed to parse the language of each answer, arguing about its import in the past, present and future world of *Trek*.

Imparting an intellectual motive to something as benignly enjoyable as a *Star Trek* convention could be seen as overreaching. The original *Star Trek* was, after all, a campy space adventure with lots of breathless "battle stations!" and hairy, alien beings threatening to squeeze the life out of the human race, one red-shirted Federation member at a time. William Shatner himself, the heroic, impulsive Captain Kirk, will never be mistaken for one of the great thespians of his generation. Yet here, too, Trekkies can turn to Socrates for the moral cover to indulge their passion for a show which, though it met an untimely end, continues to live on in the goodwill of its fans. As Plato records in "The Apology":

> Someone will say: And are you not ashamed, Socrates, of a course of life which is likely to bring you to an untimely end? To him I may fairly answer: There you are mistaken: a man who is good for anything ought not to calculate the chance of living or dying; he ought only to consider whether in doing anything he is doing right or wrong — acting the part of a good man or of a bad.[10]

FROM DIALOGUES TO STARLOGS

If, as Socrates claimed, "the unexamined life is not worth living," then every aspect of the human condition — including mass media and popular entertainment — deserves close scrutiny. And in considering *Star Trek*'s bold vision of a future free from so many of our contemporary weaknesses, we find a new reason to recall Socrates' words, for if humanity is to *really* go where no one has gone before, it will first have to answer some nagging questions which have vexed mankind since the primitive past: Why is violence so prevalent? Why are bigotry and suspicion so widespread? Will humans always approach death — and what lies beyond — with anxiety? *Star Trek* offers hope for humanity as it journeys past mere life to (in the words of Socrates) "the invisible world, to the divine and immortal and irrational — thither arriving, she is secure of bliss and is released from the error and folly of men."[11]

Gene Roddenberry couldn't have put it any better.

Appendix 1: Literary Works
(and the Chapters Where They Are Discussed)

Asimov, Isaac. *I, Robot* (18)
Barrie, J. M. *Peter Pan* (3)
Beowulf (1)
Carroll, Lewis. *Alice in Wonderland* (3)
Collodi. *Pinocchio* (3)
Crichton, Michael. *Jurassic Park* (15)
Dante. *The Divine Comedy* (22)
de Villeneuve, Gabrielle. *Beauty and the Beast* (11)
The Declaration of Independence (14)
Forrester, C.S. *Horatio Hornblower* (8)
Gilman, Charlotte Perkins. "The Yellow Wallpaper" (10)
Golding, William. *Lord of the Flies* (3)
Hawthorne, Nathaniel. *The Birthmark* (20)
Herrick, Robert. "To the Virgins" (23)
Homer. *The Odyssey* (1, 16)
Ibsen, Henrik. *A Doll's House* (11)
Joyce, James. *Finnegans Wake* (16)
Lawrence, D.H. "The Snake" (9)
_____. "Whales Weep Not!" (8)
Locke, John. "Two Treatises on Government" (14)
Marvell, Andrew. "To His Coy Mistress" (23)
Melville, Herman. *Moby Dick* (2)

Millay, Edna St. Vincent. "What Lips My Lips Have Kissed" (4)
Milton, John. *Paradise Lost* (17)
More, Thomas. *Utopia* (20)
Nabokov, Vladimir. *Lolita* (4)
Ness, Eliot. *The Untouchables* (19)
The New Testament (22)
The Old Testament (9)
Plato. *The Dialogues of Plato* (24)
Poe, Edgar Allan. *The Cask of Amontillado* (2)
_____. "The Pit and the Pendulum" (10)
Polidor, John. *The Vampyre* (13)
Remarque, Erich Maria. *All Quiet on the Western Front* (7)
"The Seafarer" (8)
Shakespeare, William. *Hamlet*
_____. *King Lear* (21)
_____. *Othello* (11)
_____. *Romeo and Juliet* (4)
Shaw, George Bernard. *Pygmalion* (12)
Shelley, Mary. *Frankenstein* (15)
Stoker, Bram. *Dracula* (13)
Tennyson, Alfred, Lord. *Ulysses* (21)
Thurber, James. "The Secret Life of Walter Mitty" (6)
Virgil. *The Aeneid* (7)
Washington, Booker T. *Up from Slavery* (12)
Wells, H.G. *The Time Machine* (6)
Wister, Owen. *The Virginian* (5)

Appendix 2:
Episodes and Films
(and the Chapters Where They Are Discussed)

STAR TREK: ORIGINAL SERIES

Amok Time (4)
City on the Edge of Forever (4)
The Conscience of the King (2)
The Deadly Years (21)
The Devil in the Dark (9)
Let That Be Your Last Battlefield (14)
The Man Trap (13)
The Menagerie (23)

Miri (3)
A Piece of the Action (19)
Space Seed (2, 20)
Spectre of a Gun (5)
A Taste of Armageddon (7)
What Are Little Girls Made Of? (12)
Where No Man Has Gone Before (1)

STAR TREK: THE NEXT GENERATION

All Good Things... (6)
Darmok (9)
Datalore (18)
The Dauphin (11)
Encounter at Farpoint (3, 16)
Frame of Mind (10)
Hollow Pursuits (16)

The Inner Light (23)
The Masterpiece Society (20)
The Measure of a Man (14)
The Next Phase (22)
Redemption (18)
Sub Rosa (13)

STAR TREK: DEEP SPACE NINE

Badda-Bing, Badda-Bang (19)
Captive Pursuit (14)
The Cardassians (7)
The Emissary (22)
Move Along Home (3)
The Nagus (12)
Our Man Bashir (16)

STAR TREK: VOYAGER

Dreadnought (15)
Lifesigns (11)

STAR TREK: ENTERPRISE:

Chosen Realm (17)
North Star (5)
Similitude (12)

STAR TREK MOVIES

Star Trek: The Motion Picture (18)
Star Trek II: The Wrath of Khan (2, 8, 15, 20)
Star Trek III: The Search for Spock (15)
Star Trek IV: The Voyage Home (4, 8)
Star Trek V: The Final Frontier (8, 17)
Star Trek VI: The Undiscovered Country (7, 10)
Star Trek: VII: Generations (3, 16)
Star Trek VIII: First Contact (13)
Star Trek IX: Insurrection (15)
Star Trek X: Nemesis (2, 12)

Chapter Notes

Introduction

1. "The Visitor." *Deep Space Nine* episode #76.
2. Jacqueline Lichtenberg, Sondra Marshak and Joan Winston, *Star Trek Lives!* (New York: Bantam, 1975), 134.
3. See especially Yvonne Fern's *Gene Roddenberry: The Last Conversation* (Berkeley: University of California Press, 1994).
4. *Star Trek V: The Final Frontier.*
5. Given the immense amount of interpretation of various aspects of *Star Trek* in books, journals, fan magazines and websites, both official and unofficial, it is possible to acknowledge only a small swath of prevalent opinion. Like *Trek* itself, I expect to echo much of what has been written, and contradict countless other interpretations.

Chapter One

1. A thoughtful exploration of Kirk's flaws, as well as his heroism, can be found in James Devon's article "Walking on Water and Other Things James Kirk Can't Do," from the *Best of the Best of Trek II*, ed. by Walter Irwin and G.B. Love (New York: Penguin, 1992), 158– 67.
2. For good examples of this emphasis on the deceitful nature of Odysseus, see Euripedes' *The Cyclops* and Sophocles' *Philoctetes.*
3. Stephen Whitfield and Gene Roddenberry, *The Making of Star Trek* (New York: Ballantine, 1968), 22.
4. The list of all nominees, culled from 100 years of film, can be found on the American Film Institute website, www.aft.com.
5. Stephen Whitfield and Gene Roddenberry, *The Making of Star Trek*, 28.
6. *Ibid.*, 28–29.
7. "Where No Man Has Gone Before." *Star Trek,* episode #2.

Chapter Two

1. Elizabethan writers were interested in both Greek and Roman theater. However, most scholars of the period agree that Shakespeare and his contemporaries were drawing from Roman, not Greek models of revenge tragedy. The dramatic works of Seneca were widely circulated and available to dramatists in the age of Elizabeth I in a way that Seneca's forebears were not. Many of the "classic" Greek tragedies had not yet been translated from Greek into the far more accessible Latin. See 323–34 of A.C.

Bradley's *Shakespearean Tragedy* (New York: Fawcett Premier, 1965) and 38–40 of F.E. Halliday's *Shakespeare in His Age* (New York: Thomas Yoseloff, 1965).

2. The "problem" of Hamlet's indecision has been most famously argued by T.S. Eliot in the essay on *Hamlet* in his 1920 collection of literary criticism, *The Sacred Wood*; some modern critics, however, such as Harold Bloom, have argued that Hamlet is one of the most active and focused characters in all of literature. See 383–431 in Bloom's *Shakespeare: The Invention of the Human* (New York: Riverhead Books, 1998).

3. For a fuller discussion of Shakespeare in *Star Trek*, see Douglas Lanier's *Shakespeare and Popular Culture* (Oxford UP, 2002), 1–20.

4. The "Prime Directive" (also known as "Starfleet General Order #1") dictates non-interference in the development of other cultures — even if the behavior of those cultures is anathema to Starfleet personnel.

5. See 1 Kings 16:29–22:40; 2 Kings 9:30–37.

6. Herman Melville, *Moby Dick* (New York: Barnes & Noble, 1993), 423.

7. A helpful introduction to this topic can be found in Marc Swanson's "Ishmael in Space: Literary Allusions in *The Wrath of Khan*" in the *Best of Trek 12* (New York: Penguin, 1986), 113–117.

8. *Star Trek: Nemesis.*

Chapter Three

1. Gene Roddenberry frequently protested the notion that his series was about aliens, strange worlds or space-age technology, claiming instead that it was always about humanity. As he noted in his discussion about the gruesome, menacing "Horta" in the episode "The Devil in the Dark": "If you can learn to feel for a Horta, you may also be learning to understand and feel for other humans of different cultures, ways and beliefs" (*The Making of Star Trek*, 36).

2. "Encounter at Farpoint." *The Next Generation*, episodes #1-2.

3. As critic Jerome Bump has noted, "[T]he most appropriate perspective for understanding Charles Dodgson is that of a child, because Dodgson's life was devoted to perpetuating childhood," (from the Foreword to Lisa Bassett's *Very Truly Yours, Charles Dodgson, Alias Lewis Carroll* [New York: Lothrop, Lee & Shepard Books, 1987]).

4. Lewis Carroll, *Alice in Wonderland* (New York: Clarkson N. Potter, Inc., 1973), 108.

Chapter Four

1. Herbert Solow and Robert Justman, *Inside Star Trek: The Real Story* (New York: Pocket Books, 1996), 235.

2. William Shakespeare, *Romeo and Juliet—The New Folger Library Edition* (New York: Washington Square Press, 1992), 83.

3. "Amok Time." *Star Trek*, episode #34.

4. All quotations taken from the Everyman Library edition of *Lolita* (New York: Knopf, 1992).

5. Fern, *Gene Roddenberry: The Last Conversation*, 72.

6. This untitled poem can be found in many anthologies. I've cited the text reprinted in *American Poetry: the Twentieth Century, Volume One* (New York: Library of America, 2000), 861.

7. Allan Asherman, *The Star Trek Compendium* (New York: Pocket Books, 1986), 64.

Chapter Five

1. John Q. Anderson, "Introduction," *The Virginian* (New York: Dodd, Mead & Co., 1968), vii.

2. Certainly other American writers had included the frontier in their narratives — most notably James Fenimore Cooper in his Leatherstocking Tales. However, most frontier stories prior to Wister showed protagonists struggling to adapt to life in the wild. For example, Cooper's Natty Bumppo uses his wiles to survive in the outdoors, but he remains out of his element — an awkwardly transplanted Easterner. Wister's Virginian lives in sync with the wild, choosing to live among the animals and natural elements of the plains rather than as a member of "polite society."

3. Owen Wister, "To The Reader," *The Virginian*, xiv.

4. *Ibid.*
5. *Ibid.*
6. "North Star." *Star Trek: Enterprise,* episode #61.

Chapter Six

1. See "150 Things We Love About *Star Trek*," (*Star Trek Communicator*, Issue #150, 50–61) for many testimonials from scientists, researchers and astronauts about the impact the franchise made on their career choices.
2. H.G. Wells, *The Time Machine* (New York: Ace Books, 2001), 3.
3. *Ibid.*, 126.
4. *Star Trek IV: The Voyage Home.*
5. Interested readers should consult Lawrence Krauss' *The Physics of Star Trek* (New York: HarperCollins, 1996). See especially chapter two, "Einstein Raises," 12–29.
6. H.G. Wells, *The Time Machine*, 127.
7. "All Good Things...," *The Next Generation,* episodes 177–78.

Chapter Seven

1. Gene Roddenberry wrote and spoke extensively about his hopes for a future free from traditional war-like conflict. Perhaps the clearest statement of his intention to advance this notion through *Star Trek* can be found in the final lines of the book *The Making of Star Trek*: "[*Star Trek*] has given us a legacy — a message — man *can* create a future worth living for...a future that is full of optimism, hope, excitement, and challenge. A future that proudly proclaims man's ability to survive in peace and reach the stars as his reward.
"Whither *Star Trek*?
"It really doesn't matter. We have its legacy... all we have to do is use it" (402).
2. The "Xindi" story arc, which lasted the entire third season, featured the *Enterprise*'s response to an unprovoked attack on Planet Earth by a hostile alien race. Many fans and critics drew parallels to the 9/11 terrorist attacks throughout the season.
3. Virgil, *The Aeneid* (New York: Modern Library, 1950), 142.
4. *Ibid.*, 140.
5. *Ibid.*, 214.

6. Erich Maria Remarque, *All Quiet on the Western Front* (New York: Ballantine Books, 1982), 12–13.
7. *Ibid.*, 284.
8. *Ibid.*, 296.
9. "A Taste of Armageddon." Original series, episode #23.
10. *Ibid.*
11. *Ibid.*
12. "Dreadnought." *Voyager,* episode #34.
13. Erich Maria Remarque, *All Quiet on the Western Front*, 205.
14. James Van Hise, *Trek: The Making of the Movies* (Las Vegas: Pioneer Books, 1992), 132–146.

Chapter Eight

1. See Walter Irwin's article "Boots and Starships" in *The Best of the Best of Trek II* (New York: Penguin, 1992), 22–26, for a general overview of the Hornblower-*Trek* connection.
2. The entry for the Klingon expression "GhoS!" in *The Star Trek Encyclopedia* (New York: Pocket Books, 1994), 174, explains the derivation of Picard's signature "Make it so!" command.
3. Stephen Whitfield and Gene Roddenberry, *The Making of Star Trek*, 28.
4. C.S. Forrester, *Mr. Midshipman Hornblower* (Boston: Little, Brown and Company, 1948), p.28.
5. *Ibid.*, 34–5.
6. Nicholas Meyer, director's commentary, *Star Trek II : The Wrath of Khan (Special Collector's Edition).*
7. "The Seafarer," reprinted in George Anderson's *The Literature of the Anglo-Saxons* (New York: Russell & Russell, Inc.), 160.
8. *Ibid.*
9. *Star Trek V: The Final Frontier.*
10. Dorothy Whitelock explores the affect of this last line on the overall poem in her essay on "The Seafarer" in *Old English Literature: Twenty-Two Analytical Essays,* ed. Martin Smith and Jerome Mandel (Lincoln: University of Nebraska Press), 205.
11. D.H. Lawrence, "Whales Weep Not!" Reprinted in *Modern Poems* (2nd ed), ed. by Richard Ellmann and Robert O'Clair (New York: Norton, 1980), 209.
12. *Ibid.*, 209.

Chapter Nine

1. For a good background discussion on the Tower of Babel, its origin and significance, see the article "Genesis 11: 1–9" at the website www.tribulation.com.
2. All citations from the King James Version of the Bible.
3. "Darmok." *The Next Generation,* episode #102.
4. *Ibid.*
5. *Ibid.*
6. William Shatner, who played Captain Kirk, has stated that it's *his* favorite episode as well. See Shatner's *Star Trek Memories* (New York: HarperCollins, 1993), 200.
7. Lawrence's work seems to have resounded with *Trek*'s writers; his poem "Whales Weep Not!" was quoted prominently in *Star Trek IV: The Voyage Home.*
8. D.H. Lawrence, "The Snake" (reprinted in *Modern Poems, 2nd Edition,* ed. by Ellmann and O'Clair), 205–07.
9. *Ibid.*
10. *Ibid.*
11. *Ibid.*
12. Perhaps the most famous example is Book IV of Johnathan Swift's *Gulliver's Travels.*
13. "The Devil in the Dark." Original series, episode #26.

Chapter Ten

1. See Alan M. Pavlik's "Celebrity Trials are the Opiate of the Masses?" at www.justabovesunset.com.
2. Edgar Allan Poe, "The Pit and the Pendulum." *The Gold-Bug and Other Tales* (New York: Dover, 1991), 62.
3. *Ibid.*, 68–69.
4. *Ibid.*, 73.
5. Edward Davidson, *Poe: A Critical Study.* (Harvard UP, 1957), 134.
6. Jeanine Lawall, "*The Yellow Wallpaper*: The Rest Cure as Catalyst to Insanity," at www.unix.oit.umass.edu.
7. Elaine Hedges, "Charlotte Perkins Gilman." *American Women Writers: A Critical Reference Guide from Colonial Times to the Present.* Ed. by Carol Hurd Green and Mary Mason (Farmington Hills, Mich: St. James Press, 1994), 349.
8. Charlotte Perkins Gilman, "The Yellow Wallpaper." Reprinted in *Great American Short Stories* (Pleasantville: Reader's Digest Association, 1977), 203.
9. *Ibid.*, 205.

Chapter Eleven

1. Ibsen was one of the first and most prominent writers to advocate for women's rights and worker's rights, and to portray Victorian-era conformity as a social pathology. See, for instance, *When We Dead Awaken* and *Ghosts.*
2. Larry Nemecek, *The Star Trek: The Next Generation Companion.* (New York: Pocket Books, 1992), 78.
3. "Plato's Stepchildren." Original series, episode #67.
4. "Lifesigns." *Voyager,* episode #36.

Chapter Twelve

1. A succinct summary of his life can be found in the section "New Explorations of an American Self," in the *Heath Anthology of American Literature, v.2* (Lexington, Mass: Heath, 1999), 850–853.
2. *Ibid.*, 854.
3. See the 1895 edition of *The Life and Times of Frederick Douglass* for a fuller statement of Douglass' ideology.
4. Booker T. Washington, *Up from Slavery,* excerpted in the *Heath Anthology of American Literature, v.2,* 853.
5. From William Shakespeare's *King Lear,* Act III, scene iv, line 107.
6. G.B. Shaw, *Pygmalion.* Reprinted in *Cavalcade of Comedy* (New York: Simon and Schuster, 1953), 429–30.
7. Larry Nemecek, *Star Trek: The Next Generation Companion,* 38.
8. The Godfather-Nagus connection is discussed in Terry Erdmann's *Deep Space Nine Companion* (New York: Pocket Books, 2000), 39.

Chapter Thirteen

1. There are numerous sources of vampire lore and history. One of the best and most eclectic is *The Vampire's Vault,* a website

maintained by the Gothic Society of Nova Scotia, available at www. Chebucto.ns.ca/~vampire.
  2. The "Borg" entry in *The Star Trek Encyclopedia* (New York: Pocket Books, 1999), 50–52, provides a typically comprehensive overview.
  3. John Polidori, *The Vampyre*. Reprinted in Christopher Frayling's *Vampyres: Lord Byron to Count Dracula* (London: Faber and Faber, 1991), 116.
  4. For an example of this type, see Anne Rice's serial protagonist, the vampire Lestat.
  5. Larry Nemecek, *Star Trek: The Next Generation Companion*, 280.
  6. Judith and Garfield Reeves-Stevens, *The Making of Star Trek: Deep Space Nine* (New York: Pocket Books, 1994), 179.
  7. Bram Stoker, *Dracula* (New York: Barnes & Noble Books, 2003), 75.
  8. J. Gordon Melton, *The Vampire Book: The Encyclopedia of the Undead* (Farmington Hills, MI: Visible Ink Press, 1999), xxi.

Chapter Fourteen

  1. Testimonies abound. See, for example, the discussion of Whoopi Goldberg's decision to join *The Next Generation* cast and the accompanying photo on the set with her "inspiration," Nichelle Nicols, in Larry Nemecek's *Star Trek: The Next Generation Companion* (New York: Pocket Books, 1995), 64–5.
  2. John Locke, *Two Treatises on Government*, Chapter II, sec. 4, paragraph 1.
  3. *Ibid.*, sec. 7, paragraph 1.
  4. In Locke, the exact phrase is "being equal and independent"; sec. 6, paragraph 1.
  5. "Captive Pursuit." *Deep Space Nine,* episode #6.
  6. King delivered his "I Have a Dream" speech in August 1963 on the steps of the Lincoln Memorial to a crowd of roughly a quarter of a million people.
  7. *Ibid.*
  8. "The Measure of a Man," *The Next Generation,* episode #35.
  9. *Ibid.*
  10. *Ibid.*
  11. *Ibid.*
  12. "Let That Be Your Last Battlefield," original series, episode 70.

Chapter Fifteen

  1. Mary Shelley, *Frankenstein* (New York: Bantam Books, 1981), 105.
  2. *Ibid.*, 13.
  3. *Ibid.*, 152.
  4. Michael Crichton, *Jurrasic Park* (New York: Knopf, 1990), 284.
  5. *Ibid.*, 1.
  6. *Star Trek II: The Wrath of Khan.*

Chapter Sixteen

  1. Homer, "The Lotus Eaters," from *The Odyssey.*
  2. *Star Trek VII: Generations.*
  3. For a brief, comprehensive overview of the Lotus' variable meaning, see William Rose Benet's *The Reader's Encyclopedia*, second edition (New York: Thomas Y. Crowell, 1965), 600.
  4. James Thurber, "The Secret Life of Walter Mitty," from *The Thurber Carnival* (New York: Harper & Row, 1945), 50.
  5. *Ibid.*, 49–50.
  6. Captain Picard is, ostensibly, a fan of James Joyce; he took a copy of Joyce's *Ulysses* with him on vacation in the episode "Captain's Holiday."

Chapter Seventeen

  1. As noted throughout Yvonne Fern's *Gene Roddenberry: The Last Conversation* (Berkeley: University of California Press, 1994). Roddenberry's humanism was a driving force in his work. As he stated in Fern's book, "You must free your mind of those values dearest of all to you: affection for home, your background, your country, its customs, your own culture, your religious beliefs. The more precious the belief to you, the more certainly it must go if you are to free your forebrain to use its perception and logic" (43).
  2. For more on the topic of religious beliefs in *Star Trek*, see Judith Barad and Ed Robertson, *The Ethics of Star Trek* (New York: HarperCollins, 2000).
  3. For consistency, I follow the Old Testament's usage of the singular "He" and "Him" in referring to the deity. No offense intended for those who endorse a more gender-neutral pronoun.

4. John Milton, *Paradise Lost*, from *The Poetical Works of John Milton* (London: George Routledge and Sons, 1853), 1.
5. *Star Trek V: The Final Frontier*.
6. Stephen Whitfield and Gene Roddenberry, *The Making of Star Trek* (New York: Ballantine, 1968), 112.

Chapter Eighteen

1. See "The Robot Chronicles" in *Isaac Asimov Gold* (New York: HarperCollins, 1995), 161–75.
2. Isaac Asimov, *I, Robot* (New York: Bantam, 2004), 44–45.
3. *Ibid.*, 9.
4. *Ibid.*, 14.
5. Though Data malfunctions — in fact, he goes berserk — in *Star Trek: Insurrection*, that's a result of his having been shot by phaser blasts, triggering a pre-programmed aggressive response.
6. "Redemption," *The Next Generation*, episodes #100–101.
7. A thorough account can be found in James Van Hise's *Trek: The Making of the Movies* (Las Vegas: Pioneer Books, 1992), 12–43.
8. *Ibid.*, 21.
9. Robert Moore Williams, "Robot's Return," in *Machines That Think*, ed. by Isaac Asimov, et al. (New York: Hold, Rinehart and Winston, 1983), 139.
10. *Ibid.*, 150.
11. *Ibid.*, 152.

Chapter Nineteen

1. Although the most famous, and most copied, Mafia entertainment vehicle is certainly Francis Ford Coppola's *The Godfather*, the movie was made two years *after* the original series went off the air, so the series had to draw from the plethora of earlier mob movies and TV shows.
2. Eliot Ness, *The Untouchables* (New York: Barnes & Noble Books, 1996), *Star Trek* 39–40.
3. Tim Dirks, "*Scarface: The Shame of the Nation*": A Review, @www.filmsite.org.
4. *Scarface: The Shame of the Nation*.
5. *Ibid*.
6. Eliot Ness, *The Untouchables*, 40.

7. "A Piece of the Action." The original series, episode #49.
8. *Ibid*.
9. "Badda Bing Badda Boom." *Deep Space Nine*, episode #566.

Chapter Twenty

1. More's debt to Plato is discussed in Edward Sturtz's "Introduction" to the *Selected Works of St. Thomas More: Utopia* (New Haven: Yale University Press, 1964), vii–xxx.
2. Thomas More, *The Selected Works of Thomas More: Utopia*, 52.
3. *Ibid.*, 60.
4. *Ibid.*, 146.
5. *Ibid.*, 67.
6. *Ibid.*, 91.
7. *Ibid.*, 92–93.
8. *Ibid.*, 79.
9. *Ibid.*, 79.
10. "The Masterpiece Society." *The Next Generation*, episode #113.
11. *Ibid*.
12. *Ibid*.
13. Nathaniel Hawthorne, "The Birthmark," from *Works of Nathaniel Hawthorne, Vol. III* (New York: Bigelow, Brown & Co., 1923), 37.
14. *Ibid*.
15. *Ibid.*, 47.
16. *Ibid.*, 56.
17. "Space Seed." Original series, episode #24.
18. *Ibid*.

Chapter Twenty-One

1. D.A. Traversi, *An Approach to Shakespeare, 2nd ed.* (New York: Doubleday, 1956), 182.
2. *Star Trek II: The Wrath of Khan*.
3. See the entry on "Kobayashi Maru" in Michael and Denise Okuda's *Star Trek Encyclopedia* (New York: Pocket Books, 1999), 248, for further details about this intriguing test of command.
4. Cf. Act V., Scene iii, lines 8–9.
5. Wm. Shakespeare, *King Lear*, in *The Riverside Shakespeare* (Boston: Houghton Mifflin, 1974), 1277.
6. *Star Trek II: The Wrath of Khan*.

7. Alfred Tennyson, "Ulysses," reprinted in *The Best Poems of the English Language* (New York: HarperCollins, 2004), 597–99.
8. *Ibid.*, 599.

Chapter Twenty-Two

1. For an argument that Gene Roddenberry's humanism was actually a version of pantheism, see Paul Harrison's "The Real *Star Trek* Theology: Gene Roddenberry's Pantheism" online at www.potentialsmedia.com.
2. See the "Native American" section on the Website of the National Humanities Center for more information about this concept.
3. A Sanskrit word, nirvana represents "the completion of the path of Buddhism" (www. fundamentalbuddhism.com).
4. *I Thessalonians*, 4:16–17.
5. *The Gospel of Matthew*, 13:41–43.
6. *The Book of Revelations*, 4:1–5.
7. There are many translations of Dante available. I've relied on Mark Musa's translation in *The Portable Dante* (New York: Penguin, 2003).
8. *Ibid.*, xxxv.
9. *Ibid.*, 207.
10. *Voyager*'s episode "Coda" is similar in concept, but for clarity I've limited my discussion to "The Next Phase."
11. "The Next Phase." *The Next Generation,* episode #124.
12. *The Portable Dante,* 228.
13. "Journey's End." *The Next Generation,* episode #172.

Chapter Twenty-Three

1. William Blake's "Auguries of Innocence," reprinted in *Eighteenth-Century English Literature* (New York: Harcourt Brace Jovanovich, 1969), 1506.
2. That translation comes from *The Encarta Book of Quotations* (New York: St. Martin's Press, 2000), 496.
3. As the critic Harlod Bloom notes in his anthology *The Best Poems of the English Language* (New York: harperCollins, 2004), "Herrick implicitly understood that love, shadowed by mortality, is kindled into eroticism" (157). The poem's text comes from Bloom's collection.
4. Andrew Marvell, "To His Coy Mistress," from Bloom's *Best Poems of the English Language,* 172–73.
5. "The Inner Light." *The Next Generation,* episode #125.

Chapter Twenty-Four

1. Plato's *Dialogues* were, really, *Socrates'* Dialogues. Plato played Boswell to Socrates' Johnson, if you will. Since no record from Socrates himself has come down to us, we must rely on Plato.
2. Clifton Fadimon and John S. Major, *The New Lifetime Reading Plan* (New York: Harper Perennial, 1999), 24.
3. The convention I attended in Cherry Hill, NJ, in 2004, for example, featured an in-depth panel discussion about how to improve the current state of the *Trek* franchise.
4. From Plato, "The Apology." Reprinted in *Plato: Five Great Dialogues* (New York: Grammercy Books, 1969), 41–42.
5. *Ibid.*
6. William Shatner, with Chris Kreski, *Get a Life!* (New York: Pocket Books, 1999), 23–4.
7. Herb Solow and Robert Justman, *Inside Star Trek: The Real Story* (New York: Pocket Books, 1996), 378.
8. David Gerrold, *The World of Star Trek* (New York: Ballantine, 1973), 394.
9. William Shatner, with Chris Kreski, *Get a Life!,* 96
10. Plato, "The Apology." Reprinted in *Plato: Five Great Dialogues,* 46.
11. Plato, "Phaedo." *Plato: Five Great Dialogues,* 115.

Bibliography

Aldis, Brian W. *Trillion Year Spree: The History of Science Fiction.* New York: Atheneum, 1986.
Anders, Louis, ed. *Projections: Science Fiction in Literature and Film.* Austin, Texas: Monkeybrain Books, 2004.
Asherman, Allan. *The Star Trek Compendium (special 20th anniversary edition).* New York: Pocket Books, 1986.
Asimov, Isaac. *Gold.* New York: HarperPrism, 1995.
Barad, Judith, with Ed Robertson. *The Ethics of Star Trek.* New York: HarperCollins, 2000.
Bénét, William Rose, ed. *The Reader's Encyclopedia (2nd edition).* New York: Thomas Y. Crowell, 1965.
Blish, James. *The Star Trek Reader.* New York: Dutton, 1976.
Bloom, Harold. *The Best Poems of the English Language.* New York: HarperCollins, 2004.
_____. *Shakespeare: The Invention of the Human.* New York: Riverhead Books, 1998.
Bond, Jeff. *The Music of Star Trek.* Los Angeles: Lone Eagle Publishing, 1999.
Campbell, W. John. *The Book of Great Books.* The Wonderland Press, 2000.
Careless, James. "'Don't Worry — He Was Only a Redshirt': The 'Life and Death' Prime Directive." *Star Trek Communicator* (Number 147): 42–47.
Clute, John. *Science Fiction: The Illustrated Encyclopedia.* London: Dorling Kindersley, 1995.
Dean, Leonard F. *Shakespeare: Modern Essays in Criticism (revised edition).* Oxford University Press, 1967.
Dilmore, Kevin, and Dayton Ward. "War in *Star Trek*: Reflecting the Times?" *Star Trek Communicator* (Number 149): 38–44, 95.

Ellison, Harlan. *The City on the Edge of Forever: The Original Teleplay That Became the Classic Star Trek Episode*. Clarkston, Georgia: White Wolf Publishing, 1996.
Elton, William R. *King Lear and the Gods*. Lexington: University Press of Kentucky, 1988.
Erdmann, Terry J., with Paula Block. *Star Trek: Deep Space Nine Companion*. New York: Pocket Books, 2000.
Fadiman, Clifton, and John S. Major. *The New Lifetime Reading Plan (4th edition)*. New York: HarperCollins, 1998.
Fern, Yvonne. *Gene Rodenberry: The Last Conversation*. Berkeley: University of California Press, 1994.
Gerrold, David. *The World of Star Trek*. New York: Ballantine, 1973.
Irwin, Walter, and G.B. Love, eds. *The Best of the Best of Trek*. New York: ROC, 1990.
_____. *The Best of the Best of Trek II*. New York: ROC, 1992.
Kraemer, Ross, William Cassidy and Susan L. Schwartz. *Religions of Star Trek*. Boulder: Westview Press, 2003.
Kraus, Lawrence M. *The Physics of Star Trek*. New York: HarperPerenniel, 1996.
Lanier, Douglas. *Shakespeare and Modern Popular Culture*. Oxford University Press, 2002.
LeGuin, Ursula K., and Brian Attebery, eds. *The Norton Book of Science Fiction*. New York: W.W. Norton, 1993.
Lichtenberg, Jacqueline, Sondra Marshak and Joan Winston. *Star Trek Lives!* New York: Bantam, 1975.
McTigue, Maureen. *Star Trek: Celebrations*. New York: Pocket Books, 2001.
Melton, J. Gordon. *The Vampire Book (second edition)*. Detroit: Visible Ink Press, 1999.
Nemecek, Larry. *The Star Trek: The Next Generation Companion (revised edition)*. New York: Pocket Books, 1995.
_____, ed. "150 Things We Love About Star *Trek*." *Star Trek Communicator* (Number 150): 50–56.
Nicholls, Peter, general ed. *The Science Fiction Encyclopedia*. Garden City, New York: Doubleday, 1979.
Nimoy, Leonard. *I Am Not Spock*. Millbrae, California: Celestial Arts, 1975.
Okuda, Michael and Denise, with Debbie Mirek. *The Star Trek Encyclopedia (updated and expanded edition)*. New York: Pocket Books, 1999.
Reeves-Stevens, Judith and Garfield. *The Making of Star Trek: Deep Space Nine*. New York: Pocket Books, 1994.
_____. *Star Trek: The Next Generation—The Continuing Mission*. New York: Pocket Books, 1998.
Rioux, Terry Lee. *From Sawdust to Stardust: The Biography of DeForest Kelley, Star Trek's Dr. McCoy*. New York: Pocket Books, 2005.
Ruditis, Paul. *Star Trek Voyager Companion*. New York: Pocket Books, 2003.
Schuster, Al, executive director. *International Star Trek Convention Official Program*—1975, 22 pp.
Shatner, William, with Chris Kreski. *Get a Life!* New York: Pocket Books, 1999.
_____ and _____. *Star Trek Memories*. New York: HarperCollins, 1993.

_____ and _____. *Star Trek Movie Memories*. New York: HarperCollins, 1994.
Sherwin, Jill. *Quotable Star Trek*. New York: Pocket Books, 1999.
Solow, Herbert F., and Robert Justman. *Inside Star Trek: The Real Story*. New York: Pocket Books, 1996.
Stafford, Nick, ed. *Trekkers: True Stories by Fans for Fans*. Toronto: ECW Press, 2002.
Taylor, Mary P., ed. *Star Trek: Adventures in Time and Space*. New York: Pocket Books, 1999.
Van Hise, James. *Trek: The Making of the Movies*. Las Vegas: Pioneer Books, 1992.
Westmore, Michael, et al. *Star Trek: Aliens and Artifacts*. New York: Pocket Books, 2000.
Whitfield, Stephen, and Gene Rodenberry. *The Making of Star Trek*. New York: Ballantine, 1968.
Wright, Gene. *The Science Fiction Image*. New York: Facts on File, 1983.

Index

Aeneas 9, 59
The Aeneid 58–65, 148
Aeschere 11
Aesop 25
Alecto 59
Alice in Wonderland 30–32
"All Good Things…" 55
All Quiet on the Western Front 58, 60–65
American Film Institute 12
"Amok Time" 36
Anan 61
Apollo 59
"The Apology" 206–207, 211
April, Robert T. 13
Aquinas, Sir Thomas 171, 191
Archer, Jonathon 47–48
Aristotle 8
Asimov, Isaac 154–155
"The Assignment" 194
Aylmer 177

Bacon, Francis 171
"Badda-Bing, Badda-Bang" 164, 168–170
Bajor 64, 194
The Bak'u 133–134
Barclay, Reg 104, 140–141
Barrie, J.M. 26–28
Bashir, Julian 140
Batai 201
Bates, Norman 83

Baudelaire, Charles 110
Baumer, Paul 60
Beauty and the Beast 93, 97–98
Bele 125
Beowulf 9–13
The Best of Trek 2
Bhagavad Gita 142
The Bible 62; *see also* New Testament; Old Testament
"The Birthmark" 177
Blake, William 25, 196
Boccaccio 5
Bond, James 140
The Borg 111–112, 157
Brando, Marlon 107
Brooks, Albert 147
Brooks, Avery 122
Brueghel 66
Burroughs, James 101
Burton, LeVar 119
Byron, Lord 69, 110, 112

"The Cage" 203
Camonte, Tony 165
Campbell, John 154
Capone, Al 162, 165
Captain Ahab 12, 21–23
Captain Hook 26
Captain Masters 68
"Captive Pursuit" 120–122

"The Cardassians" 61, 63–64
Carmilla 113
Carroll, Lewis 30
"The Cask of Amontillado" 23–24
The Catcher in the Rye 89
Chakotay 98
Chaucer, Geoffrey 5
Chekov, Pavel 181
Cheron 125–126
"The Children of Tama" 77
"Chosen Realm" 151
A Christmas Carol 192
"City on the Edge of Forever" 39, 54
Civil Rights Movement 7
Clanton Gang 45–47
Clark, Arthur C. 12
Cochrane, Zephram 19
Collodi 29
A Connecticut Yankee in King Arthur's Court 50
"The Conscience of the King" 19–21
"The Corbomite Maneuver" 68
Cordelia 182–183
Costillo, "Big Louis" 165
Costner, Kevin 164
The Count of Monte Cristo 24
Crater, Nancy 117
Crater, Robert 117
Crichton, Michael 128, 130–131
Crusher, Beverly 29, 114, 157
Crusher, Wesley 96, 181, 195
Cyrano de Bergerac 95

Dante 148, 189, 191–192
Darby, Kim 28, 77
Darin, James 168
"Darmok" 76–78
Data 5, 29–30, 77, 104, 112, 123, 133, 155, 193
"Datalore" 155
"The Dauphin" 96–97
"The Deadly Years" 185–186
Debussy, Claude 66
Decker, Will 160
Declaration of Independence 10, 119–120
"Deja Q" 143
DeNiro, Robert 164
DePalma, Brian 165
"The Devil in the Dark" 78–82
Dialogues of Plato 201–212
Dickens, Charles 184, 192
Disney, Walt 95

Divine Comedy 148, 189, 191–192
D'Jamat 151–152
The Doctor (aka EMH) 97–99, 157
Dr. Strangelove 127
Dodgson, Charles Lutwidge 30
A Doll's House 93–94
Doolittle, Eliza 105, 107
Douglas, Frederick 102
Dracula 109, 111, 113, 116
"Dreadnought" 61–63

Earp brothers 45–47
Earwicker, Humphrey Chimpden 143
Einstein, Albert 50, 141
Eline 201
Ellison, Harlan 39
Eloi 51
Emerson, Ralph Waldo 69
"The Emisary" 194–195
"Encounter at Farpoint" 29, 61, 138, 142
Enterprise see Starship *Enterprise*
Eyes, Frankie 169

Fadiman, Clifton 205
"The Fall of Icarus" 66
Finnegans Wake 136, 141–144
Fontaine, Vic 168–170
Ford, John 41
Forrester, C.S. 67
Fortunato 24
"Frame of Mind" 89
Frankenstein 112, 128–130, 134, 176
Freud, Sigmund 141

Genesis Project 130–133, 173
Georgiana 177
Gerrold, David 210
Get a Life! 3, 208–210
Gilman, Charlotte Perkins 84, 88–91
Gloucester 183, 185
The Godfather 107, 166
Goldberg, Whoopie 119, 124
Golding, William 26–28
Goneril 182–183
Grand Nagus 106
Grendel 11
Guinan 11, 124, 137
Gunfight at the OK Corral 45

Hamlet 2, 6, 12, 17–21, 65, 192
Hammer, Mike 24
Hawks, Howard 165

Hawthorne, Nathaniel 176
Hecht, Ben 163, 165–167
Helmer, Nora 93–94
Helmer, Torvald 93–94
Henry VIII 143
Herrick, Robert 197–198
Higgins, Henry 105
Hillyer 51
Holliday, Doc 45
"Hollow Pursuits" 140
Holmes, Sherlock 2, 7
Homer 5, 10, 17, 69, 136, 181
Horace 197–198, 203
Hornblower, Horatio 5, 67–69
Horta 81–82
Hubbard, Jamie 96
Huckleberry Finn 43
Hugo, Victor 95
Humbert Humbert 37–38
Hunchback of Notre Dame 95
Hurston, Zora Neale 25
Huxley, Aldous 171
Hythloday, Raphael 173

I Am Not Spock 3
I, Robot 154–155
Ibsen, Henrik 93–95
The Iliad 10, 17, 148
Ilya 160
"The Inner Light" 30, 197, 200–202
Inside Star Trek: The Real Story 209
Irving, Washington 50
Irwin, Walter 3

James, Henry 42, 89
Janeway, Captain 6, 15, 16, 59, 63, 143
Jason 9
Jefferson, Thomas 119, 120
Jesus Christ 189–190, 194
Joyce, James 25, 136, 141–144
Jurassic Park 128, 130–131
Justman, Robert 3, 209

Kaamin 201–202
Kahless 151
Kahn 22, 131–133, 176, 178–179
Karidian 20
Kataan 201
Keeler, Edith 39–40
Kes 98, 181
King, Martin Luther 122–123
King Arthur 9
King Lear 104, 181–183

Kirk, James Tiberius 5, 6, 9, 10, 12–16, 20, 22, 35, 36, 37, 39–40, 43, 45, 46, 58, 59, 61, 64–65, 71, 81, 86–88, 132, 137, 145, 149, 150, 161, 167–168, 178, 181–187, 208
Klingons 64, 86–88
Krako, Jojo 167
Kreski, Chris 208

LaForge, Geordi 140, 176, 193
Laren, Ensign Ro 193
Lawrence, D.H. 6, 73, 79
Lawrence, Friar 37
Leaves of Grass 2
LeFanu, Joseph Sheridan 113
Leone, Sergio 41
"Let That Be Your Last Battlefield" 125–126
"Lifesigns" 97–99
Locke, John 119–120
Lokai 125
Lolita 37–39
Lord of the Flies 27–28
Love, G.B. 3
Lovecraft, H.P. 5, 110
Lovo, Johnny 166
Luther, Martin (*95 Theses*) 142

Macbeth 19
The Mad Hercules 18
The Making of Star Trek 3, 67, 152
"The Man Trap" 116
Marcus, Carol 131
Marvell, Andrew 197–199
Masefield, John 71
"The Masterpiece Society" 174–176
McCoy, Dr. 31, 35, 36, 39–40, 46, 71, 78, 82, 86–88, 132, 150, 157, 168, 186
"The Measure of a Man" 123
Melton, J. Gordon 117
Melville, Herman 5, 17, 21, 23, 69, 71
"The Menagerie" 197, 202–203
"La Mer" 66
Meyer, Nicholas 68
Michelangelo 147
Millay, Edna St. Vincent 34, 38–40
Milton, John 17, 23, 69, 129
"Miri" 27
Mitchell, Gary 14
Moby Dick 2, 21–23, 66, 71, 154
Montalban, Ricardo 183
More, Sir Thomas 171

Morlocks 51
"Move Along Home" 31
My Fair Lady 104

Nabokov, Vladimir 34, 37–39
"The Nagus" 106
Ness, Eliot 163–165
The New Testament 189–191
"The Next Phase" 192
Nicols, Nichelle 119
Nimoy, Leonard 3, 33, 36, 211
Nog 169
"North Star" 47

O'Brien, Keiko 194
O'Brien, Miles 121–122, 194
The Odd Couple 92
"Odes" of Horace 197
Odo 16, 113, 115–116
Odysseus 9, 10, 13
The Odyssey 10, 69, 114, 136–138, 148
Oedipus 18
Old Testament 5, 75–76, 146–148
Orwell, George 8, 171
Othello 93–96
"Our Man Bashir" 141
Oxmyx, Bela 167

Pah Wraiths 59, 194
Paradise Lost 129, 146, 148–149
Paradise Regained 148
Paris, Tom 98
Parsifal 9
Pel, Denara 98–99
Penelope 10
Pequod 21
Peter Pan 26–28
Picard, Jean Luc 6, 15, 16, 23, 24, 30, 59, 67, 76–78, 103, 112, 114, 123, 133–134, 137, 140, 143, 156, 175–176, 187, 200–202
Picasso, Pablo 142
Pickering, Colonel 105
"A Piece of the Action" 164
Pike, Christopher 13, 202
Pinocchio 28–30
"The Pit and the Pendulum" 85–86
Plato 25, 171, 204
Plutarch 171
Poe, Edgar Allan 5, 23–24, 84–86, 110
Polidori, John 112, 113
Popeye 104
A Portrait of the Artist as a Young Man 25

"The Prelude" 25
The Prime Directive 19
Puzo, Mario 166
Pygmalion 101, 104–106
"Q" 6, 8, 55–56, 59, 136, 141–144
Quark 16, 31, 106

"Redemption" 156
Regan 182–183
Remans 23
Remarque, Erich Maria 60
The Republic 171–172
Riker, Will 29, 90–91, 140, 143
"Rip Van Winkle" 50
Rites of Osiris and Isis 142
Robbie the Robot 155
Robin Hood 55
"Robot's Return" 158
Rodenberry, Gene 3, 7, 8, 12, 38, 43, 52, 56, 64, 67, 74, 110, 119, 125, 134, 144, 149, 172, 174, 181, 189, 195, 209, 212
Romeo and Juliet 34
Romulans 23, 156
Ronin 114
Roosevelt, Theodore 42
Rostand, Edward 95
Ruthven Lord 112

Saint Matthew 190
Saint Paul 190
Salia 96
Salinger, J.D. 89
The Salt Vampire 116
Sarek 181
Satan 96, 115, 195
Scarface: Shame of the Nation 165–166
Scarfo, Nicky 162
Schultz, Dutch 162
Scotty 168
"The Seafarer" 69–70
"The Secret Life of Walter Mitty" 136, 138–140
Seneca 17
Serling, Rod 83
Sha Ka Ree 72, 149–150
Shakespeare, William 5, 6, 7, 34, 35, 69, 93, 142, 180, 192
Shatner, William 3, 7, 208–209, 211
Shaw, George Bernard 101
Shelley, Mary 112, 128–130, 176
Shinzon 23, 102–104
"Shore Leave" 31
"Similitude" 108

Simpson 68
Sisko, Benjamin 6, 15, 16, 121–122, 194
Sisko, Jake 6, 169, 181
Skagorans 47–48
"The Snake" 79–80
Socrates 204–212
Solow, Herb 3, 209
The Son'a 133
Songs of Innocence and Experience 25
Soran, Doctor 187
"Space Seed" 178–179
"Spectre of a Gun" 45
Spillane, Mickey 24
Spock 8, 14, 33–40, 46, 71, 78, 81, 104, 132, 149, 160–161, 167, 179, 184–185, 202
Stack, Robert 164
Star Trek Communicator 2
Star Trek: Deep Space Nine 3, 6, 31, 54, 59, 106, 116, 143, 164, 168, 193–194
Star Trek: Enterprise 3, 47–48, 108, 158
Star Trek Lives 7
Star Trek Memories 3
Star Trek Movie Memories 3
Star Trek: The Next Generation 3, 29, 55–56, 106, 138, 156, 174
Star Trek: The Motion Picture 158, 160–161
Star Trek: Original Series 1–3, 6–7, 12–13, 57–58, 83, 84, 108, 119, 164
Star Trek: Phase Two 159, 204
Star Trek: Voyager 3, 6, 97, 143, 156, 168
Star Trek II 68, 130, 176, 178, 181–185, 187
Star Trek III 53, 86, 130, 206
Star Trek IV 6, 53–55, 72–73
Star Trek V 7, 70–71, 73, 149
Star Trek VI 64–65, 86–88, 187
Star Trek VII 29, 137–138, 187, 208
Star Trek VIII 157
Star Trek IX 133
Star Trek X 23, 30, 102–104
Starship *Enterprise* 8, 15, 57, 71, 78, 87, 90–91, 108, 109, 114, 128, 134, 149, 150, 161, 162, 175, 178, 179, 184–185, 200
Stoker, Bram 116
Sybok 72, 149–150

A Tale of Two Cities 184
"A Taste of Armageddon" 61
Telemachus 10
Tennyson, Alfred Lord 181, 186–187
Tepes, Vlad 116

The Thessalonians 190
Thurber, James 136, 138–140
Tibetan Book of the Dead 142
The Time Machine 49–52, 56
"To His Coy Mistress" 197–199
"To the Virgins, to Make Much of Time" 197–198
Torres, B'Elana 63
Tosk 121
Troi, Deanna 77, 140, 175–176
The Trojan War 10, 92, 136
The Trojan Women 18
"The Trouble with Tribbles" 210
Tuskegee Institute 101–102
Twain, Mark 2, 7
The Twilight Zone 83
2001: A Space Odyssey 63

"Ulysses" 181, 186–187
The Untouchables 163–165
Up from Slavery 101–103
Utopia 171–175

The Vampyre 112–113
Vietnam War 7, 57
Villeneuve, Gabrielle de 95
Virgil 58, 192
The Virginian 42–48
"The Visitor" 54

Wagon Train 12, 43
Washington, Booker T. 101–103
Wells, H.G. 49–52, 56, 171
"Whales Weep Not" 6, 73
"What Are Little Girls Made Of?" 108
"What Lips My Lips Have Kissed" 38–40
"Where No Man Has Gone Before" 13
Whitman, Walt 2, 70
"Who Mourns for Adonais?" 145
Wiglaf 11
Williams, Robert Moore 158
Wister, Owen 42
Witfield, Stephen 3
Woolf, Virginia 5, 69
Wordsworth, William 25, 70
Worf 29, 151
The World of Star Trek 210

Xindi 48

Yeats, William Butler 69
"The Yellow Wallpaper" 88–90